Brief En

C000268926

Brief Encounters

Lesbians and Gays
in British Cinema
1930–1971

Stephen Bourne

CASSELL PLC

CASSELL

Cassell
Wellington House
125 Strand
London WC2R 0BB

127 West 24th Street
New York, NY 10011

© Stephen Bourne 1996

All rights reserved. No part of this publication may be reproduced or transmitted in any form or by any means, electronic or mechanical including photocopying, recording or any information storage or retrieval system, without prior permission in writing from the publishers.

First published 1996

British Library Cataloguing-in-Publication Data

A catalogue record for this book is available from the British Library.

Library of Congress Cataloging-in-Publication Data

Bourne, Stephen.
    Brief encounters : lesbians and gays in British cinema 1930–1971 / Stephen Bourne.
        p.   cm.
    Includes bibliographical references and index.
    ISBN 0-304-33283-6.—ISBN 0-304-33286-0
    1. Homosexuality in motion pictures. 2. Motion pictures—Great Britain—History. I Title.
PN1995.9.H55B68 1996
791.43'653—dc20   96-13881
                                                                          CIP

ISBN 0 304 33283 6 (hardback)

      0 304 33286 0 (paperback)

Cover still: Celia Johnson and Trevor Howard in *Brief Encounter* (1945). Courtesy of National Film Archive London.

Designed and Typeset by Ben Cracknell Studios.

Printed and bound in Great Britain by Biddles Ltd, Guildford and King's Lynn.

Contents

About the Author

Stephen Bourne left his secondary modern school in South London at the age of sixteen with no qualifications. The jobs that followed included sales assistant in a shoe shop in Peckham, working for the DHSS, nursery officer, library assistant, kitchen porter and cinema usher, but he continued to pursue his childhood dream of writing film books. Untrained, he began contributing articles and reviews to black publications, including *The Voice*, in the early 1980s. He feels the turning point was graduating in 1988. Since then he hasn't looked back. His work on race and representation in film and television has included compiling a number of successful and ground-breaking retrospectives for the National Film Theatre. He also worked as one of the researchers on *Black and White in Colour*, a two-part BBC documentary about the history of black people in British television. In 1992 Stephen shared the Raymond Williams Prize for Community Publishing with his Aunt Esther for *Aunt Esther's Story*, the autobiography of a working-class black woman born in London before the First World War. Since then he has received two *Race in the Media* awards from the Commission for Racial Equality. Stephen lives in South London and describes himself as a gay member of the community in which he lives. In 1994 Stephen helped pioneer work with his local council and police on the issue of homophobic violence. Stephen's third book, *Black in the British Frame*, a history of black people in British film and television, will be published by Cassell in 1997.

Foreword

by Keith Howes

Most sensible people used to think the Earth was flat, until one of those crackpot fellows came along and proved it wasn't. At the dawning of cinema's second century, Stephen Bourne shows us that we have not yet reached the limits of the screen world. For too long British cinema has been depicted as sexless, featureless and passionless: an Old Dark House. No surprise then that queer (non-100 per cent heterosexual) British cinema, with a few exceptions, always used the servant's entrance. Because of prejudices and misconceptions, this vast pink and lavender arena has mostly escaped the attentions of the orthodox critic and historian. Yet in *Brief Encounters* Stephen Bourne reveals a cinema more various, more vital and more sensuous than we could ever have imagined in our most Oscar Wildest, most technicolored dreams. And definitely, irridescently queer!

Free of reductive jargon and theory, this fluent chronology of films famous, half remembered and forgotten is a true illumination. Now we can no longer deny how much gays and lesbians have contributed to this country's cinema culture. Stephen uncovers many extraordinary intimacies, playful ironies and unconventional couplings, most of which have not been highlighted before. There is still a reticence about discussing this area of life, reinforced by the shadowland that exists around British cinema itself, save for repeated excursions into the worlds of Hitchcock, Ealing, Powell and Pressburger, David Lean, the *Carry On's*, and Hammer horror. The almost complete blackout on discussion of homoemotional and homoerotic cinema outside the United States has been, and continues to be, actively encouraged by the contagious indifference of lesbian, gay and bisexual editors, writers, reviewers and cultural historians (not to mention television producers, media studies professors and film programmers).

For the first time we see laid out before us an exhilarating gallery of heroes and heroines. In front of the cameras: Cicely Courtneidge (drawing the crowds as an out-and-out lesbian thirty years before *The L-Shaped Room*); Esmé Percy (Hitchcock's 'half-caste' but all-queer in *Murder*); Emlyn Williams (Caligula in a little 'cocktail number'); the incomparable, darkly brilliant and rooftop-shouting lesbian Mary Morris; Judith Furse (once softly, if heftily, femme in *Goodbye Mr Chips* and beyond, and then post-war, irrevocably, immoveably, bull-dykey); majestic Anton Walbrook (mesmerizingly misogynist or tenderly gay); Eric Portman (equally convincing sturdy or silky); Michael Ward (who never played a 'straight' role); Dennis Price (who occasionally tried to) . . . and many more. Stars, leads, featured, supports, bit parts . . .

Behind the cameras there's a former Prime Minister's son in a boiler suit; John Ford's cousin who liked a bit of rough; the man who created Frankenstein's monster for the ages, but died mysteriously and forgotten in Hollywood; Sir Terry and Sir Noel, the twin darlings of Shaftesbury Avenue; and the selectively uncompromising, frequently leather-clad bisexual Oscar winner who never came out, not even in his award-winning autobiography, discovered in his 'closet' after his death. I know of no other openly gay writer who could so effortlessly and accessibly glide through such a dazzling array of diverse talent, white and black, across forty years, lifting, almost in passing, the 'other' Forces sweetheart on to her own small, but secure lesbian icon pedestal.

Here then is a British cinema history that deftly and, always, politely argues so persuasively for homoeroticism in every genre, throughout each decade. Until the revolution in the late 1960s, all under the noses of the censors, and even – until he was replaced by accountants – J. Arthur Rank himself (whose own name, in certain disreputable quarters, is still a euphemism for that which some continue to believe is a threat to male eyesight).

I was too young (thirteen) to see *Victim* upon its initial release, but I knew all about it. You almost couldn't avoid doing so. A major production, the film received coverage (always discreetly avoiding the actual reason for the blackmail) on radio and television. Every major newspaper carried (much franker) reviews, and there were print interviews with the man Mum rapturously called 'my Dirk'. Of the film itself, my mother said nothing. She certainly didn't go and see it. But she still called its star 'my Dirk' until he gave those post-*Death in Venice* interviews on television in the 1970s. By the early 1980s she had completely erased him from her conversation.

That the film *Victim* had made an impact was obvious to me. It was, after all, 'controversial' and, despite repeated subtle belittlings of it in various British film histories (but not this one), it remains a fine piece of work. Acting, photography, direction, and most of the script are pointed and involving (only the music and the glaring censorship demands of the time jar). *Victim* is a film I have seen many times, and continue to enjoy viewing: alone, with my lover Peter, with friends or with (predominantly non-gay) audiences at adult education film courses. The reaction can usually be summed up as: how did they manage to make such an honest film in such a hostile climate? However, until I read the superbly detailed and moving pieces written by gay men who went to see *Victim* in 1961 – the most precious gems in this book's crown – I hadn't realized just how personal a film could be, how meaningful, how strengthening. For some, just by going into a cinema where *Victim* was playing and watching that film with other people was a brave act of coming out. To others, it was the rallying call for a change in a disgusting and hypocritical law.

Above all, *Victim* was part of the ebb and flow of contemporary movie-going. A coming attraction. A continuous performance. Something to enjoy and think about all the next week. And *Victim* was *British*! It was *ours* and, for the very first time, about *us*, and it was introduced by that comforting, glistening, semi-naked man with the gong!

In 1971 – when this book regrettably ends (sequel soon, please) – I was a journalist for a popular national magazine for women. It fearlessly dealt with subjects taboo in other publications, except for its mid-1960s rival, *Nova*. However, when I interviewed Murray Head on the set of *Sunday, Bloody Sunday* I was so nervous of the film's theme that I bashfully tried to sidestep it. Finally I plucked up the courage to address the character the young actor was playing. 'In this story you are playing a bbbbbisexual . . .'. Red hot flush and collapse of interview's subject into amused concern, and the offer of a soothing glass of water.

At that time I fully supported showbiz's culture of denial. I was an obedient heterosexual propagandist along with everyone else in the mainstream. With the notable exception of Derek Jarman, I did not knowingly meet, on a professional level, a twenty-four-hour-a-day openly gay or lesbian actor, writer, director or producer in my fifteen years in and around the British film industry. Neither as a show business reporter and interviewer (for non-gay and gay audiences), nor as features editor of *Gay News*, the newspaper by and for lesbians and gays from the mid-1970s. Certainly not as co-director of British Film Year in 1985, a million-pound campaign designed to promote the industry overseas, and woo the British public back into the near-deserted cinemas.

I suspect that, even with the changes in the post-AIDS era, the philosophy of 'Deny! Deny! Deny!' lives on. For every closet door that opens, another two are nailed tight shut. Because, darlings, the public wouldn't accept it, the producer wouldn't like it, the Americans would feel uncomfortable, and you'll never work again. As for the films that comprise our British cultural heritage, well, my dears, they continue to stereotype (John Sessions pitching camp in *In the Bleak Midwinter*) and to sweep under the carpet (Emma Thompson, hetero rather than accurately bi in, and as, *Carrington*).

I grew up with my nose pressed against the window of British cinema. My parents talked of Ivor Novello, Will Hay, Jessie Matthews and honorary Brit Paul Robeson. They were major personalities to me, revered and loved even though I had never seen them in a film. In the early 1950s there was no regular supply on television, and no video. Growing up in a different era my sister Joy, fourteen years my senior, and a teenager swooning over Stewart Granger and James Mason, vividly related the plots of *The Wicked Lady*, *Dead of Night*, *Kind Hearts and Coronets*, *The Third Man* and other classics. Scene by scene, and – at my excited request – over and over again. These were my bedtime stories! Later, with the advent of the forbidden X film, I would urge Joy to give me a blow-by-blow account of *Room at the Top*, *Saturday Night and Sunday Morning* and – ears pricking, wheels turning madly here – of the two Oscar Wilde films and *Victim*! Then, having by subterfuge gained entry to my first 'adults only' film (*The Innocents* – most of whose perversions went straight over my head), I was free to roam and to safely graze in the dark.

I realize, courtesy of *Brief Encounters*, that I never *consciously* saw most of what was really going on in all those U- and A-certificate homegrown films that I trooped along to see at the Broadway (posh) and Palace (fleapit) cinemas, Letchworth Garden City, Hertfordshire. Now the doors of perception are wide open to me. I've fallen in love with my country's cinema all over again.

Most things are easy when someone has shown you how.

Thanks Stephen.

Preface

It began ten years ago in 1985 when I participated in a summer school about British cinema at the Watershed Arts Centre in Bristol. The object of the exercise was to compare British films of the 1940s with British films of the 1980s. Included among them was *Dead of Night* (1945) in which Michael Redgrave played Maxwell Frere, a ventriloquist who is obsessed with his dummy. Afterwards I joined a discussion group and became annoyed when one of the members said that he felt the tortured, obsessed ventriloquist, who attempts to murder a rival, was a repressed gay man. He likened him to the mother-obsessed killer Norman Bates in Hitchcock's *Psycho*! As the only openly gay member of the group, this made me feel very uncomfortable and self-conscious. Subsequently I rejected the suggestion that Frere and Bates were gay. I was concerned that the other members of the group might think that all gay men were psychopaths. But looking back I realize I was refusing to open my eyes to the wide range of images of lesbians and gays in British cinema. Even so, I had been aware of our existence on film since I was a young child. I have never forgotten when *The L-Shaped Room* was shown for the first time on television. It was 1968, I was ten years old, and Cicely Courtneidge – as the retired music hall player Mavis – gently, movingly revealed to Jane (Leslie Caron) that the woman in the photograph was her lesbian 'friend'. 'It takes all sorts, dear,' she explained. Even at that tender age, I knew what she meant.

The same year in which I took part in the summer school in Bristol, I eagerly commenced a Bachelor of Arts Degree in Film and Television at the London College of Printing (now the London Institute). It was here I began to open my eyes to the existence of a gay and lesbian cinema in Britain before *Victim* (1961) and *The Killing of Sister George* (1969). However, I faced indifference and resistance from tutors and students when I identified myself as a working-class gay man. I already knew that the film course had an enviable reputation in film-study circles for being unconventional, and helping 'minorities'. It had a radical, left-wing and Marxist bias in Thatcher's Britain, and actively discouraged students from working in the 'mainstream'. Instead it encouraged students to be independent, political and 'experimental'. Most students I met from other film schools expressed envy because we had tutors like the highly-respected film theorist Laura Mulvey, and one of our external examiners was the radical, left-wing film director Ken Loach. However, I found the climate very hostile, and alienating. Lesbian and gay sexuality was definitely *not* on anyone's political agenda! Though I have a great deal of admiration for Mr Loach, who has always worked against the grain, I can't remember ever seeing a gay man or a lesbian in one of his films. Or, for that matter, black people either. So by just being openly gay I felt I was going against *their* grain. My aims and objectives were neither understood, nor taken seriously. I was completely isolated and, ironically, often felt I was being a disruptive influence. Against the odds, in my final year, I wrote a thesis about the gay Hollywood director James Whale called *James Whale – Hollywood's Gay Auteur?*, and made a short video called *Where There Was Silence*, which included gay men's reminiscences about the ground-breaking British film *Victim*.

After graduating in the summer of 1988, *Where There Was Silence* received enthusiastic reviews from the gay press, in particular Pas Paschali in *Capital Gay* and Rupert Smith in *The Pink Paper*. However, the late film critic Jack Babuscio refused to look at it. 'I don't review student productions and certainly not videos!', he explained. Not one to give up easily, I persisted and, eventually, he agreed to view the tape. Consequently he included a favourable review in his *Gay Times* film column! I also received encouragement and support from the late film director Stuart Marshall. So I had good reason to feel optimistic about the future, and confident that I could make a career for myself as a gay film and video maker. But only for a short time. My confidence took a battering when *Where There Was Silence* was turned down for *A Queer Feeling When I Look at You*, the third London Lesbian and Gay Film Festival. This rejection was unbearable and it made me question whether there was such a thing as 'gay solidarity'. This was something I desperately needed after the isolation I experienced at film school for three years. It also made me realize how much British film history, gay and straight, is unappreciated and marginalized in this country. This is not the case with American cinema. What made the situation worse –

adding insult to my painful injury – was that I was helping to review the Lesbian and Gay Film Festival for *The Pink Paper*. I had to attend press screenings of films and videos I felt were far less worthy of attention than my own. However, a few months later, *Where There Was Silence* found its way into Frameline's 1989 San Francisco Lesbian and Gay Film Festival, and I was thrilled that *someone* was being given an opportunity to view my modest production!

My confidence was given another boost at the beginning of 1990 when Peter Burton, the arts editor of *Gay Times*, invited me to become the magazine's film critic. Sadly, Jack Babuscio had passed away and a replacement was needed. I held this position for almost two and a half years and enjoyed every minute. I was proud to be associated with a popular gay magazine, and welcomed the chance to develop as a writer. Two years later, with the support of the TV Unit of the British Film Institute, I began to explore our television past when I programmed *Out of the Archives*, the first lesbian and gay television retrospective, for the National Film Theatre and Museum of the Moving Image. Since then, *Out of the Archives* has happily become an annual event.

When Peter Burton encouraged me to write features for *Gay Times*, I contributed several which related to British films and filmmakers including *Dangerously Indiscreet – James Whale in Hollywood* (December 1988), *Victim – Thirty Years On* (July 1991) and, in March 1992, *Brief Encounters*, a 'tie-in' with a presentation I gave in the sixth London Lesbian and Gay Film Festival. In *Brief Encounters* I looked at some of the ways lesbians and gays had been portrayed in early British films, and one of the extracts I used to illustrate my talk was Michael Redgrave as the obsessed ventriloquist in *Dead of Night*. After the presentation I had a revealing brief encounter of my own with an elderly gentleman. He informed me that, as a young man in 1945, on seeing *Dead of Night* for the first time, he felt there was a gay subtext to the story.

Very few gay writers have tackled this subject in any depth. America's Vito Russo (1946–91) published what, for many of us, is the definitive book about lesbian and gay cinema, *The Celluloid Closet* (Harper & Row, 1981; revised in 1987). But Russo's emphasis was on Hollywood cinema, and his knowledge of lesbians and gays in British cinema before the 1960s was almost non-existent. Keith Howes's marvellous *Broadcasting It: An Encyclopaedia of Homosexuality on Film, Radio and Television in the UK 1923–1993* (Cassell, 1993) has opened up the subject in more ways than one.

My passion for British cinema began in the 1960s. As a young child, growing up in a working-class family in a council flat in Peckham, I was given almost unlimited access to television by my parents. I particularly looked forward to seeing old films on Sunday afternoon. After roast beef and Yorkshire pudding, I'd sit with my family and watch some of the glories of British cinema. Anna Neagle and Michael Wilding Maytiming in Mayfair, Dennis Price being bad as Lord Byron, John Mills and Sylvia Syms dreaming of that ice-cold beer in Alex, Gracie Fields being the pride of her alley. How I relished the black-and-white wonders of the war films, when heroes like Kenneth More were shot down over enemy territory, the Gainsborough melodramas, the Ealing comedies, the not quite Hollywood but still fascinating musicals. I fell in love with their originality, atmosphere and modesty! Above all, I felt the best of them had a glorious honesty, a human glow. None more so than the film whose title I have pluralized for this book, Noel Coward's unforgettable *Brief Encounter*.

After giving my talk in 1992 I decided that the subject required greater attention and exploration; however, this book could not possibly be the *definitive*, history, and include every British film which contains a lesbian or gay presence. It has also – for obvious reasons – been impossible for me to give a lesbian perspective on the subject. So I hope this book will inspire someone to take this on board. Finally, because my interest in British cinema has always been primarily with the pre-1970s 'talkie' period, I have focused the book on 1930–71, beginning and ending with films by two British gay directors: James Whale's *Journey's End* and John Schlesinger's *Sunday, Bloody Sunday*. Schlesinger's landmark film was released just before other openly gay directors (Derek Jarman, Ron Peck) began making an impact in British cinema. But that's another story.

Stephen Bourne
London, 1996

Acknowledgements

Brief Encounters would not have been possible without the existence of Denis Gifford's *The British Film Catalogue 1895–1985*; Parker Tyler's *Screening the Sexes*; Jack Babuscio's *Screen Gays* series in *Gay News*; Vito Russo's *The Celluloid Closet*; Richard Dyer's BFI 'Film Classic' *Brief Encounter* and his work on Charles Hawtrey; Andrea Weiss's *Vampires and Violets: Lesbians in the Cinema*; and Keith Howes's encyclopaedia *Broadcasting It*. I would also like to mention Andy Medhurst's work on *Brief Encounter*, the *Carry Ons*, Dirk Bogarde and *Victim*.

Thanks to Robin Baker, Terry Bolas, Peter Burton, Rose Collis, Steve Cook and Jane Greenwood at Cassell, Mark Gatiss, Gillian Rodgerson (former editor of *Capital Gay*) and Andrea Weiss.

Finally, *Brief Encounters* could not have been written without the assistance, support and enthusiasm of Keith Howes and Ken Rhodes, and all the gay men who kindly took the trouble to share with me their memories of seeing *Victim* at the time of its release.

For photographic stills reproduced in this book, we thank BFI Stills, Posters and Designs.

Though every care has been taken, if, through inadvertence or failure to trace the present owners, we have included any copyright material without acknowledgement or permission, we offer our apologies to all concerned.

1930

James Whale and *Journey's End*

James Whale, a gay man, was responsible for directing the war drama *Journey's End*. Set in the claustrophobic world of the trenches in 1918, the film explores the relationships of a group of British officers sharing a dugout just before a German attack. This was Whale's first film as a director, and it is a considerable achievement. Through Whale, *Journey's End* becomes a haunting, poetic vision of male-bonding.

For many years it was difficult to assess the films of James Whale (1889–1957) because of the unavailability of many of his productions. Also, because Whale retired from film directing in 1941, and became something of a recluse, very little attention was given to him. Most writers have concentrated on his quartet of stylish horror films (*Frankenstein*, *The Old Dark House*, *The Invisible Man* and *Bride of Frankenstein*), but until Mark Gatiss's well-researched and informative *James Whale: A Biography*, published by Cassell in 1995, there were hardly any references to Whale being gay, and no explorations of gay subtexts in his films. It remained a 'secret' though, unlike other gay and bisexual directors working in Hollywood in the 1930s, Whale did not hide his gay sexuality,

James Whale came from a working-class background. Born in Dudley, Worcestershire, actress Elsa Lanchester said: 'He came from a poverty-stricken English family, and I heard him describe the tiny little grate in the rooms where he was brought up'.[1]

Trained in graphic art, Whale spent most of the First World War interned in a prisoner-of-war camp in Germany. After the war, he became an actor, but later turned to directing. He enjoyed commercial and critical success with the London and New York stage versions of R. C. Sherriff's anti-war play *Journey's End*. He then directed the film version, a British production made in Hollywood. Sherriff's anti-war message is related in part by the tortured, helpless and confused Captain Stanhope (Colin Clive). Lieutenant Albert Osborne (Ian MacLaren), affectionately known as 'Uncle', is described as 'a very level-headed chap' and members of the company look to him for advice and support. There's also the young Second Lieutenant, Harry Raleigh (David Manners), who went to the same school as Stanhope, and has hero-worshipped him ever since.

Considering that Whale was gay, and Sherriff never married (he called his autobiography, published in 1968, *No Leading Lady*), one can only speculate how far Whale's gay sexuality and Sherriff's life-long single status influenced their perception of men and male relationships. Though gay sexuality is not *explicit* in *Journey's End*, one can identify a gay subtext. Also, Whale's gay sensibility enriched the drama and militated against the usual conception of the story as male heterosexual war drama.

When he started work on the film version of *Journey's End*, Whale knew exactly what he wanted. He said:

> When it comes to human emotions people are the same. . . and the simpler a big situation is presented to them the harder it strikes. The whole foundation of *Journey's End*, to my mind, is that it presents an unusual situation in a most appealing way. Some critics have said that it violates the ethics of the drama. It does not, because the essential element in all drama is truth.[2]

One of the most striking features of *Journey's End* is the intimacy in the relationships of some of its male characters. Stanhope, an alcoholic, has spent three traumatic years at the Front. He looks to the older Osborne or 'Uncle', for comfort and reassurance. The male-bonding of Stanhope and 'Uncle' is developed throughout the story. Their friendship is more than it seems. They share a close, intimate union within the confines of the dugout and this occasionally brings to the surface deeper feelings and emotions. For example, at the beginning of the film a captain, in conversation with 'Uncle', criticizes Stanhope. 'How is the dear young boy? Drinking like a fish as usual?' he asks. 'Uncle' immediately defends his friend: 'He's by far the best Company Commander we've got. You don't know him as I do. I love that fellow. I'd go to hell with him.' Taken aback, the captain responds sarcastically: 'Oh, you sweet sentimental old darling.'

Throughout the film there are several intimate and tender exchanges between 'Uncle' and Stanhope. This freedom of expression is made possible by the constant interplay between the male characters, and the camaraderie they enjoy. In one scene an extremely drunk Stanhope complains that the trenches need cleaning up. 'Dear Uncle,' he says, 'clean trenches up with a little dustpan and broom, eh? I'll make you a little white apron with lace on it.' There follows a request by Stanhope for 'Uncle' to tuck him up in bed. 'Kiss me Uncle!' he adds. 'Kiss you be hanged,' Uncle replies.

Stanhope is angered by the arrival of Raleigh, and worried by the young Second Lieutenant's hero-worship of him. Stanhope treats Raleigh with contempt, and this creates further tension in the dugout. However, after 'Uncle' is killed in a raid, Stanhope suffers a breakdown, and subjects Raleigh to an hysterical outburst after the young man has accused him of not caring about 'Uncle's' death: 'You think I don't care?' he cries, 'The one man I could trust. My best friend. The one man I could talk to as man to man, who understood everything. And you think I don't care. . . . You little fool.' It is an outburst one would expect to hear from someone who has lost a lover, not a fellow officer in wartime. After Raleigh leaves the room, Stanhope breaks down and sobs uncontrollably. It is the film's most powerful and emotional moment, with Stanhope's sense of loss, confusion, helplessness and desperation beautifully expressed by Colin Clive. The pain of war has finally taken its toll, and so has the loss of his companion.

The impact of the scene is heightened by Clive's performance. The role of Stanhope was perfectly suited to Clive, a complex and confused man who, like Stanhope, was an alcoholic. This was caused partly because of his inability to come to terms with his bisexuality. In fact he had been deliberately cast in the role of Stanhope by Whale because of the close parallels of his tortured and unhappy private life, and the character he portrayed. The tensions which surface in Clive's performance can also be identified in other troubled gay and bisexual actors, such as Charles Laughton and Eric Portman who failed, for one reason or another, to fully come to terms with their sexuality.

Making his film debut as Raleigh in *Journey's End* was David Manners. He later recalled Colin Clive's personality:

To me, his face was a tragic mask. I know he was a tortured man. There seemed to be a split in his personality: one side that was soft, kind and gentle; the other, a man who took to alcohol to hide from the world his true nature. . . . Today he would find help. Everyone of us wanted to help then, but when he was on the bottle, which was most of the time, he put on the mask of a person who repelled help and jeered at his own softness. He was a fantastically sensitive actor – and, as with many great actors, this sensitivity bred addiction to drugs or alcohol in order to cope with the very insensitive world around them.[3]

After making *Journey's End*, Whale worked in Hollywood for over a decade and directed an impressive range of films in different genres. A recurring theme in Whale's films is the plight of social outcasts and perhaps the most famous example of this is Frankenstein's 'monster'. But there are others, such as the tragic streetwalker Myra in *Waterloo Bridge* (1931), and Julie, who is discovered passing for a white, and subjected to virulent racism in America's Deep South, in the musical *Show Boat* (1936). Along with Captain Stanhope in *Journey's End*, these characters reveal Whale's understanding of people who are victims of other people's fear and prejudice, and who better to relate to them than a gay man? Ironically, by the 1940s, Whale became a victim himself. Homophobia reared its ugly head but, unlike his closeted lesbian, gay and bisexual contemporaries (George Cukor, Edmund Goulding, Dorothy Arzner, Mitchell Leisen), he remained dangerously indiscreet. Says film director Robert Aldrich:

Jimmy Whale was the first guy who refused to stay in the closet. Mitchell Leisen and all those other guys played it straight, and they were onboard, but Whale said 'Fuck it, I'm a great director and I don't have to put up with this bullshit' – and he *was* a great director. . . . And he was unemployed after that – never worked again.[4]

Murder

Lesbian and gay characters can often be found in the films of Alfred Hitchcock. For example, there's Mrs Danvers in *Rebecca* (1940), the killers in *Rope* (1948) and Bruno Anthony in *Strangers on a Train* (1951). However, Hitchcock's lesbians and gays have often been criticized for being lamentable, perverse figures. An early example can be found in one of his pre-Hollywood British films, *Murder* (1930), which director François Truffaut once described as 'a thinly disguised story about homosexuality'. In *Murder* Esmé Percy plays Handel Fane, an effeminate transvestite trapeze artist who commits homicide. In a memorable but disturbing performance, Percy embodies the unnatural and perverse characteristics often associated with cinematic depictions of gay men. His portrayal of Fane adds to the evil atmosphere of the film. However, gay writer Andrew Britton has challenged the view that Fane is a 'negative' stereotype:

> Because the killer in *Murder* is a transvestite, the film has sometimes been cited as an example of Hitchcock's allegedly conservative sexual attitudes. Such criticisms ignore his consistently astringent, critical and pessimistic treatment of heterosexual relations, and no more than in *Rope* is 'perverse' sexuality identified with viciousness. Rather, Hitchcock's interest focuses, typically, on the male protagonist's defensive fear of femininity.[5]

Borderline

Shot in Switzerland by Pool Films, a tiny English production company, *Borderline* is a classic of the avant-garde. An experimental narrative integrates the montage theories of Eisenstein and the psychoanalytical ideas of Hanns Sachs. It was written and directed by bisexual Kenneth MacPherson, a member of the Zurich-based avant-garde group associated with the film journal *Close-Up*. The film is notable not only for its experimental narrative, but also for its cast of expatriate artists. They include lesbian poet H. D. (Hilda Doolittle) and her real-life lover Winifred Bryher. They play Swiss innkeepers who become involved in sexual and psychological game-playing with several visitors. These include two black American expatriates, played by singer, actor and political activist Paul Robeson and his wife, Eslanda.

Without sound or dialogue, the cinematic style of *Borderline* is influenced by the gay Russian director Sergei Eisenstein. It's a film with complex themes of loneliness, rejection and racism, as well as strong homoerotic undercurrents. Lesbian and gay characters exist on the periphery of the story including H. D. as the cigar-smoking owner of the bistro who is seen with her arm around her lover, the barmaid (Bryher). There's also the slim, elegant, over-anxious pianist, played by Robert Herring (MacPherson's real-life lover), who expresses an unrequited love for Paul Robeson. This is revealed by the photograph he keeps of Robeson on his piano.

Hutch

In 1930 bisexual singer–pianist Leslie 'Hutch' Hutchinson, the 'darling' of café society, made his film debut with a guest appearance in *Big Business*. This popular cabaret star was befriended and lionized by the pre-war rich and famous, and equally loved by the public. His trademark was a white handkerchief which he used to mop his brow and for many years Hutch was the supreme interpreter of Cole Porter, recording and helping to popularise most of his great songs. But the private lives of black lesbian and gay performers of the 1920s and 1930s have always been shrouded in mystery, and they remain the most secret of all. Though the bisexuality of down-to-earth 'classic' blues singers like Bessie Smith, Gertrude 'Ma' Rainey and Ethel Waters has been documented, today there is still a reticence from survivors of the era to talk about the lesbian and gay sexuality of black singers and entertainers who enjoyed mainstream popularity. Many of these performing artists rose to fame in the 1920s when New York experienced an explosion of creative energy and artistic expression, an event known as the Harlem Renaissance. Throughout the decade, many of these artists were active in Britain too, for example, Ethel Waters topped the bill at the London Palladium in 1929. While working in this country most of them associated with the upper classes, and such friendships suggest a degree of social acceptance in a society where some people of wealth and influence expressed liberal views on relations between whites and non-whites. However, this would be a superficial view for black entertainers were rarely accepted as individuals, only as symbols, including two of the most famous black people in Britain at that time: Hutch and Paul Robeson.

Sophisticated nightclub entertainer Hutch differed from Robeson in more ways than one. Unlike Robeson, in his professional life, Hutch wouldn't have taken an artistic risk by acting in an experimental film like *Borderline*. When Hutch associated with the upper classes he avoided rocking any boats, unlike Robeson who preferred to sink them by turning his back on the 'smart set' and embracing left-wing politics. However, like Robeson, Hutch posed a threat to white male supremacy and sexuality in 1930s Britain, especially with his sexual liaisons.

Hutch was born in 1900 in a tiny fishing village on the west coast of Grenada. Before the end of the First World War he'd set off to study medicine in New York and began playing piano at parties. After turning professional he was so alarmed by the Ku Klux Klan during an engagement in Palm Beach, that he decided to leave America for good. In Paris Hutch was 'adopted' by the rich and famous 'smart set', and met Cole Porter, the gay songwriter who was to become his friend and musical alter-ego. Hutch became Porter's favourite pianist, and best-loved interpreter of his songs. There was even a joke that said Hutch knew the lyrics before Cole Porter had written them!

In 1927, when Hutch was brought to London by the impresario, Charles B. Cochran, he quickly became London's most sought-after accompanist, and a true celebrity. Several West End stage appearances included Noel Coward's *This Year of Grace* and Cole Porter's *Wake Up and Dream*. Charlotte Breese, the author of a forthcoming biography of Hutch, describes the legend:

> Hutch was a remarkably elegant man. Outwardly he conformed entirely and he became part of the set that were his clients. He was certainly invited to their houses at weekends although of course it would have been different at official functions in London where he was still expected to enter by the tradesman's entrance. For a man with as much pride as Hutch it must have been extraordinarily humiliating. He was a walking threat in a kind of way because he was so good-looking.
>
> Hutch's bisexuality was known in Paris, where it was acceptable and ubiquitous amongst the smart set in the 1920s, but when he came to London he observed a different set of rules. His affairs with men were covert in Britain and, like many gay men, he conducted affairs when abroad. My impression is that Hutch's bisexuality was rooted in his relaxed view of sex

generally, and a long-lasting belief that 'anything goes'. He was promiscuous and experimental all his life, and often forgot that this attitude was unacceptable amongst many of his friends in Britain. Like-minded lovers enjoyed his blatant bisexuality, others were never aware of it![6]

At the height of his popularity in Britain in the 1930s and 1940s, Hutch made numerous appearances in newsreel films, and his elegant cabaret persona enlivened several feature films. As himself, Hutch made guest appearances in such productions as *Cock O' the North* (1935), *Beloved Imposter* (1936) and *Happidrome* (1943). After the Second World War Hutch's style of performing was no longer in fashion, and his health deteriorated. Though he continued performing, he only occasionally recaptured the level of popularity he had enjoyed in pre-war Britain. He died in 1969.

Other films of interest released in 1930

Alf's Button featured ballet dancer Anton Dolin in an Arabian Nights sequence; in *The Shaming of the True,* revue artist and female impersonator Douglas Byng made a rare film appearance. This five-minute comedy was produced by Charles B. Cochran for his aborted feature *Charles B. Cochran's 1930 Revue*; *Symphony in Two Flats* was a melodrama based on the play by Ivor Novello in which he also starred as a blind composer. This was his first sound film. A friend rang him and said: 'It's very good, isn't it?' Ivor replied: 'No.'

Notes

1. Elsa Lanchester, *Elsa Lanchester Herself* (Michael Joseph, 1983), p.135.
2. *New York Times*, 8 September 1929.
3. Gregory Mank, 'Colin Clive 1900–1937' in *Films in Review,* vol. 31, no. 5, May 1980, p. 259.
4. Vito Russo, *The Celluloid Closet: Homosexuality in the Movies* (Harper & Row, 1981, revised 1987), p. 50.
5. Andrew Britton, National Film Theatre programme notes for *Changing Gear: Cross-Dressing in the Cinema*, September/October 1990.
6. Charlotte Breese, interview with the author, London, April 1995.

1931

Anthony Asquith

In the Edwardian romance *Dance Pretty Lady* (1931) a ballet dancer believes her artist lover has deserted her. This is the second sound film directed by Anthony Asquith, and we find him at his most visually delicate, successfully integrating music, movement and camera in the exquisite ballet sequences. There's also a brief but memorable scene at the stage door where an effeminate autograph hunter, with pencilled eyebrows and heavy lipstick, waits patiently for a ballerina to leave the theatre. Pulling out a mirror, he runs his finger across his eyebrows. It's a rare *explicit* glimpse of 'gay life' in an Asquith film, though afterwards a gay sensibility or subtext could be found in his work.

Charming, gentle and effeminate, Anthony Asquith was affectionately known to his colleagues as 'Puffin'. In her autobiography, Ingrid Bergman remembered her first encounter with Asquith:

> I was on the set of *The Yellow Rolls-Royce* and John O'Gorman was making me up, when along came this very shabby little man in frayed blue overalls and an old shirt, carrying a bunch of flowers which he handed to me saying, 'Welcome. I'm so pleased to see you.' 'Thank you. How kind of you,' I said. He went away. I turned to John. 'I suppose I have met him on an earlier picture; he must have been a stagehand or one of the electricians?' 'Ingrid!' John said patiently. 'That was your director.' It was Anthony Asquith. . . . He was the kindest and most polite director I have ever known. He was so polite that if he stumbled over a cable he would turn back and say, 'Oh, please forgive me.' When he needed the extras he would say, 'Ladies and gentlemen I don't want to disturb you – please finish your tea by all means – but when you have a few moments would you please come up and

stand in the background, because I need a few people there. Don't rush.'[1]

Asquith was the son of Lord Herbert Asquith, the first Earl of Oxford and Asquith, the Liberal statesman, and Britain's Prime Minister from 1908–16. Born in 1902, Asquith was a tiny, delicate baby with curly blond hair, and a hooked nose, hence the nickname, 'Puffin'. A schoolboy 'aesthete' who described himself as 'hopelessly incompetent' at sport, he was educated at Winchester and Balliol, and later went to Oxford. A radical who was always ready to take up the cause of the underdog (for thirty-one years he was president of the film technicians' trade union ACCT), with a kind, gentle and considerate nature, Asquith's films sometimes included public school boys of a similar disposition, such as Ronnie Winslow in *The Winslow Boy* (see 1948) and Taplow in *The Browning Version* (see 1951).

At Oxford Asquith belonged to a literary group who called themselves the 'Aesthetes'. A fellow student, Richard Crossman, who was later a cabinet minister in Harold Wilson's government, once recalled:

> In college we had two groups – the Aesthetes and the Athletes – We (the Aesthetes) had readings of plays, drawing on world literature. . . we read in fact an astonishing amount of modern drama; the small boys took the female parts. . . . I was tremendously influenced by Puffin – indeed all of us were. He never beat a fag nor would he allow any other Aesthete to beat us. But the Athletes not only beat their own fags but beat us too. . . . Puff had at that time a shrill high-pitched voice and his Adam's apple stuck out. . . . He was sensitive, an epicure, snobbish only so far as books were concerned. . . . The Aesthetes had a special way of dressing up. They used to wear mauve shirts and flowing ties and took a delight in flaunting their get-up before the Athletes.[2]

At Oxford Asquith showed an enthusiasm for cinema and in 1925 he became a founder member of the original Film Society along with such distinguished people as George Bernard Shaw and H. G. Wells. After submitting a script to British International, he was taken on by that studio and given his first chance to direct in 1928, a light comedy called

Shooting Stars.

From the 1920s to the 1960s Asquith divided his time between directing semi-documentaries and adaptations of drama and literature. He made films in a range of genres, including thrillers, war films, musicals, historical films and comedies. His many film successes included several polished film adaptations of drama classics, such as George Bernard Shaw's *Pygmalion* (see 1938), *The Doctor's Dilemma* (1959) and *The Millionairess* (1960). His screen version of Oscar Wilde's *The Importance of Being Earnest* (see 1952) captured most of the sparkle of the author's wit. In the 1930s Asquith was considered Britain's leading film director along with Alfred Hitchcock, before he departed for Hollywood at the end of the decade. Says Roy Armes in *A Critical History of British Cinema*:

> Since 1939 the achievements of Alfred Hitchcock and Anthony Asquith have diverged sharply, but until that date there were many points of contact between them and for many years their careers ran parallel. Both began at the bottom – Hitchcock designing titles at Islington and Asquith working as odd-job man at Cricklewood – but quickly found their talents recognized. By the end of the 1920s both had established a reputation based on a clear appreciation of the narrative potential of the silent cinema . . . . Though both had low points in their mid-1930s careers, each had demonstrated a total professionalism and had discovered his mature style by the end of the decade.[3]

Very little attention has been given to Asquith's gay sexuality. It is something he concealed and repressed, while friends and colleagues tactfully avoided the subject. Asquith's biographer, R. J. Minney, offers a celebratory and glowing appraisal of the man and his work, but touches only briefly, and discreetly, on the director's sexuality. He even quotes a denial from Asquith's collaborator, writer Terence Rattigan:

> Some thought that Puffin never married because he had homosexual tendencies. Others denied it emphatically. 'There was,' Terence Rattigan told me, 'an impenetrable side to Puff, however close one was to him. He certainly liked being with young men, but it never went further than talking or going to a concert, or playing cards.'[4]

Considering that Rattigan was also a troubled, 'self-conscious' gay man, it is hardly surprising he denies Asquith was gay. Film student Nicholas Thomas elaborates:

> Terence Rattigan defends Asquith fiercely in Minney's biography against 'accusations' that his friend might have been gay. To say that many of his films are essentially 'feminine' in appeal is not, of course, 'evidence' of his homosexuality, although one (gay) member of the Film Studies MA group was moved to observe that, 'you only have to see one of his films to know that he was gay'. These two views are reconcilable if we suggest that Asquith, though possibly gay, was, as the term has it, 'not practising'. . . . But all the evidence suggests that for most of his career he did not actually have a private life to speak of, since his union activities, his film-making and his writing took up all his time. In an article in *Picturegoer* in 1933 he offered some interesting advice to young people wanting to enter the film world. *'Give up something that's pretty important to you; then associate the need for the thing you've sacrificed with your desire, whatever that is. Do you see the plan? You make the simple need work for you so that your desire becomes as simple, as natural, as essential.'* In Asquith's example, he talks about giving up smoking, and channelling the need for cigarettes into a desire to become a great actor. But a simple Freudian reading of this passage would see it as a prescription for the sublimation of an artist's sexuality into his work, which is what Asquith, following his own advice, appeared to do. And that is why it is of interest in looking at his career.[5]

While Asquith repressed his sexuality, he found great pleasure and enjoyment in the company of lorry drivers. In 1950 the *Daily Mirror* 'outed' Asquith when they published an article which revealed Asquith's 'secret life':

> To the lorry drivers on the Great North Road, the dish washer in Joe's transport cafe is just Tony. . . . For when Mr Asquith gets bored with the beauty of film stars and cocktails at film premieres, he turns into [a] dishwasher. Vic Dossor said Tony met Joe Jones, the cafe owner, at Vic's pub. 'Tony was here making *The Way to the Stars*. . . Joe, an ex-regimental sergeant-major,

told Tony in army language what he thought of his dart playing. After that, they were inseparable.' Joe said: 'We have a lot in common, and we both like a pint of wallop. He often rings me up from London and talks to my wife and three kids. He often comes here at weekends and sleeps in our spare bedroom. He gets up at 6.30 to deliver the papers and then serves the lorry men with breakfasts.' Mr Asquith's explanation is: 'I enjoy myself here. It is a complete change from the film work I do and the lorry drivers I meet are grand fellows.'[6]

It is interesting to look at Asquith's films from a gay perspective. For example, in some of his films, like the war drama *We Dive at Dawn* (see 1943), Asquith successfully explored the theme of male-bonding. However, in most of his films, Asquith seems preoccupied with the breakdown of heterosexual relationships, for example, in *Carrington VC* (1954) and *The VIP's* (1963). Occasionally, in films like *The Woman in Question* (1950) and *The Browning Version*, Asquith focused on the way in which women can disrupt the lives of men. Also, in any study of Asquith, it is important to look at the films in which he collaborated with Sir Terence Rattigan, CBE (1911–77).

Asquith's association with Rattigan began with *French Without Tears* in 1939. Though Rattigan's gay sexuality was not obvious, he made no secret of it, but sometimes it made him feel ashamed. Here were two gay men with an emotional attachment to each other. Sometimes they found expression for it in their work, giving revealing insights into male relationships. For example, on the surface *The Way to the Stars* (see 1945) is a film about an RAF station in wartime, but it often movingly portrays the pilots trying to cope with their emotions in the face of almost certain death. Later, in *The Browning Version*, a friendly public schoolboy unleashes all kinds of emotions when his kind gesture towards an unpopular headmaster shatters the master's rigid self-control. These films contain two of Michael Redgrave's finest screen performances, with the troubled bisexual actor giving depth to his characters.

Asquith's association with Rattigan was a long and happy one. Rattigan later remembered their first meeting:

The positively enchanting, delightful character he seemed to be was wild with enthusiasm about what he was going to do. . . . He also seemed to be wildly enthusiastic about meeting me. . . . I couldn't believe this was the great Anthony Asquith and frankly at that moment I more or less fell for him – fell for his personality, fell for his charm, fell for his enthusiasm and for his eagerness, for his way of life. . . . This led to a friendship which lasted until his death.[7]

However, unlike Asquith, Rattigan did have sexual relationships with other men. One with Kenneth Morgan, that ended in tragedy (suicide), inspired one of Rattigan's most famous works, *The Deep Blue Sea*. Of course the relationship in the play, and film version starring Vivien Leigh and Kenneth More, had to be heterosexual but, says Rattigan's biographer Geoffrey Wansell: 'Rattigan's own experience coloured every line of the play. He saw Kenneth Morgan in Hester Collyer, and himself in her devoted husband, Sir William.'[8]

Sadly, in the late 1950s, Asquith and Rattigan were unsuccessful in bringing what might have been their greatest collaboration to the screen, their version of *Lawrence of Arabia* with Dirk Bogarde. Asquith worked very closely with Bogarde on the development of the Lawrence project. He also gave the young actor some insight into his sexuality:

With some hesitation Dirk then asked Puffin a very personal question about Lawrence – 'out of the blue', to use his own phrase. 'Puff, tell me really and truly, now we have it all before us, was Lawrence homosexual?'

'Puffin's face,' Dirk told me, 'was a study in white horror. The cigarette dropped its ash; with an unsteady hand he removed it, then stubbing it out, he replied. "Not practising." I know that I should not have asked it.'[9]

Bogarde later recalled: 'Ten days before we were due to shoot Rank pulled the plug. It destroyed Asquith and it practically destroyed me. Rattigan then turned what remained of his work into a play called *Ross*.'[10]

In *Sixty Voices*, several actors who recall the 'golden age' of British cinema remember Asquith with love and affection. John Mills says he was 'wonderful, very sympathetic and totally charming. He loved actors, loved movies.' Stewart Granger remembered him as 'a sweet man' and Margaretta Scott described him as 'the most wonderful director. He was quite firm but with such charm. . . Puffin always wore trousers that were a bit too short, sort of cut-down dungarees; I remember him having a party with the crew. He was rather precious and one would have thought that the lads mightn't have gone to the party, but they adored him.' Jean Kent, who was seen in *Fanny by Gaslight* (see 1944), says 'He was the only director who actually introduced members of the cast to each other! He used to wear this blue boiler-suit and sit like a little pixie under the camera.' Unlike Asquith's actors, Sir Anthony Havelock-Allan, producer of Asquith's *The Young Lovers* (see 1954) and *Orders to Kill* (1958), offers a more critical appraisal of the director: 'Puffin was never quite a great director – perhaps not ruthless enough – but he was a very, very good one.'[11]

Anthony Asquith died in 1968 after a battle with cancer. A memorial service, held later at St Margaret's, Westminster, was attended by the elite of film and theatre in Britain including Dame Edith Evans, Dirk Bogarde, Rex Harrison, Cecil Beaton, Michael Balcon and Victor Saville. The lessons were read by Sir Michael Redgrave and Sir Laurence Olivier. At the end of the service, when Yehudi Menuhin played Bach's *Chaconne* (Partita in D Minor), many in the congregation wept.

Other films of interest released in 1931

Glamour, a romantic drama starring Seymour Hicks (who also directed) and his wife Ellaline Terriss, included rare acting roles for gay playwright, journalist and broadcaster Beverley Nichols, and lesbian novelist and broadcaster Naomi Jacob.

Notes

1. Ingrid Bergman and Alan Burgess, *Ingrid Bergman: My Story* (Michael Joseph, 1980), pp. 440–41.
2. R. J. Minney, *Puffin Asquith* (Leslie Frewin, 1973), pp. 34–5.
3. Roy Armes, *A Critical History of British Cinema* (Secker & Warburg, 1978), p. 97.
4. Minney, p. 163.
5. Nicholas Thomas, *The Contribution of Anthony Asquith to British Film Culture*, unpublished MA dissertation, University of East Anglia, 1988, p. 32.
6. *Daily Mirror*, 30 May 1950.
7. Minney, pp. 123–4.
8. Geoffrey Wansell, *Terence Rattigan: A Biography* (Fourth Estate, 1995), p. 217.
9. Minney, p. 174.
10. Brian McFarlane (ed.), *Sixty Voices: Celebrities Recall the Golden Age of British Cinema* (British Film Institute, 1992), pp. 26–7.
11. *Ibid.*, pp. 103, 119, 147, 169, 196.

1932

Ernest Thesiger and *The Old Dark House*

The Old Dark House, from J. B. Priestley's novel, is often considered to be among the great horror films but it is also one of the funniest black comedies ever made. With this production, director James Whale took a classic situation and injected it with his perverse sense of humour. When a group of travellers take refuge in a strange old house during a terrible storm, they encounter some bizarre characters during their night of terror. *The Old Dark House* is an American production but it is included here for two reasons: it is set in Wales, and contains a flamboyant performance by the British gay actor Ernest Thesiger. When he died in 1961 at the age of eighty-one, an obituary in *The Observer* described Thesiger as:

> An eccentric blend of satanic impishness and good breeding; he suggested the intellectual black-sheep of a titled family (he was, in fact, the son of the Hon. Sir Edward Thesiger). He never moved without grace or spoke without elegance, but implicit in his performance there was a quizzical mockery of these qualities. It was a contradiction that gave his work its ironic edge.[1]

Off-screen Thesiger's recreations included needlework, and he was expert at working tapestries, cushion covers, chair backs and even carpets. He published a book on the subject under the title *Adventures in Embroidery* and, in 1927, an autobiography called *Practically True*. Thesiger once complained to dramatist W. Somerset Maugham about his never having written a part for him. 'But I am always writing parts for you, Ernest,' Maugham replied. 'The trouble is that somebody called Gladys Cooper will insist on playing them!' He sometimes wore outlandish garb including strings of pearls, green-painted toenails and blue velvet shorts with matching blouse. 'I have the perfect skin for healing pearls,' he once said. In *The Pink Plaque Guide to London*, Michael Elliman and Frederick Roll's indispensable collection of biographies of famous lesbians and gays, Thesiger is described as:

A founder member of the Men's Dress Reform Society [who] designed many of his own clothes. He was very proud of his legs and enjoyed showing them off in pale moleskin shorts or in a blue velvet pair with matching silk blouse and muffler. . . . In later life he modelled himself on Queen Mary [*they were reported to have embroidered together*] and grew more and more to resemble her, with his pursed lips, regal bearing and haughtiness of manner.[2]

Witty, skeletal Ernest Thesiger was by far the most eccentric gay actor around in the 1930s and 1940s, and he made two of his most explicitly gay appearances in *The Old Dark House* and as the sinister Dr Pretorius in *The Bride of Frankenstein* (1935), also directed by James Whale. In *The Old Dark House* Thesiger plays the sarcastic, weak and effeminate Horace Femm, member of a strange and grotesque family who live in isolation with a number of skeletons in their closet. Says William K. Everson:

It's unquestionably Thesiger's best role, and I'm not forgetting his colourful Dr Pretorius in *Bride of Frankenstein*. There's just the right mixture of fear, pride, potential insanity and mordant sense of humour. While the camerawork and specific angles stress his thin, bird-like body and features as he walks into the camera, his contempt for the characters surrounding him seems to extend to the film crew and theatre audience as well!. . . However, none of his marvellous lines match the combination of contempt, miserliness and distrust that he manages to inject into the simple line, 'Have a potato', as he hosts his uninvited guests to a singularly frugal meal.[3]

Horace Femm makes his first appearance descending a staircase and making an announcement to the travellers in an imperious and haughty manner, 'My name is Femm. Horace Femm.' In some ways he embodies the characteristics of the asexual 'sissy' comic stereotype of gay men, often seen in films of the period. However, there is a nasty streak in Femm's personality. For instance, after acknowledging his guests' introductions ('Charmed, I'm sure'), he walks to the fireplace and picks up a bouquet of flowers. 'My sister was on the point of arranging these flowers,' he says, and then casually tosses them into the fire. This action reveals Femm's cruelty, and casual dismissal of his sister's feelings.

Handsome Roger Penderel, played by Melvyn Douglas, is one of the travellers who takes refuge in the Femm household. Though presented as heterosexual (he becomes romantically involved with one of the women), he seems unthreatened by Horace Femm, and relaxed in his presence, engaging in witty dialogue with the older man. For example, one conversation between the two men includes gay innuendo and double-meanings. Femm offers Penderel a toast of gin to 'illusion', believing the younger man will not appreciate it. Penderel responds by pointing out that he is 'precisely the right age for *that* toast'. The reference to illusion is interesting, and could be read as two men pretending to be something they are not to the outside world.

At the end of the film, Horace Femm appears at the front door as the travellers depart after experiencing a night of terror in his house. 'Goodbye,' he says condescendingly: '*So* happy to have met you.' Nothing could be camper than the sight of Femm giving a Queen Mary-like royal wave to his 'guests'. It is Ernest Thesiger and James Whale's camp sense of humour at its very best.

In Britain Thesiger made numerous memorable film appearances. In Laurence Olivier's version of Shakespeare's *Henry V* (1944) he appeared as the bejewelled and beautifully gowned Duke of Berri. In the film version of George Bernard Shaw's *Caesar and Cleopatra* (1945) he was the haughty Theodotus, the king's tutor, stealing the film from under the noses of its stars, Claude Rains and Vivien Leigh, especially when he screamed 'Woah! Alas! I *must* save the library!' In Anthony Asquith's *The Winslow Boy* (1948) he was the vain and snobbish Mr Ridgeley-Pierce who claims to be 'the greatest handwriting expert in the country,' but whose 'evidence' in the trial is quickly destroyed. He played the ghoulish undertaker in Brian Desmond Hurst's much-admired version of Dickens's *Scrooge* (1951), and the skeletal industrialist in *The Man in the White Suit* (1951), a brilliant performance, symbolizing all that is rotten with management. In D. H. Lawrence's *Sons and Lovers* (1960) he appeared in the small but memorable role of Paul Morel's patron.

Unlike the screen persona of someone like Charles Hawtrey from the *Carry On* comedies, Thesiger used his eccentricity in a variety of roles.

He embodied intelligence with wit and, occasionally, like a hostile alien in a horror film, he could instil sheer terror in an audience. In 1960, a few months before he died, Thesiger was created a Commander of the British Empire. He should have been created a Dame.

Other films of interest released in 1932

One year after she directed the German classic *Mädchen in Uniform* – about lesbianism in a girls' school – Leontine Sagan came to Britain to make *Men of Tomorrow*, a romantic drama for producer Alexander Korda.

Notes

1. *The Observer,* 15 January 1961.
2. Michael Elliman and Frederick Roll, *The Pink Plaque Guide to London* (Gay Men's Press, 1986), p. 202.
3. William K. Everson, *Classics of the Horror Film* (Citadel Press, 1974), p. 83.

1933

Soldiers of the King

Vivacious, ebullient, uninhibited comedienne Cicely Courtneidge revelled in eccentric roles, some of which involved cross-dressing or 'butch' behaviour. Later in her career, helped by Bryan Forbes's sensitive direction, she gave a memorable, understated performance in a character role as cat-loving Mavis, the ex-music hall player, in *The L-Shaped Room* (see 1962). This was one of the first explicitly lesbian film roles. However, thirty years earlier she appeared in *Soldiers of the King* in which she gave an intriguing performance as Maisy, a boyish male impersonator, expressing tenderness to the ingenue, and showing very little interest in men, especially Edward Everett Horton, her prissy leading man.

In *Soldiers of the King* Cicely plays the dual roles of retired music hall artist Jenny Marvello and her daughter Maisy. They're members of the 'Royal family of music hall players descended from Nell Gwynn', but the film is really nothing more than an excuse for Cicely to show off her gifts as a male impersonator. Dressed in a soldier's uniform, with a twitching moustache, plenty of thigh-slapping, and an excess of grimacing, she opens the film with the patriotic, show-stopping title song. However, nothing can prepare us for the shock of seeing Maisy *without* her soldier's uniform. At a family gathering, when Jenny passes on her crown of 'Queen of the Marvellos' to her daughter, Maisy has her back to the camera. But when she turns round, revealing a strikingly masculine look and bobbed-hair, and launches into a chorus of 'I'm a jolly good fellow!', it's lesbiana more or less unashamed!

When pretty young Judy (Dorothy Hyson) is offered a lift in a car by an admirer, Maisy hijacks her. 'You get into *my* car,' she commands. 'You and I are going to work very hard together. You can have admirers, but there must never be any really serious affair. I had one years ago and gave it up.' Later, when the admirer visits Judy in her dressing-room he discovers flowers have been sent to her from a rival suitor. 'You'd better not let Maisy see you smiling at men,' he warns, 'It's not the Marvello tradition!' He later adds: 'I hear Maisy's very fond of you.'

When Maisy performs a song called 'The Moment I Saw You' at the music hall in top hat and tails, she is completely at ease with herself, and sings revealingly: 'You were the girl I was meant to adore/I knew it the moment I saw you.' After the show, when Edward Everett Horton invites her to supper, she responds: 'Don't be silly. Go away.' Throughout most of the film, Maisy seems uncomfortable around men, though she does admit to Judy (with her arms stretched across the young woman's legs!) she once had a 'little romance' with a soldier.

When Maisy discovers Judy is being courted by a handsome young soldier, played by dishy Anthony Bushell, she confronts him, saying: 'Judy belongs to *me*. She doesn't go out with you even if I have to keep her under lock and key!' After Judy has defied Maisy, and been dismissed from the troupe by Jenny for going out with the soldier, Maisy has a showdown in her dressing-room with her mother. In the film's dramatic highlight Maisy prepares to leave the family and consequently break up the act. Dressed as a man she runs out of the theatre in pursuit of Judy.

At the end of the film, everything is sorted out, the troupe is saved, Judy gets her soldier, and Maisy remains the object of Edward Everett Horton's dubious affections. After all, this *was* family entertainment – and a major box office success of its time. Even so, the climax finds Maisy performing Noel Gay's rousing 'There's Something about a Soldier'. In later films, even those co-starring her husband Jack Hulbert, she's still on parade, with her military bearing, gruff voice, forever one of the principal boys. But strictly only 'in performance', not in her private life.

Tiger Bay

In *Tiger Bay* the beautiful Chinese–American star Anna May Wong plays Lui Cheng, owner of a dockside restaurant. The original script located the story in London, but censors demanded that the film be set in South America. Like Courtneidge's Maisy in *Soldiers of the King*, Lui

Cheng is very protective of a younger woman. In *Tiger Bay* she takes good care of her 'ward', Letty (Rene Ray), protecting her from the unwanted attentions of her brutal customers. These are described in the film as the 'riff-raff of the Seven Seas'. But the love and care Lui Cheng lavishes on the young woman is more than maternal, and one cannot help but detect a hint of lesbian feeling in her relationship with Letty. In most of her films Anna May Wong was either murdered or committed suicide in the final reel. Such was the fate of the first Chinese–American movie star! *Tiger Bay* is no exception and in keeping with convention, Lui Cheng sacrifices herself to save Letty, knowing that she will live happily ever after with the hero. The difference between *Tiger Bay* and Anna May Wong's other movies is that she dies at the end of this film to save the life of a *woman*.

Other films of interest released in 1933

Herbert Wilcox produced and directed Noel Coward's operetta *Bitter Sweet* with Anna Neagle; Emlyn Williams contributed to the screenplay of *Friday the Thirteenth* and appeared as the blackmailer in the segment entitled 'Blake, Gentleman of Fortune'; in *The Good Companions* John Gielgud was an unlikely leading man to Jessie Matthews in a comedy about a concert party; the war drama *I Was a Spy*, starring the popular German actor Conrad Veidt, won the *Film Weekly* award; weedy-looking Charles Hawtrey made an early film appearance in the comedy *The Melody Maker*; musical-comedy star Billy Milton appeared in *Three Men in a Boat*, a comedy about the misadventures of three friends on a boating holiday; producer Alexander Korda enjoyed an international success with his lavish historical drama *The Private Life of Henry VIII* and his star, Charles Laughton, won a Best Actor Oscar.

1934

Say it with Flowers

Images of lesbians in early British films are rare and easily overlooked, so if you blink you'll miss flower seller Kate's brief encounter with a beautiful, smartly dressed, but stereotypically mannish lesbian in the low-budget but charming comedy *Say it with Flowers*. Set in a street market in the Old Kent Road, she strides up to Kate's flower stall, dressed in a suit, tie, wide-brimmed hat and cane. 'Good morning, Sir,' says Kate, played by Mary Clare, not realizing the gender of her customer. The camera cuts to a shot of the lesbian with a surprised look on her face. Immediately Kate gulps an apology: 'Good morning, *Miss.*' The lesbian asks for a red rose (in a deep voice!) and, after she has left, Kate is then approached by a giggling, effeminate sissy who greets Kate cheerily: 'Hello. Good morning, Kate. Could I have a buttonhole?' Kate replies: 'Well, I haven't any pansies. A few violets?' Says the sissy: 'That'll do nicely.' Bursting into a fit of giggles he adds: 'Do you mind if I pay you on Thursday?' After he has departed, Kate turns to her friend Sam and exclaims: '*Struth*. What do you make of *that*, Sam? Well, boys will be girls, and girls will be boys!' This brief inclusion of a lesbian and gay man in the film is an unexpected acknowledgement of our existence, even if we are caricatured.

My Song for You

My Song for You is a musical set in Vienna and stars the Polish tenor Jan Kiepura. In the film this most unusual leading man enjoys a close friendship with his business manager, played by Sonnie Hale. There is a frivolity in Kiepura's screen persona which is appealing. He doesn't take himself too seriously and thus establishes tremendous rapport with Hale who is wonderfully unselfconscious as an uninhibited fairy. There is one particularly delightful sequence when the two men come together in a most revealing way. First, Kiepura pinches Hale's bum and begins serenading him with a song called 'I'd Do the Same For You.' Hale responds by clasping his hands to his heart while Kiepura drops to his knees, continuing to serenade his friend. Finally, Kiepura slaps Hale on the behind, and the two men prance around the room with joyful abandon!

Nina Mae McKinney and Alberta Hunter

In 1929 sixteen-year-old Nina Mae McKinney was 'discovered' in the chorus line of the Broadway revue *Blackbirds of 1928* , and transported to Hollywood. Here she made an impressive screen debut in *Hallelujah*, one of the first films to feature a black cast. Energetic and strikingly beautiful, McKinney was an overnight sensation. She was acknowledged as America's first black movie star, and critic Richard Watts Jr described her as 'assuredly one of the most beautiful women of our time'. He even named her 'The Black Garbo'. A blues shouter in the tradition of Gertrude 'Ma' Rainey and Bessie Smith, Nina's moment of Hollywood glory was brief. In the early 1930s black actors who became movie stars were expected to play comic servants, and within a few years Nina found herself struggling to find movie roles of integrity.

Throughout the 1920s and 1930s, some black American entertainers pursued their careers in Europe where they experienced less racism and more hospitality than in the United States. Among them was blues singer Alberta Hunter who co-starred with Paul Robeson in the London version of the musical *Show Boat* (1928). She later recalled: 'The Negro artists went to Europe because we were recognized and given a chance. In Europe they had your name up in lights. People in the United States would not give us that chance.'[1]

During the 1920s and 1930s, women like Alberta Hunter, Josephine Baker, Adelaide Hall and Elisabeth Welch found Europe offered more possibilities for work and acclaim, and they captured the continent with their songs, beauty, elegance and style. In 1932 Nina travelled to Paris with her pianist, black gay Garland Wilson, and the following year they made their London debut. In 1934 Nina made her first British film appearance as a guest artiste in the musical finale of *Kentucky*

Minstrels. In 1935 Nina starred opposite Paul Robeson in the adventure-drama *Sanders of the River*, but her performance as an African was not convincing. Said *Film Weekly* : 'Miss McKinney is just about as much at home in the jungle as, say, a Harlem nightclub entertainer. Sophistication is written all over her personality.' In 1938 Nina made her final British film appearance in *On Velvet*. Unused footage, possibly from *Kentucky Minstrels*, featuring Nina and her accompanist Garland Wilson, was incorporated into this low-budget comedy.

Off-screen, Nina led a troubled existence. Married to Jimmy Monroe (later the husband of Billie Holiday), she became addicted to drugs. She also had many affairs with men and women. In a recent biography of Josephine Baker, black American singer and dancer Maude Russell describes one of the reasons why women like Nina were drawn into relationships with other women at that time:

> Many of us had been kind of abused by producers, directors, leading men – if they liked girls. In those days, men only wanted what they wanted, they didn't care about pleasing a girl.
> And girls needed tenderness, so we had girl friendships, the famous lady lovers, but lesbians weren't well accepted in show business, they were called bull dykers. I guess we were bisexual, is what you would call it today.[2]

However, although there is very little knowledge available about Nina's affairs with women (though rumour has it she once had a 'liaison' with silent Hollywood star Clara Bow), Donald Clarke's recent biography of Billie Holiday, *Wishing on the Moon*, reveals that by the late 1930s Nina 'had turned lesbian'. In the 1940s Nina attempted a Hollywood comeback but the only roles available to her were bit parts as maids. When she died in obscurity in 1967 at the age of fifty-four, not even *Variety* published an obituary.

In 1934 Nina was announced as one of the many guest stars of the musical extravaganza *Radio Parade of 1935*, released in December 1934. However, for reasons which have not come to light, she was replaced by Alberta Hunter. In the 1920s Alberta projected an image of a tough woman who could take care of herself. Mostly she sang about anguished love affairs and these had a special resonance for gay audiences. Incredibly, Alberta made only one screen appearance in her entire career. In *Radio Parade of 1935* she makes a memorable appearance in the film's finale dressed in a white robe singing 'Black Shadows Are Haunting Me' with John Payne and his Negro Choir. Her biography says:

> Alberta was a lesbian (but) she grew up in an era that did not permit discussion of sexuality, much less acceptance of homosexuality. The subject matter remained one she refused to discuss. But she went further. Alberta did everything to conceal this preference all her life. In her mind lesbianism tarnished the image of propriety and respectability she struggled so hard to achieve.[3]

Brian Desmond Hurst

Film director Brian Desmond Hurst was the son of a distinguished surgeon. Born in 1895 in south Belfast, he was christened Hans Moore Hawthorn Hurst but changed his name during the First World War because Hans was a German name. Educated at Westminster, Hurst enjoyed an adventurous and varied career before becoming a film director. At the age of fourteen-and-a-half he ran away from his Belfast school and joined the army. At fifteen-and-a-half he was in Gallipoli with the Royal Irish Rifles and, at the end of the war, having survived being a prisoner of war, a bayonet wound and malaria, he retired from army life – a captain.

In his unpublished autobiography, Hurst is quite open about his gay sexuality, and recalls his first sexual experience at the age of sixteen:

> I was in an alleyway with a boy called Robert Montgomery. It was so nice and exciting that I made him do it again the very next night. We went for walks after that into the wasteland round about where we lived. I'm not sure whether I did the same to him or not, but I certainly used to feel him in those dark places.[4]

Undecided about what to do after leaving the army, Hurst studied medicine but dropped that in favour of newspaper reporting. On a trip to Canada in 1922 he worked as a lumberjack, and then took up art. After studying art in Paris at L'Ecole des Beaux Arts and L'Académie Julien, he migrated to America and became a fashionable painter of portraits and murals. In 1925 a lucrative commission took him to California and, while in Los Angeles, he met his cousin, film director and fellow Irishman, John Ford. Hurst acted as his assistant and art director on a number of silent films. Years later, film critic David Robinson was a guest at a dinner party in a London restaurant attended by John Ford. He recalls: 'Ford asked someone to call his cousin, Brian Desmond Hurst, and invite him to join the party. One of the guests made a remark about Hurst being gay and Ford responded: "So what if he is? Doesn't *everyone* have a gay cousin?"'[5]

When he returned to Britain, Hurst was determined to become a film director in his own right. He began directing films in 1934, beginning with *Riders of the Sea* and *The Tell Tale Heart*. Until the 1960s he found regular work in a variety of genres, everything from Ivor Novello's lavish musical *Glamorous Night* (1937) to *Simba* (1955), a powerful drama about the Mau Mau uprising starring Dirk Bogarde. Hurst has never acquired the status of other British film directors, including his contemporaries, Hitchcock, David Lean and Carol Reed. So perhaps the time has come for a reassessment of his career. In some ways he is difficult to pigeon-hole, because he worked in different genres. But he did excel at making melodramas, in which he often cast gay actors, or included gay characters, such as the popular wartime classic *Dangerous Moonlight* (see 1941) starring Anton Walbrook, *Hungry Hill* (1947), based on the novel by Daphne du Maurier and starring Dennis Price, and *The Mark of Cain* (see 1948) starring Eric Portman. In his prison drama *Prison Without Bars* (see 1938) lesbian actress Mary Morris registered in a strong supporting role, and there are some queer goings-on in his crime thriller *Alibi* (see 1942). Hurst was also responsible for a much-admired wartime documentary, *Theirs is the Glory* (1945), a record of the landings at Arnhem in 1944 and the subsequent battle for the Rhine bridge. He later made the delightful musical *Trottie True* (1949), starring Jean Kent as a Gaiety girl from the music halls who marries a duke; *Scrooge* (1951), a highly praised version of Dickens's *A Christmas Carol* starring Alistair Sim; and the war drama *The Malta Story* (1953) starring Alec Guinness.

Off-screen, Hurst had a reputation for being something of a bully on the set of his films. A young Ian Carmichael started his film career as a bit player in the late 1940s, and later recalled Hurst's treatment of him:

I remember being on location in Camden Town for *Trottie True*. The director was Brian Desmond Hurst and, at one point, the cameraman asked me 'What are you doing here?' and I said, 'Well, the director's just told me I've got to do so-and-so, but in this bit of script they sent me I do something else.' Hurst heard this, turned round, and absolutely snapped my head off with, 'Will you bloody well learn to do as you're told?' I never looked favourably on Brian Desmond Hurst from that day onwards.[6]

In 1942 Hurst featured his friend and neighbour, singer Elisabeth Welch, as a Parisian cabaret entertainer in *Alibi*. Elisabeth came to London in 1933 and visited friends like Brian and Hermione Gingold in Knightsbridge. She recalls:

I met him some years before we made *Alibi*. He gave fantastic parties and everybody came, including Ivor Novello. Everybody knew Brian as a director who was very important in the film world. He lived in a private mews in a beautiful studio which had a gallery all around the inside. He always had plenty of money. Brian and Hermione were lovely people and persuaded me to move into a flat there. That's how we became neighbours. It was a well-known and very exclusive artist's residential section of Knighstbridge. Many big names lived there. We had pianists, musicians, painters – a real 'colony' of creative, elegant people. I suppose you could say it was the Greenwich Village of London! A lot of people envied us. It was a wonderful place to live – secluded, respectable, but fun.[7]

Hurst never hid the fact that he was gay, at least amongst the 'safe' film and theatre colony. However, before the 1967 Sexual Offences Act partially decriminalized gay sexuality, it seems incredible that Hurst was never caught and arrested. A few years before he died, film actress and 1950s 'blonde bombshell' Diana Dors gave this revealing insight into Hurst's private life and outrageous personality:

Brian Desmond Hurst was very prominent in the industry. Brian was, and still is, one of the most colourful characters I have ever met. He lived in great splendour amidst wealth inherited from his Irish ancestors with, amongst other things, carved wooden saints around his bedhead, and stained glass windows depicting

religious scenes in the bedroom, for he was a devout Catholic.
His conversation was always spiced with acid witticisms, and his
impersonation of Queen Victoria on the lavatory. . . was unsur-
passed, and famous throughout show business.

He always had a penchant for beautiful boys, loving to have
them around all the time. Brian always insisted that in order to
gain his favour, *everybody* must be 'pretty, witty or rich'! Brian's
social gatherings were always amusing, and inevitably one could
be sure of a great deal of enjoyment at his home. One summer
afternoon, while we were all sipping champagne, he drew my
attention to a young labourer who was working outside his
window. . . he was stripped to the waist and sported a beautiful
brown chest above his tightly fitting jeans. 'Go and get him,'
ordered the wicked old rogue. . . and the boy was ceremoniously
ushered into his elegant drawing room. Offering him a glass of
bubbly. . . Brian waited until he had drunk the champagne and
remarked lecherously, his eyes fixed on the lower half of the boy's
anatomy, 'Right, we've all seen what you have on display in the
shop window, now let's find out what you've got at the back of
the store!'[8]

Hurst also made an impression on the young actor and writer Bryan
Forbes when the latter was working as an actor in *The Black Tent*
(1956). William MacQuitty, the film's producer, asked Forbes to rewrite
Robin Maugham's first draft screenplay. Forbes remembers Hurst as:

an amiable but wicked old queen who did not take kindly to my
employment. Bill MacQuitty had forewarned me that I would
meet with a hostile reception and urged me to answer in kind.
Sure enough when I encountered Brian for the first time, he
immediately went on the attack. 'Why have they given me a third-
rate writer like you?' he said in his thick Irish brogue. Thanks to
Bill I was prepared for this. 'Probably because you're a third-rate
director,' I said. From that moment on we got on famously.[9]

William Roache, who is famous for his continuing role on British
television as Ken Barlow in the long-running drama series *Coronation
Street*, was a young, inexperienced actor in the late 1950s when Hurst
invited him to his mews house in Belgravia:

I was shown into a long room whose walls were covered with paintings. Very expensive statues and a profusion of *objets d'art* were scattered everywhere. At the far end, sitting in a massive chair behind an ornate antique desk, was Brian Desmond Hurst. He was a big man, both physically and in personality.[10]

After fixing him up with a small part in his film *Behind the Mask*, Hurst propositioned Roache:

'Right, you've got the part. Now, I don't mind telling you I'd like to go to bed with you. But don't worry about it. I never force myself on anybody.' My jaw dropped and I stared at him. 'Don't make up your mind now,' he said. 'It's open house here every evening; you're very welcome to come along and meet some famous people. Off you go now, and I'll see you on Monday for the filming.' I walked out of there in a daze. . . . As for his proposition, it was never mentioned again, and you were all right as long as you made sure you weren't the last to leave. . . . I was extremely grateful to Brian Desmond Hurst for giving me that first break. But I found later that you never mentioned you had made a film for him, because it was automatically assumed you had got it for the wrong reasons.[11]

The legendary film magnate J. Arthur Rank expected everyone connected with his organization to behave in a respectable manner, and yet he showed unexpected tolerance towards Hurst's gay sexuality. In his unpublished autobiography, Hurst recalled an encounter he had with Rank sometime in the late 1940s:

After lunch, Arthur Rank took me for a walk in his garden. He showed me a beautiful bank of daffodils. 'How many daffodils do you think there are growing on that bank?' Thinking to be very flattering, I said: 'Well, Arthur, there must be quite sixteen thousand.' He replied: 'Thirty-six thousand.' Then he told me about a sermon he had preached to the boys at bible class that morning. I admired the espaliered apple trees on the garden walls. Suddenly he paused and turned to me. He said in his slightly Northern accent: 'I've heard some peculiar things about you, lad.' 'There's no doubt about that,' I replied. 'Arthur, I am as God made me.' He patted me on the shoulder and said: 'I understand you.' The next morning I signed a three-year contract with the Rank Organization.[12]

It seems Hurst was a reliable journeyman film director who rarely aspired to the great heights of a David Lean or Carol Reed. He could also grow tired of a project if his heart wasn't in it. Says actress Muriel Pavlow, who appeared in *The Malta Story*: 'I thought he was very talented and I liked his direction, but he was inclined to get a bit bored with a project. Towards the end of the film you could see that his interest was waning.'[13]

However, there were at least two film projects, both about famous historical figures who were gay, which Hurst was involved with, and enthusiastic about. Sadly, neither materialized. One was the story of T. E. Lawrence, the legendary Lawrence of Arabia, which he was going to direct for the internationally-acclaimed producer Alexander Korda. However, in *The Making of David Lean's Lawrence of Arabia*, Adrian Turner says that Hurst was not a good choice,

> despite his knowledge of Arabic and his acquaintance with Lawrence himself. Then there was the casting of Lawrence. . .
>
> The initial casting choice was Walter Hudd, who did several screen and costume tests in 1936. Hudd had also been casually recommended by Lawrence, since the actor already played a thinly-disguised Lawrence – Private Meek in Bernard Shaw's play *Too Good To Be Good*. Then John Clements did a test, followed by Clifford Evans, Laurence Olivier, Robert Donat and Leslie Howard.[14]

In 1936, while Hurst was scouting locations in Jerusalem, Korda abruptly cancelled the project. In 1952 Hurst's dream of making *The Last Romantic*, a film about Ludwig II, the so-called 'mad' King of Bavaria, got underway, but the production was quickly abandoned. A project close to his heart, it was never realized. He later said:

> Though I made a lot of preparation for the film, the (Bavarian) Royal Family didn't want any mention whatsoever of the King's homosexuality so it became pointless to continue with it. A year or so later, Count von Molo. . . made a film about Ludwig, which was not a success. Neither was the more recent version by Visconti.[15]

In 1962 Hurst directed his final film, *Playboy of the Western World*, and retired. He died on 26 September 1986 at the age of 91. In the 1930s, at the beginning of his film career, he said:

> A film director, like a novelist, must be a man of wide sympathies, of great experience. He must see humanity as individuals, not as a collective mass; he must understand their problems and have an imagination vivid enough to share their point of view. That is an ideal to aim at but one which few of us attain.[16]

Other films of interest released in 1934

In *Autumn Crocus* Ivor Novello starred in a romantic drama about a spinster school teacher on holiday in the Tyrol who falls in love with a dashing innkeeper. It was his last screen appearance. 'I love seeing films,' he said. 'But I hate doing them.'; the musical *Evensong*, with a screenplay based on a novel by Beverley Nichols, had a cast that included Emlyn Williams, and an enchanting leading lady in Evelyn Laye. She starred as an Irish prima donna who gives up love for a career. The film was full of music, including operatic excerpts from *La Bohème* and *La Traviata*, as well as Ivor Novello's 'Keep the Home Fires Burning'; America's Lorenz Hart provided the lyrics to three Jessie Matthews' songs in the delightful musical *Evergreen*. Emlyn Williams contributed to the screenplay; German leading lady Dolly Haas came to Britain to star in *Girls Will Be Boys*, a comedy about a girl who poses as the grandson of a noble misogynist; Christopher Isherwood contributed to the screenplay of *Little Friend*, a drama about a child's attempted suicide which stops her parents' divorce; ballet dancer Anton Dolin choreographed the lavish musical *Chu Chin Chow* which included a spectacular dance arrangement for Anna May Wong and ensemble in the film's finale.

Notes

1. Frank C. Taylor with Gerald Cook, *Alberta: A Celebration in Blues* (McGraw-Hill, 1987), p. 88.
2. Jean-Claude Baker and Chris Chase, *Josephine: The Hungry Heart* (Adams Media Corporation, 1993), p. 63–4.
3. Taylor with Cook, pp. 42–4.
4. Brian Desmond Hurst, *Travelling the Road*, unpublished autobiography, BFI archives, p. 14.
5. David Robinson, interview with the author, 1995.
6. Brian McFarlane (ed.), *Sixty Voices: Celebrities Recall the Golden Age of British Cinema* (British Film Institute, 1992), p. 55.
7. Elisabeth Welch, interview with the author, 1995.
8. Diana Dors, *Behind Closed Dors* (A Star Book, 1979), pp. 99–100.
9. Bryan Forbes, *A Divided Life: Memoirs* (Heinemann, 1992), pp. 307–8.
10. William Roache, *Ken and Me* (Simon & Schuster, 1993), pp. 98–100.
11. *Ibid.* p. xx.
12. Hurst, p. 141.
13. McFarlane, p. 185.
14. Adrian Turner, *The Making of David Lean's Lawrence of Arabia* (Dragon's World, 1994), pp. 28–9.
15. Hurst, p. 175.
16. Press release for *Prison Without Bars*. August 1938.

1935

First a Girl

First a Girl is a spectacular and sophisticated musical extravanganza, directed by Victor Saville, in which the divine Jessie Matthews confuses her co-stars, Anna Lee (as the Princess) and Griffith Jones (as Robert) by cross-dressing and smoking a cigar. She plays a shopgirl who becomes a star by pretending to be a male female impersonator called Bill. At the beginning of the film there is a lovely, playful sequence in which Jessie, dancing with the shopgirls, suddenly takes centre stage with her famous high-kicks. Jessie then grabs one of the women and forces her to dance with her, but their fun ends when the women pretend to become *too* intimate and slap each other.

At first Robert thinks Bill is a weak and effeminate man. He says to the Princess: 'I dislike men who make marvellous girls.' However, he quickly realizes that Bill is really a woman in disguise. There follows a delightful scene in which Bill's mentor, played by Sonnie Hale, Jessie's husband and frequent collaborator, teaches 'him' how to smile like a man: 'At the Princess, *not* the Prince!' The film was a remake of a German comedy called *Viktor und Viktoria* and four decades later Blake Edwards directed this classic as a lavish if vulgar musical vehicle for his wife Julie Andrews. *First a Girl* is a charming study of role reversal with Jessie at her most entrancing. When Jessie masquerades as a man, her image has lesbian overtones, but inevitably the film treads carefully around the lesbian and gay implications in the story. Other British films of the 1930s which have similar themes of this playful, high-spirited androgyny include a version of Shakespeare's *As You Like It* (1936), starring Elisabeth Bergner as Rosalind, and *Wings of the Morning* (1937), a romantic comedy starring Annabella as a Spanish gypsy princess posing as a boy.

Music Hath Charms

Music Hath Charms is a modest musical revue built around the talents of the popular bandleader Henry Hall. Preparing one of his famous weekly broadcasts he is thrown into a state of panic when he discovers that his BBC Dance Orchestra is caught in a traffic jam. One by one the members arrive, to Hall's relief, and join in the programme. Other members are seen at various stages of travelling through the streets of London. While Hall and the orchestra play 'Just Little Bits and Pieces' on the soundtrack, a tall, lanky but rather queer looking policeman is seen directing traffic in the middle of the road. Suddenly he begins to bob up and down to the music. Unexpectedly the policeman gives a high kick in the air, one that Jessie Matthews would be proud of, and gyrates in a most provocative manner, to the amusement of passers by! He ends this delightfully silly dance by wiggling his body and swivelling his hips.

Benjamin Britten

A graduate of the Royal College of Music, Benjamin Britten (1913–76) became one of the most famous and influential composers of his time. He composed songs, documentary film music, operas and musical epics such as his *War Requiem*, and much of his output was written for his lover, tenor Peter Pears (1910–86). Britten's gay sexuality had an important effect upon his work. In *The Pink Plaque Guide to London*, Michael Elliman and Frederick Roll quote the musicologist Hans Keller who referred to 'the enormous creative advantage of Britten's homosexuality' which 'placed him in the privileged position of discovering and musically defining new truths which otherwise might not have been accessible to him.' Elliman and Roll also identify 'an underlying theme of homoeroticism' running through Britten's major operas, *Peter Grimes*, *The Turn of the Screw*, *Billy Budd* and *Death in Venice*.[1]

Britten's professional music career began in 1935 when he joined the GPO Film Unit. This was headed by producer John Grierson who believed that film could be used as the most important tool in educating people about democracy, and as a way of gaining an understanding about how society worked. Grierson was passionate about creating a new art form, the 'documentary', and some of his films were influenced by the gay Russian film director Sergei Eisenstein. The meanings of Grierson's films were also enhanced by the employment of Britten, who provided musical settings for the verse commentary of the gay poet W. H. Auden (1907–73). *Coal Face* (1935) was the first of several Britten–Auden collaborations, and the start of a long-lasting friendship between the two men. However, while Grierson's documentaries were among the first to depict the lives of working-class people, and provide a 'realism' not often seen in British cinema, the treatment of the subject matter was something else altogether. The films often romanticized their subject matter, and the middle-class 'high art' approach, including the contributions of Britten and Auden, could be very distracting.

Coal Face

Coal Face was put together mainly from library material, and supplemented by film shot (but not used) by director Robert Flaherty for another documentary project, *Industrial Britain* (1933). New location footage was shot inside coal mines by various members of Grierson's GPO Film Unit, and the studio work was directed by Alberto Cavalcanti. He was also responsible for assembling the film and supervising the highly experimental soundtrack. While *Coal Face* stressed the importance of the coalmining industry to the British economy, and criticized its accident record, it failed to show the lives of the miners. For example, the major social and political issues of the 1920s and 1930s, including low wages, unemployment, and the fight against fascism, were hardly dealt with by Grierson and his team who worked within a system of state sponsorship.

From a gay perspective, the music and poetry of Britten and Auden provide an interesting dimension to *Coal Face*, but it is the film's homoeroticism which has caught the attention of some gay observers. For example, film-maker Jeff Cole has described *Coal Face* as embodying a homoerotic undercurrent in the way the bodies of coal miners are filmed:

> In *Coal Face* we see the sweaty miners hacking away at the coal seam, their naked torsos in full frame and it cannot be escaped that there is a certain aestheticization of their bodies. . . there is a homoeroticism to the sequence exemplified by one of the miners

taking off his shirt to reveal his proud torso at the beginning of the sequence, in a way that is used coyly and provocatively, because we don't then go straight to the shots of the miners digging but to a short informative section on lamps in the mine.[2]

The men who worked for Grierson in the GPO Film Unit viewed themselves as left-wing propagandists with social messages to convey. Though not many of them were communists, they were influenced by Russian revolutionary film-makers, studied their work on montage and propaganda, and admired the way they portrayed the heroic worker in their films.

In Britain middle-class gays have sometimes been attracted to young, muscular working-class men and this found expression in E. M. Forster's only gay novel, *Maurice*, written in 1914, but not published until after his death in 1970. Jeff Cole suggests that a connection can be made between the desires of some of the middle-class men involved in the British Documentary Movement, and the images they portrayed of working-class masculinity in their films. He says they were men from the same class background and education process of public school and then Oxford or Cambridge University, worlds where women were excluded and rather despised:

> It was in this context that they worked for what was considered by them very little money (for people of the professional classes), but they were fired by the enthusiasm for the work and the camaraderie in making films. Says director Harry Watt: 'The other extraordinary atmosphere about the office was the absolute monasticism of it. We were all normal, pretty well, but we were absolutely forbidden to get married, and even the fact of having girl friends was rather kept in the background.' The very discreet reference to the homosexuality of some members of the Unit by Watt is the only one I have found from members of the British Documentary Movement, and yet the whole background of public schools, men's colleges at Cambridge and then the male atmosphere of the units, absolutely stinks of repressed homosexuality. Not necessarily repressed homosexuality of the individuals in the group, but certainly of their society at the time . . . . Both Auden and Britten were gay men and although they were not necessarily open about it they were clearly very much a

part of the world which went out to make these films. Their work was used in a way so as to aestheticize the films and give them credence as 'a work of art'.[3]

Other films of interest released in 1935

In *The Passing of the Third Floor Back* Conrad Veidt gave a memorable performance as the Christ-like stranger whose presence alters the unpleasant atmosphere of a Bloomsbury boarding house.

Notes

1. Michael Elliman and Frederick Roll, *The Pink Plaque Guide to London* (Gay Men's Press, 1986), p. 26.

2. Jeff Cole, unpublished essay (London College of Printing, 1989).

3. *Ibid.*

1936

It's Love Again

Following the success of *Evergreen* and *First a Girl*, Jessie Matthews and Victor Saville collaborated again on their third musical *It's Love Again*. In this enjoyably witty creation, Jessie gives one of her best performances as an ambitious, aspiring stage actress who hopes to become famous by impersonating a big-game hunter.

In the supporting cast is the wonderful American-born actor Ernest Milton, who was equally adept at Shakespearean tragedy and light comedy. He made occasional appearances in British films as 'sissy' types. In *It's Love Again* he plays an impresario called Archibald Raymond. Jessie's leading man, Robert Young, imported from Hollywood, refers to Archibald as a 'queer duck'. The description is accurate. Very commanding and draped in a hooded robe, Archibald is a temperamental and flamboyant queen bee with a deadly sting. When he is greeted by an ageing actress called Francine, Archibald's pianist describes her to a curious Jessie as 'Raymond's star before she started dodging mother parts in Hollywood'. Says Archibald to Francine: 'You've saved my life. I was about to enter a convent.' Quickly correcting himself he adds 'a monastery'. Archibald and Francine also join together at the piano for a rousing rendition of 'When You Wore a Tulip'.

Song of Freedom

Another flamboyant gay impresario appears in *Song of Freedom*, a melodrama with songs. Here Esmé Percy (previously seen as Handel Fane in Hitchcock's *Murder*) plays Gabriel Donozetti, an uninhibited, hysterical Italian who is not impressed with Britain's aspiring opera singers. 'In this country there are hundreds either roaring like lions, or cooing like gentlemen from the harem!' he complains in a high-pitched voice. On his arrival in London by ship he hears a black dockworker singing, and later insists on returning to the docks to find him. His assistant isn't impressed: 'He's *only* a coloured man.' But the dockworker, John Zinga, is played by Paul Robeson, often billed as 'the greatest singing star of the age', and Donozetti knows there is talent there. He responds to his assistant, with great passion: 'What's the matter of the colour of his skin when he has colour in his voice – power, beauty. I go to find him – I cannot *live* until I find him.' After finding Zinga singing in a pub, Donozetti offers him a contract, and launches him on a career as an opera singer.

Jury's Evidence

Jury's Evidence is an above-average crime thriller starring Margaret Lockwood, who later became Britain's Wicked Lady, as a typist who is unwittingly involved in murder. The cast also features an hilarious performance from Jane Millican as a butch lesbian called Agatha, dressed in tweed suits and ties. She is forever slapping Lockwood on the back, or trying to entice her on a weekend camping trip. 'Two days under canvas with me will make a man of you!' she says.

Calling the Tune

Not only does the musical *Calling the Tune* include 'dresses by Norman Hartnell', but in a scene set in RADA, a portrait of Charles Laughton appears on the wall. Later, elegant black gay pianist Reginald Foresythe appears briefly, entertaining in a posh restaurant with a piano solo he composed for the film called 'Evergreen Restaurant'. When the star of the film, Adèle Dixon, posing as a Russian princess, enters the restaurant and orders a meal, she is quickly observed by two swishy gays gossiping at a nearby table. 'How do you pronounce *her* name?' asks one of the woopsies, mincing while munching on a breadstick. 'You can't without a flute,' his intimate companion replies bitchily. Their exchange is followed by brief scenes of other couples in the restaurant trying to guess what the 'Russian' Adèle is going to do for a living. Says the wrist-flapping, breadstick-munching gay, tapping his friend on the hand: 'She's going to open an opera house!'

Reginald Foresythe

Reginald Foresythe was an audacious pianist and bandleader who was also an innovative composer bringing classical techniques and a rare musical wit to jazz. Born in London in 1907, he was the son of a Yoruba (Nigerian) barrister and German mother. The family lived in the small West African community in the Shepherd's Bush area of London. Foresythe received a public-school education, and studied piano and composition. Throughout his life Foresythe used his upper-class British accent to achieve some measure of acceptance in an otherwise racially segregated world. In the 1930s in Britain he won respect in jazz circles for his bold and dazzling compositions such as 'Serenade for a Wealthy Widow' and 'Dodging a Divorcee'. Jazz giants, including Louis Armstrong and Fats Waller, admired him and recorded his compositions.

At the height of his popularity in the 1930s Foresythe made several guest appearances in films including *Jimmy Boy* (1935), *The Big Noise* (1936) and *Calling the Tune* (1936). In *Crackerjack* (1938) Burton Pierce dances to Foresythe's 'Dodging a Divorcee'.

When the American singer Elisabeth Welch settled in London in 1933, she began looking for an accompanist. She recalls:

> When I arrived in London I was offered cabaret and variety engagements, but I didn't know anyone who could accompany me. I was given Reggie's name and of course I'd heard about him in America and Paris. He was a sweet, simple, charming person. Immaculate and elegant. He loved good food and always talked with that wonderful English upper-class accent. We used to send him up but he didn't mind at all. He had a great sense of humour about himself. We all loved him. I used to go almost two or three times a week to see him perform his famous 'New Music' at the 400 Club, a very chic place in Leicester Square. Reggie was a very distinguished-looking person, and always wore a coat with a huge fur collar.[1]

Foresythe worked in Mayfair clubs until the beginning of the war. When the war broke out he was over-age for active service, but volunteered for the RAF anyway. Drafted into the RAF, he became an Intelligence Officer. A 'confirmed bachelor', no woman was ever associated with him. His gay liaisons were always discreet. He lived alone and, sadly, became an alcoholic.

In the 1930s Foresythe had been ahead of his time, but after the war time seemed to have passed him by. He was soon leading bands in obscure West Country hotels, and playing solo piano in drinking clubs around the West End. His career ended in obscurity and he died tragically young at the age of fifty-one in 1958.

Just before the coronation of Queen Elizabeth Foresythe received word from the Queen herself that his ballad 'Importune Me No More' – to words by a sixteenth-century Elizabethan lyricist – had been officially accepted for use by the Queen's own regiment. It was played at state functions and other court and military concerts, taking its place among the great English folk tunes.

Other films of interest released in 1936

Hitchcock's *The Secret Agent*, based on two of Somerset Maugham's *Ashenden* adventure stories, starred Robert Young as a villain who is superficially heterosexual, but displays an obvious interest in the straight hero, John Gielgud; two gay Americans visited Britain to take starring roles: Cary Grant in *The Amazing Quest of Ernest Bliss* and Douglass Montgomery in *Tropical Trouble* and *Everything is Thunder*. Montgomery had already been directed in Hollywood by James Whale in *Waterloo Bridge* and George Cukor in *Little Women*. After the war, in 1945, he returned to Britain for Anthony Asquith's *The Way to the Stars* and several other roles.

Notes
1. Elisabeth Welch, interview with the author, London, April 1995.

1937

I, Claudius

I, Claudius was Alexander Korda's ambitious but ill-fated attempt at filming Robert Graves's classic story of murder, lust and intrigue of Ancient Rome. Directed by Josef Von Sternberg, the film was abandoned after only a few weeks shooting when one of its stars, Merle Oberon, was involved in an automobile accident. Almost thirty years later the rushes were rediscovered and pieced together for inclusion in a fascinating BBC television documentary, narrated by Dirk Bogarde, called *The Epic That Never Was* (1965). Among the cast members included in the footage were Charles Laughton in the difficult, challenging role of the physically disabled, stammering Claudius ('nature never quite finished me'); Emlyn Williams as the effeminate psychopath Caligula; Flora Robson as the ageing Empress Olivia; and Merle Oberon as the depraved, immoral Messalina.

In *The Epic That Never Was*, Emlyn Williams described Caligula as 'a marvellous part' and recalled his first meeting with director Von Sternberg who told him: 'The part is a very cruel, degenerate man, perhaps a little bit sissy – not too much.' Williams continued: 'I was glad of that because I had had my fittings for the costumes which looked to me a little bit like two hostess gowns, a couple of short cocktail numbers and a false fringe. So I had to say to myself – watch out!'

The footage that exists of Williams's performance is most revealing. He plays Caligula as a beautiful but evil queen, and it is hardly surprising Empress Olivia describes him in one scene as 'the vilest, most despicable little reptile that the Gods ever created'. *The Epic That Never Was* also preserves examples of Laughton's magnificent performance as Claudius, including a scene on his farm with his effeminate, blond, curly-haired slave, Narcissus. Narrator Dirk Bogarde says when we watch Laughton's performance we experience 'his extraordinary sense of humility and shame . . . his wonderful sense of humanity, humour and strength.' After the death of Caligula, Claudius addresses the senate and condemns the evil and corrupt government of Rome. Says Bogarde: 'This is one of the most moving, beautiful and powerful speeches I have ever seen on the screen. It ranks in greatness and splendour to my mind with Olivier's Crispin Day speech in *Henry V*, and on another plane it has the humour, honesty and pain of Judy Garland's dressing-room scene in *A Star is Born*. Laughton here proves that he was kissed with genius.'

Over the Moon

Alexander Korda had better luck with his next project, the sparkling romantic comedy *Over the Moon* starring Merle Oberon as Jane, an heiress who takes off on a madcap spending spree. She is befriended and 'adopted' by Julia, a sophisticated fortune-hunter (a gloriously camp performance by Zena Dare) who takes innocent Jane under her wing. First, Julia persuades Jane to bring her stuffy fiancé, played by Rex Harrison, to a fashion parade in Lapelle, a classy department store in Grosvenor Square. The models include a swishy gay called François whose outrageous, effeminate posturing horrifies the macho Harrison. Next, Julia encourages Jane to throw a lavish party and enlists the help of her friend, Lord Petcliffe, played by Peter Haddon. Before Jane meets him, Julia describes him to her as 'an interior decorator by profession, a social organizer by choice and, well, never mind, dear, you'll see.'

Haddon steals every scene he appears in as the gay fortune-hunter and hanger-on, an upper-class sissy who is also a bit of a silly ass. Lord Petcliffe is first seen languishing in his extravagantly furnished bedroom wearing fluffy pink slippers and complaining to Julia on the telephone: 'We had a pageant last night. I wore myself to a positive shadow over some dreadful charity.' But he soon brightens up when Julia invites him to help Jane spend some of her millions!

Other films of interest released in 1937

In the crime thriller *Non-Stop New York* heavyweight character actors Francis L. Sullivan and Peter Bull played a couple of sinister queer villains. Bull was particularly creepy as a blackmailing hotel waiter; composer Benjamin Britten scored the feature *Love from a Stranger*, a crime drama based on an Agatha Christie novel starring Ann Harding and Basil Rathbone; Brian Desmond Hurst directed a screen version of Ivor Novello's Drury Lane musical hit *Glamorous Night*; Marlene Dietrich left Hollywood to come to Britain to star opposite Robert Donat in Korda's *Knight Without Armour*; music-hall star Arthur Lucan dragged up for the first time on screen as Old Mother Riley, the first of a long-running and popular series; Anton Walbrook starred in a sound remake of Ivor Novello's silent classic *The Rat*.

1938

Pygmalion

In George Bernard Shaw's 1913 stage play, *Pygmalion*, the Cockney speech patterns of flower seller Eliza Doolittle fascinate Henry Higgins, a bachelor professor of phonetics. On the basis of a wager made by his friend, Colonel Pickering, another confirmed bachelor, the professor agrees to teach Eliza the speech and deportment of a lady, vowing that she will be accepted by English high society. This plan is subsequently implemented at a grand ball with great success.

When it was announced that a screen version was going to be made, directed by Anthony Asquith and starring Wendy Hiller as Eliza, Shaw disapproved of the casting of Leslie Howard as Higgins. He preferred Charles Laughton, rejecting the idea that the film would lose the tenderness Howard would provide. Shaw said it was not a tender part, and not a love story. While the film was being made, he wrote to Gabiel Pascal, the film's producer, and said: 'It is amazing how hopelessly wrong Leslie is. However, the public will like him, and probably want him to marry Eliza, which is just what I don't want.'

It is interesting to look at *Pygmalion* from a gay perspective. Apart from Mrs Pearce (Jean Cadell), the elderly housekeeper, women do not figure in the lives of bossy, overbearing Higgins and kind, sensitive Pickering. Says Higgins to Pickering: 'I'm a confirmed old bachelor and likely to remain one!. . . I've taught scores of American millionairesses to speak English. . . the best-looking women in the world. . . they might just as well be blocks of wood!' When Eliza enters their lives, her relationship with Higgins remains platonic, and Pickering is very protective of her, reminding his friend after he has upset her: 'Doesn't it occur to you, Higgins, that the girl has some feelings?'

In one of the film's many enchanting and intimate moments, Higgins and Pickering demonstrate to Eliza how to dance at the ball. In Asquith's capable hands, as we observe the two men swirling around the room in each other's arms, it's presented as the most natural thing in the world.

Later, when Eliza is being prepared for her appearance at the ball, a scene begins with the angry face of Mrs Pearce looking straight towards the camera exclaiming: 'Did you ever see the like!' The camera then reveals a couple of gay hairdressers in conversation. They include the young Anthony Quayle who is billed on the end credits as 'French hairdresser'.

The grand ball sequence is among the film's alterations of Shaw's original play. Written by Shaw himself, it allows the audience to witness Eliza's triumph. At the ball, Higgins is concerned about the presence of the effeminate, long-haired ('if I cut my hair, nobody notices me!') but dangerous Count Aristid Karpathy (Esmé Percy) who, he fears, might expose Eliza. The Count is portrayed as a threat, a blackmailing queer. The ballroom sequence also includes an appearance by a tall, strident, monocled lesbian called Perfide (played by Viola Tree, who died shortly after this film was released. She was the daughter of Sir Herbert Beerbohm Tree), a journalist who writes for the *Globe*. She is accompanied by her small, fluffy blonde companion Ysabel (Iris Hoey), who writes for the *Sun*. Perfide and Ysabel have an air of writer Gertrude Stein and her companion Alice B. Toklas about them. Could Shaw or Asquith be acknowledging the existence of the most famous lesbian couple of the 1930s? The word perfidious means treacherous and dishonest but, unlike her friend, the Count, Perfide is sympathetically drawn. She's not a monster. When she introduces herself to Higgins, giving him a manly handshake, their encounter is observed by the Duchess (Irene Browne) who turns to Eliza and says: 'What *extraordinary* people seem to get in everywhere nowadays!'

Wendy Hiller had no doubts about the importance of Shaw's text. In an interview she gave to *Radio Times* in 1973 she said: 'Shaw quite simply wrote the most brilliant anti-romantic comedy of the century. To me there was never any question of her marrying or being in love with Higgins. Those who want that sort of ending are running absolutely counter to the author. We've all been brainwashed, if you like, into wanting conventional, happy-ever-after endings. So we get them.'

Mary Morris

Mary Morris was quite unlike any other British actress. With her authority and supreme self-assurance, she always stood out from the crowd, but she made only a handful of appearances in films, often in small roles which barely gave her an opportunity to shine. Off-stage (and screen) Morris's private life was rarely commented on by the press. So when Peter Noble described her in his book *Profiles and Personalities* in 1946, we were given a fascinating insight into the life of one of our most accomplished actresses. He said:

> Petite, large-eyed, gaminesque, Mary Morris is one of the most striking and unusual personalities on the English stage. Neither in appearance, outlook nor acting style does she resemble any other British actress. Like all great theatre personalities she is unique, and added to this she is independent, highly intelligent, sometimes arrogant. . . . Living in an artist's studio in Notting Hill Gate, she has solved the furniture shortage by making most of the furniture with her own hands. Beds, chairs, table, dresser – all these were made by Mary and her friend, Cecile Krog, daughter of a Norwegian playwright, who shares her flat with he . . . . Mary Morris does not fit easily into any category. Neither does she want to. She is distinctive, sometimes aggressive, Leftist, idealistic, sincere, talkative, talented, likeable. She is an Orson Welles fan, a chain smoker, likes wearing slacks and staying in bed until lunch.[1]

An out lesbian, Morris was greatly loved and respected within theatre circles. A regular theatregoer, often accompanied by Ivor Novello and his boyfriend, she never turned down a challenge. Once, having bet Noel Coward, she raced him to their respective theatres. Not only did she win, but had time to park her car and deliver a bunch of flowers to Noel *before* he reached his stage door!

Born at Suva in the Fiji Islands in 1915, Mary Morris was educated in a Sussex convent school and impressed the nuns with an unusual interpretation of Richard III. In 1936, after studying at the Royal Academy of Dramatic Art, she formed her own repertory company, Stranger Players, at the Barn Theatre in Oxted where she acted, directed and painted the scenery. In 1937 she went to Hollywood under contract to MGM. Unconventional Morris walked around the backlot wearing a boyish cap, plus-fours and pumps. Spencer Tracy affectionately nicknamed her 'Little Clarkie', after Clark Gable, but after six idle months, she returned to Britain. Her talent was recognized by the film producer Alexander Korda who signed her to a contract with London Films. She made her screen debut as Renée, the reform school inmate in *Prison Without Bars* (1938), and then Korda cast her in the small but memorable roles of the Nazi chauffeuse who assists with a kidnapping in *The Spy in Black* (1939), and the sorcerer's henchwoman in *The Thief of Bagdad* (1940).

Though Morris enjoyed a long and successful stage career in Britain, playing a wide range of parts, everything from Juliet to Saint Joan, Greek tragedy to Peter Pan, she made only rare film appearances. Difficult to cast because of her 'exotic' looks, there were few openings for her in films, though she gave impressive performances in *Pimpernel Smith* (1941), *Undercover* (1943), *Train of Events* (1949) and *High Treason* (1951).

Morris may have enjoyed a more productive career in films if director Michael Powell had cast her as the psychotic and sexually repressed nun, Sister Ruth, in his celebrated film version of Rumer Godden's novel, *Black Narcissus* (1947). Powell had already directed Morris in *The Spy in Black* and *The Thief of Bagdad*, and should have cast her in *Black Narcissus*. He later recalled:

> During the war, Mary Morris had come to me with a book which she thought would make a wonderful film. She also said that it had a wonderful part for Mary Morris. It was by an author new to me at that time, Rumer Godden. . . . This young nun, Sister Ruth, was the part Mary Morris coveted, very naturally. . . . She had a most unusual personality, and there was no doubting her extraordinary talent. She was small, compact, agile, black-haired, large-eyed, and she had the high cheekbones and Asiatic looks that would appeal to the Korda brothers. She was an exotic. . . she came to me in the middle of the war, entreating me to make a film of *Black Narcissus* and beseeching me to let her play Sister Ruth, the young nun whose lack of vocation and untimely death breaks up the community and drives them into retreat.[2]

Sadly, when Powell filmed *Black Narcissus* after the war, for reasons he does not reveal in his autobiography, he rejected Morris for the role of Sister Ruth in favour of Kathleen Byron.

Another role coveted by Morris was Cleopatra, and she played this with great success on BBC television in 1963. Many acknowledged that Morris gave the definitive portrayal of Cleopatra of her generation. Said critic Maurice Richardson in *The Observer*: 'No kitten, she went all out for a no longer young but still taut-muscled gypsy interpretation, with an elaborate stock of star-quality hysterics in reserve.'

Throughout her career, Morris retained a clearly defined lesbian persona. She was an extraordinary woman who wasn't glamorous and made no attempt to hide the advancing years. As a film actress Morris was capable of giving big performances in small roles, and maybe that was her problem. Her personality was just *too* big for British cinema of the 1940s and 1950s, and maybe this is why Michael Powell decided not to cast her in *Black Narcissus*.

For many years she was seen quite regularly on television and never received a bad review for any of her performances. Like her Hollywood contemporary, Barbara Stanwyck, she did not seek publicity. There was no gossip about her because she was so open about her sexuality, so nobody bothered her. Some people can be *too* obvious. Yet she had this vibrant sexuality which, in hindsight, could have been quite threatening to producers.

In 1978, when Morris appeared on BBC television as the beautiful Countess in *Anna Karenina*, you just forgot the rest of the cast's attempts to pretend they're nineteenth-century Russians. Morris wiped them off the screen! She was a natural actress and, given more opportunities in films, she could have been the British Bette Davis.

In her private life, Morris was immensely practical. A portrait painter, carpenter, upholsterer, plumber and electrician, she converted a seventeenth-century cowshed – almost single-handed – into a beautiful chalet in the Swiss mountains. One of Mary Morris's last public appearances occurred in May 1988 when she arrived at the Museum of London on a motorbike dressed in black leather to attend a screening of one of her films, *The Man from Morocco*, made in 1945 and starring the handsome gay Austrian-born star Anton Walbrook. A few months later she died at her home in Aigle, Switzerland aged 72.

Prison Without Bars

Based on a French play, *Prison Without Bars* was directed by Brian Desmond Hurst, and starred Corinne Luchaire as Susanne, a girl sent to a French reform school. Here she falls in love with the school's doctor who is secretly engaged to the new superintendent. The supporting cast includes Mary Morris in her first screen role as Renée, another inmate of the reform school. With unruly dark hair, and strikingly beautiful, large, expressive eyes, she is one of the most interesting actresses in the predominantly female cast of this film. It is a part well-suited to the young Morris. Renée is outspoken, feisty and a lesbian. Her affection for a fellow inmate, Alice, played by Lorraine Clewes, is noticeable. In one revealing scene Renée takes a big risk when she steals cigarettes for Alice. In another, an inmate taunts Renée by saying: 'You get angry when anyone as much as looks at your darling Alice!'

Finally, at the end of the film, when Susanne's attraction to the doctor has been revealed, one of the members of staff remarks to her colleagues: 'Anyone in their right senses would want to kiss Susanne.'

Other films of interest released in 1938

Charles Laughton starred in *Vessel of Wrath*, based on the novel by Somerset Maugham; Michael Redgrave made his film debut in Hitchcock's *The Lady Vanishes*.

Notes

1. Peter Noble, *Profiles and Personalities* (Brownlee, 1946), pp. 68–72.

2. Michael Powell, *A Life in Movies: An Autobiography* (Heinemann, 1986), pp. 558–9.

1939

Traitor Spy

In the crime drama *Traitor Spy*, described in the pubicity handout as a 'thrilling story of Nazi spies in England', there is a sequence set in Smoky Joe's nightclub. The black gay bandleader Ken 'Snakehips' Johnson and his West Indian Band are listed on the credits of this film, but sadly he does not appear. For reasons which have not come to light, his place as bandleader is taken by uncredited Jamaican trumpet player and band member, Leslie 'Jiver' Hutchinson, who conducts the band in the background (they're playing 'It's Strange Meeting You Again') while various 'low-life' types mix together and dance. They include mannish lesbians, effeminate gay men, racially mixed couples, prostitutes and gangsters. This sequence is described in the script as having 'Lots of mirrors, screened corners, low lighting, a Negro band tucked away in a corner, and a place for a floor show and dancing. The place is crowded. The underworld is represented, the lesser theatre, boxers, refugees, ladies of less than easy virtue. Society is there too taking a shivering delight in it all. The atmosphere is heavy with smoke.'

Other films of interest released in 1939

After the football match in *The Arsenal Stadium Mystery* there is male camaraderie and high jinks in the changing room with brief, homoerotic glimpses of semi-naked men; Charles Laughton starred in the film version of Daphne du Maurier's *Jamaica Inn*; in *Shipyard Sally*, the last film Gracie Fields made in Britain before she left for Hollywood, the star impersonated a cigar-smoking gentleman in a suit and bow-tie in order to gain entry to an all-male club.

1940

The Thief of Bagdad

In the late 1930s Alexander Korda gave a banquet at the Savoy to celebrate the opening of his film *The Drum*, which starred his protégé, Indian child actor Sabu. Douglas Fairbanks Snr., the legendary silent-screen actor and star of the classic 1924 Arabian Nights fantasy *The Thief of Bagdad*, was there. Korda wanted the film rights of *The Thief* to star Sabu, and didn't encounter any problems with Fairbanks who took one look at Sabu and said: 'He's ideal. You can have the rights.' With *The Thief of Bagdad*, Korda created an exotic and camp Technicolor spectacle. Surrounded by flying horses and magic carpets, athletic, asexual Sabu gave an entrancing performance as the little thief whose sole ambition in life is to 'be a sailor sailing out to sea'. At the end of the film he is transformed into a beautiful little prince. Sabu and his companion, the attractive, romantic hero John Justin, are physically affectionate and protective of each other throughout. Semi-naked too! But nothing could be camper than the awesome sight of the towering genie, magnificently played by Rex Ingram. Here is a strikingly handsome, muscular hunk complete with fancy finger and toe nails, chinese top-knot and pink nappy. He steals the film from right under the noses of his co-stars.

Other films of interest released in 1940

Anton Walbrook gave one of his best performances in *Gaslight* as the sadistic, jewel-obsessed husband of Diana Wynyard; gay Scottish actor Simon Lack gave an impressive performance as the coal miner's son, opposite Paul Robeson, in *The Proud Valley*.

1941

Dangerous Moonlight

Dangerous Moonlight, an emotional Brian Desmond Hurst melodrama, was one of the biggest box office hits of the Second World War, and a gay 'classic', judging by the number of gay men who worked on it. It has a script co-authored by Hurst and Rodney Ackland, gowns by Cecil Beaton, music composed by Richard Addinsell, and Anton Walbrook as the leading man. Addinsell's stirring, passionate 'Warsaw Concerto', played on the soundtrack by pianist Louis Kentner with the London Symphony Orchestra, has become one of the best-loved movie themes of all time. Walbrook, playing Stefan Radetzky, a Polish airman, is a beautiful, sexy, gentle, kind, comforting hero. He also has the most seductive 'come-to-bed' eyes ever seen on the silver screen. Also featured is Keneth Kent as André de Guise, a monocled, flower-wearing, gay French impresario. Though temperamental and flamboyant, he unexpectedly shows great sympathy for Stefan when the pianist asks to cancel his concert tour and return to active service. In a revealing 'coming-out' scene André tells Stefan he isn't what he appears: 'I'm no more a Frenchman than you are. I'm English. That surprises you, doesn't it. I know you all thought of me as a fake with a phoney accent, and you were right. But for years I worked as Gussie Ginns and got nowhere at all. Suddenly one day I became André de Guise, the great impresario!'

Walbrook was unhappy during the filming of *Dangerous Moonlight*. He was Austrian, and the authorities had taken away his car and radio. To add to his misery, his Norwegian boyfriend had been sent to Canada. When he sat at the piano to play in the film's opening sequence, and his leading lady Sally Gray entered the house and came up into the room, Walbrook had to say to her, 'I'm handsome, full of charm and a wonderful musician.' Hurst thought he was doing this in an extremely effeminate way and tried every word he could to explain that to him. The term 'camp' was not yet in popular use. Walbrook pretended not to understand. The cameraman, trying to avoid the situation, hid himself in the black cloth so Hurst walked over to him, pulled him out, and said: 'You go and tell him it's too sissy.' 'But I've never addressed a star in my life,' he replied. Finally Hurst had to explain to Walbrook it was too 'sissy'. Walbrook said, 'No.' Hurst said, 'Yes.' Hurst got his way and Walbrook ended up playing the scene very well.

Richard Addinsell (1904–77) read law at Oxford but was more interested in music and the theatre. He studied briefly at the Royal College of Music, and then in Berlin and Vienna. During the 1920s he contributed music to revues and shows in London's West End, and for the next thirty years continued writing for the theatre, often in collaboration with the entertainer Joyce Grenfell. However, it is for his work as a film composer that Addinsell is probably best remembered. From 1936 to the early 1960s he wrote music for numerous British films, including over twenty government documentary films during the Second World War, and several classics (*Fire Over England*, *Goodbye Mr Chips*, *Gaslight*, *Love on the Dole*, *Blithe Spirit*, *Scrooge*).

49th Parallel

49th Parallel (released in America as *The Invaders*), made by Michael Powell and Emeric Pressburger, is superficially wartime propaganda. Lieutenant Hirth (Eric Portman, in a role originally intended for Michael Redgrave), a Nazi U-boat commander, and four of his men are stranded in Canada, and they have to get to the border. The film episodically introduces them to a number of people who represent various qualities, some useful, and others dangerous in wartime. Laurence Olivier plays the devil-may-care but naive French–Canadian trapper whose lack of vigilance costs him his life. Anton Walbrook shines as Peter, the gentle religious sect leader and spiritual idealist, fine in his way, very noble, but in the long run no help in winning a war. As with so many Walbrook roles, he seems to be acting out his own personal outsider status with the full encouragement of Powell and Pressburger. His intimate scene with Vogel (Niall MacGinnis), the decent, sensitive Nazi (who is also rather ethereal), has a definite ring to it. Finally, there's Leslie Howard as the novelist Philip Armstrong Scott, who seems to be saying 'a plague on both your houses'. Ian Christie describes him as 'a whimsical English anthropologist and aesthete who maintains that "wars may come and men may go, but art goes on for ever"'.[1] He lives close to the Indians in a tent in the wilderness, with paintings by Picasso and Matisse, and a copy of Thomas Mann's *Magic Mountain*. Scott is an artistic outsider who makes merry with quips and – in one scene – with a direct sexual invitation to Lohrmann (John Chandos), one of Portman's men (who seems to have a thing for his leader). Howard is the film's biggest surprise. Summoning up bits of his roles in *The Scarlet Pimpernel*, *The Petrified Forest* and *Pygmalion*, he delivers a high comedy turn, making mincemeat of Hirth and Lohrmann. As with the Walbrook character, Howard is seen as a wanderer, with no need of women, just the wilderness and the Indians. Sussing the gay Nazi, he fixes him with a potent gaze, holds it for a while, then provocatively says just one word: 'Interested?'

With Powell and Pressburger at the helm, Portman, Walbrook and Howard on the screen, and Rodney Ackland contributing to the script, easy judgements are not made. It preserves Powell and Pressburger's reputation for decency and honour in the depiction of Germans and English. It also confirms them, just before their 'great' period, as completely original film makers, with a faerie quality that allows them to treat lightly some terrible, dark themes.

In America Anton Walbrook received a Best Acting award from the National Board of Review. Emeric Pressburger won an Oscar for his Original Story, and he also received an additional nomination (with Rodney Ackland) for Best Screenplay.

Other films of interest released in 1941

Charles Hawtrey made a memorable appearance as a snooty schoolboy in the Will Hay comedy *The Ghost of St Michael's*.

Notes

1. Ian Christie, *Arrows of Desire: The Films of Michael Powell and Emeric Pressburger* (Faber, 1994), p. 38.

1942

In Which We Serve

Noel Coward made quite a contribution to the patriotic war drama *In Which We Serve*: producer, co-director, screenwriter, music score and star. Highly regarded at home and abroad, in America it received the prestigious New York Film Critics Best Film award, and Coward was honoured with a special Oscar for his 'outstanding production achievement'. He was also nominated for his original screenplay.

In Which We Serve movingly charts the story of a destroyer, the HMS *Torrin*, and the men who served on her during the early years of the war. Coward's screenplay was inspired by his friend, Lord Louis Mountbatten, who described to him the service record of his own British destroyer. Captain Kinross, the character played by Coward, is based on Mountbatten, but not everyone was happy with this somewhat unlikely piece of casting. While Mountbatten was happy to be immortalized on the screen by Coward, the Ministry of Information resisted the idea. Coward was famous for his light-hearted, witty comedies. His public image was that of a sophisticated entertainer, at home in café society. Hardly the sort of chap one would expect to captain a destroyer in wartime. On reflection, in spite of the film's enormous popularity (curiously Coward's performance appears to have been convincing to wartime audiences), the major flaw of *In Which We Serve* is Coward's Captain Kinross. The character desperately needs a dashing, manly and sympathetic actor, a Laurence Olivier, to be believable. Coward is totally unsympathetic in the part. He lacks warmth, his body language is all wrong (awkward, uncomfortable). It is a wholly unconvincing performance. As Captain Kinross, Coward goes to war in an irritatingly sporty, jolly, almost casual manner. He seems to be saying: 'Let's play cricket on Wednesday, and go into battle on

Thursday.' He addresses his men like a gym mistress briefing her girls as they are about to go into battle on the hockey pitch. For Coward, this performance may have established his credentials as a 'heterosexual' in wartime, but today it is a monumental piece of miscasting, and a poor performance too. Even in his 'love' scene with his wife, played by Celia Johnson, he wears a hat *over* his face!

Coward stereotypes the working-class characters. The film should have been called *The Huggetts Go to War* for, whenever they appear, 'Roll Out the Barrel' always seems to be playing in the background. However, the film's strength lies in several great scenes such as the survivors of the torpedo attack being shot at by German airmen while they cling to a raft, or John Mills informing his friend Bernard Miles of the death of the latter's wife. The superb, believable supporting players, especially Mills and Miles, lack the artificiality of Coward, and bring reality and truth to the screen as working-class men in low-key performances. Mills is comforting and supportive to the sailors, whereas Coward is cold and aloof.

As for Lord Mountbatten, for years there were rumours that he was gay and had an affair with Coward. But his daughter, Lady Pamela Hicks, is not convinced. In the television documentary *Secret Lives: Mountbatten*, shown on Channel 4 in March 1995, she said:

> I was surprised the first time they suggested that he might be gay. He was a great friend of people like Noel Coward and he had a lot of gay friends. Therefore the writers seemed to indicate that he must have been gay himself because he was very fond of Noel. But he liked Noel because Noel was fun. He didn't happen to have the same fancies.

Perhaps *In Which We Serve* is best summed up by Coward himself who, as Captain Kinross, describes Britain in wartime as 'not exactly smug, not exactly warlike, either.'

The Black Sheep of Whitehall

In the comedy *The Black Sheep of Whitehall* Will Hay, in one of his funniest roles, plays the bungling Professor Davis who is mistaken for an economics expert. When he gets involved in a Nazi plot to sabotage a trade agreement, the Professor drags up as Sister Plunkett and, with her 'patient' Bobby (John Mills), infiltrates a nursing home run by Nazi spies. Inside the nursing home, Bobby pretends he is suffering from amnesia. Says Sister Plunkett to the doctor: 'It happened in the blackout. He was in the park one night and he forgot himself. It's a very puzzling case.' This is a typical example of the kind of humour in *The Black Sheep of Whitehall*, and Hay's lovely performance as Sister Plunkett is a splendid example of the tradition of female impersonation associated with British music hall. Later, Sister Plunkett is taken by matron to the nurse's rest room where she is befriended by jolly Sister Spooner (Barbara Valerie). 'I see you're Bart's,' says Sister Spooner, 'I'm Middlesex myself. As a probationer I spent five years under the matron there. Then I went into the maternity ward and had sixteen children in two weeks. And then I passed out.' Replies Sister Plunkett: 'I'm not surprised!'

Other films of interest released in 1942

Set in pre-war Paris, Brian Desmond Hurst's thriller *Alibi*, a remake of the French classic *L'Alibi*, stars Margaret Lockwood as a nightclub hostess who helps an inspector to trap a murderous mindreader. Raymond Lovell plays Erich Von Stroheim's old part, a sinister gay character called Winkler, the 'brains' behind a wave of crimes. His assistant and confidante, Fritz, is played by gay writer/actor Rodney Ackland. Says Winkler to Fritz: 'I'm sure you'll do anything for me.'

1943

The Life and Death of Colonel Blimp

Conceived along epic lines, *The Life and Death of Colonel Blimp* is one of the great British films. It has never lost its freshness or depth. That such a film, with its anti-militarist sentiments, should be made at the height of the war says much for the cleverness and daring of its creative team, The Archers (Michael Powell and Emeric Pressburger, see also *49th Parallel*, 1941; *A Canterbury Tale*, 1944; *I Know Where I'm Going*, 1945; *A Matter of Life and Death*, 1946 and *The Red Shoes*, 1948). But it seems hard to believe that in 1943 the *Daily Mail* denounced the film as 'disastrously bad propaganda in time of war' and Sir Winston Churchill temporarily banned it from being shown abroad (it took nearly two years to reach America, but only in a cut-down version). For every swipe at British obstinacy, narrow mindedness and lack of imagination, there are two at German militarianism and cruelty. *The Life and Death of Colonel Blimp* is also one of the great British gay films. Gay film maker Derek Jarman later said:

> There is only one English feature director whose work is in the first rank. Michael Powell is the only director to make a clear political analysis in his films, his work is unequalled. *The Life and Death of Colonel Blimp* is the finest English feature, and *A Canterbury Tale* and *A Matter of Life and Death* are not far behind. When he made these films he was heavily criticized for his treatment of serious themes. *Blimp* was banned by Churchill and remained in a savaged version for nearly forty years, a plea for tolerance and regard for the enemy as human made at the height of the war – there is no more courageous English film.[1]

Clive Candy, VC (Roger Livesey) is a professional soldier whom we encounter at various stages of his long career, from 1902 to 1943. Dramatic conflicts are provided by his life-long, love–hate relationship with the unlikeliest of people, a Prussian officer, Theo Kretschmar–Schuldorff (Anton Walbrook). Their friendship begins in Berlin with a duel. Preparations for the duel itself take up fifteen minutes of screen time, culminating in an overhead shot with a Busby Berkleyesque arrangement of the duellists and their supporters. The 'ballet' begins. Walbrook moves towards Livesey and then, to our great surprise, Powell cuts away to the outside of the gymnasium, prettily covered in snow. Inside a waiting carriage are two people who love Candy – the priggish suffragette Edith Hunter (Deborah Kerr, in the first of three roles), and his effeminate schoolfriend 'Babyface' Fitzroy (played by the gay actor, and later openly gay director, Frith Banbury). This sequence is indicative of Powell and Pressburger's attitude to the story and its characters. People who love each other are more interesting than people who fight. Love transcends gender, age and nationality. The two-and-a-half-hour film ends with Candy, a dinosaur in the modern world, having found his final role (as an organizer of the Home Guard), visiting the bombed-out house he lived in with his wife. He walks towards the ruin, arm-in-arm with Theo, the German who is now classed as an 'enemy alien', adrift and alone, save for this 'Englander'.

The casting of Walbrook – whose appearance is cunningly delayed – gives the central relationship its sharp, emotional edge, though Livesey is (in superbly convincing make-up) not far behind. While both actors communicate with astonishing power and precision, Walbrook is mesmerizing. He delivers a speech (to a cold and untypically malevolent A. E. Matthews as the president of the tribunal), about the destruction of his life by the Nazis in a continuous five minute take. In its colour and intensity this must rank as one of the greatest pieces of screen acting ever. What the words mirror in the actor's own life as a gay man adds another few layers of pain and passion to this scene. What makes the film so extraordinary is that Walbrook is presented in the most sympathetic light throughout. He looks gorgeous, through youth and age, he is intelligent and sensitive. And he ends up with the guy!

While Livesey is supposed to be a caricature (his role is based on David Low's cartoon Colonel Blimp), the man is fully drawn. He may be insensitive, humourless, a colonialist and big game hunter, but he is also a man of honour and integrity. True to his nickname 'Sugar', he is a 'sweetie', and believably transcends the prejudices which would have been rife during – and between – the two world wars against the Huns. However, Livesey's subtle body language immediately transmits his racism against the black soldier (Norris Smith) who drives him to the convent across no-man's land.

Apart from the homoemotional relationship of the two central characters, there are all manner of queer references throughout the film. For example, 'Babyface', the character played by Frith Banbury, is a Wildean dandy, and another gay actor, Robert Harris, surfaces as the embassy secretary in suits which are always adorned by carnations. There are mentions of Holmes and Watson, of a play called *The Last of the Dandys*, and of an aria from *Mignon* (mignon was a French slang term for homosexual). Walbrook's proposal to Deborah Kerr finds him – and Livesey – wearing women's hats! Allan Gray's music strikes up a lilting waltz theme for Walbrook and Livesey's first meeting after the duel.

Throughout the film the maleness of Candy's world is stressed: the camaraderie on the battlefield, the Turkish baths, a men-only dinner party, sleeping at the club, ex-public school allegiances. The acceptability of this culture makes the film's central relationship both more acceptable to censors and audiences, and more invisible. Because of Deborah Kerr's triple presence in the film, it is easy for people to ignore the heart of the matter. As Candy says of the Indian Rope Trick: 'You hear about something. And then you "see it".' Audiences (and critics) have been trained to see heterosexuality. So they always see it.

Striking exactly the right balance between picaresque satire and lyric romance (mainly male–male), Powell and Pressburger created a film for all time, and all nations. The timelessness of this film was perfectly caught by Chris Peachment in *Time Out* when he said 'Like much of Powell and Pressburger's work, it is a salute to all that is paradoxical about the English: no one else has captured their romanticism banked down beneath emotional reticence and honour. And it is marked by an enormous generosity of spirit: in the history of the British cinema there is nothing to touch it.'[2]

We Dive at Dawn

Anthony Asquith's exciting, gripping Second World War drama, *We Dive at Dawn*, is set in the confined space of a submarine, the *Sea Tiger*.

Filmed in a documentary style, primarily the film is about action, not dialogue, but it's an interesting study of male bonding too. Men from different regional and class backgrounds pull together when confronting danger, but some of them also reveal ambivalent attitudes towards women, and heterosexuality. The star of the film, John Mills, is never seen with a woman, but most of the attention is given to handsome, moody Eric Portman as Hobson: 'I like to look at the petty officers now and again. It's good for discipline,' he says. Hobson is bitter about women as a result of his wife's desertion: 'You mugs make me sick,' he says to the crew. 'Have you anything else to think about but leave, females, smart dames, homework?' The crew also includes Niall MacGinnis as Mike, a rugged Irishman who is reluctant to wed, and tries everything he can to avoid his impending marriage. Needless to say, in keeping with the mood of the times, at the end of the film Niall marries his fiancée, and Eric is reunited with his wife.

From time to time homoeroticism surfaces in this film. The camera does not shy away from the semi-naked bodies of some of the men. Niall MacGinnis is not only seen sitting naked in a bath, his attractive, muscular body (with a towel wrapped conveniently round his waist) is also displayed. Also, the camera lingers on semi-naked John Mills while he is being massaged.

Off-screen Eric Portman was an unhappy, closeted, self-loathing gay man, and most of his film performances are marked by the edgy, tense manner he reveals in *We Dive at Dawn*. He has a sad, haunted look on his face, similar to that of troubled bisexual actor Michael Redgrave. Drama critic Kenneth Tynan later recalled a meeting with Portman in the 1950s:

> A year or so later (after Peter Wildeblood's trial) I had another strange insight into what it was like to be a homosexual when I went to interview Eric Portman who was appearing in *Separate Tables*. My wife and I went to dinner at his flat in Chelsea after the play and Portman began to drink quite heavily. I mentioned that he had been to school, and been quite friendly, with the murderer Christie. Suddenly Portman erupted. He banged the table and shouted that I was trying to worm out his secret life and put him into jail. The paranoia of decades emptied all over the supper table. I told him that I wasn't interested in his sex life but

he continued to shout. Obviously by mentioning a criminal, he thought I was trying to associate him with criminal acts. His manservant took me to one side and said that there was no point in trying to reason with him. Sometimes when things got really bad, Portman would go down to his country cottage and smash all the mirrors because he felt such guilt.[3]

Miss London Ltd

During the war the British public flocked to see escapist musicals like *Miss London Ltd*, and this is one of the queerest of them all. Arthur Askey stars, and he's at his most outrageous. There's a script peppered with *double entendres*, and a memorable performance by vocalist Anne Shelton.

Miss London Ltd opens at Waterloo Station with deep-voiced, hefty Anne Shelton, smartly clad in a uniform and tie as a railway station announcer, singing 'The Eight Fifty Choo Choo from Waterloo'. This appealing musical has some nice tunes, an abundance of innocence and charm, and plenty of bad jokes from Arthur 'Hallo Playmates' Askey, one of Britain's most popular funny men, who introduces himself: 'Arthur Bowden is my name – single is my station.'

Askey plays the manager of Miss London Ltd, a failing escort agency, which is unexpectedly visited, and rejuvenated, by its pretty American owner, played by Evelyn Dall. Also featured are Jack Train as Askey's campy right-hand man, Max Bacon as an hilariously coy head waiter, and Richard Hearne as a jitterbugging naval commodore. Also in the cast is Peter Graves, the tall, handsome star of several Ivor Novello musicals.

At the agency Dall interviews several young women as possible escorts including sophisticated, haughty Iris, a showgirl and firewatcher, who is game for practically anything. 'That sounds like the voice of experience talking!' says Dall. Replies Iris, laughing suggestively, 'You're not kidding!' Enter Anne Shelton, who is also interviewed as a possible escort. 'I'm not the type you want,' she says. 'If they want company, I'm game, but *only* for company!'

In *Miss London Ltd* Arthur Askey performs at his gayest and campest. In most of his previous films, including *Charley's Big-Hearted*

Aunt, I Thank You and *King Arthur Was a Gentleman*, he gave marvellous performances in drag. But, though he doesn't wear women's clothes in this film, nothing has prepared us for the outrageously camp performance he gives here.

Wearing white gloves, he performs a delightful song about a 'moth' (reminiscent of his famous 'bee' song) to an amused Max Bacon. Prancing about the room like a screaming queen, he sings: 'Fluttering round a candle/Frightened to go near/Sitting on your chaise/And feeling very queer.' As Askey flits past Bacon, he touches him while singing the line 'feeling very queer'. The song continues: 'Light and airy/Just like a fairy/Chewing up yards of cloth. . .'. It is one of the campest moments in British film history and Askey, clearly enjoying every minute, is at his silliest, and most endearing.

Towards the end of the film Richard Hearne appears as the bearded naval Commodore Wellington at a party. Waiting alone in a room outside, he hears music playing and suddenly takes off round the room, waltzing by himself. As head waiter Max Bacon enters the room, Hearne grabs him and waltzes *him* around the room. After the music stops he says: 'I'm sorry about the dancing. Music affects me like this.' As Bacon guides him into the party, the music starts playing again. Panic-stricken, Bacon looks in horror at Hearne who lunges at him, but Bacon manages to run away, chased by Hearne, who then trips and falls on the stairs, allowing Bacon to escape.

At the end of the film Arthur receives his 'call up' papers and joins the Navy. He is escorted to Waterloo Station by two sailors, one of whom is played by Ronald Shiner, soon to become a favourite with British moviegoers. At the station one of the sailors disappears to find a travel voucher. Evelyn Dall approaches Askey and Shiner, and there follows an hilarious exchange between Askey and Dall after Shiner refuses to give them permission to speak. Says Dall to Shiner: 'Well, we can talk to *you*, can't we?' Taking Shiner by the arm, and playing what is perhaps the first 'love' scene between two men on the screen, Askey says affectionately (and not unconvincingly): 'While I'm away, be true to me.'

In the final scene, as Askey is departing on the train and saying goodbye to Dall, she says to the jitterbugging Commodore Wellington: 'I'll dance with you again if you take care of Arthur in the Navy.' Retorts Arthur: 'Never. I wouldn't take refuge underneath another man's arches!'

Notes

1. Derek Jarman, *Dancing Ledge* (Quartet, 1984), p. 216.
2. Chris Peachment, *The Time Out Film Guide*, edited by Tom Milne (Penguin, 1989).
3. Kenneth Tynan, *Gay News*, no. 106, 4–17 November 1976, p. 25.

1944

Two Thousand Women

Several British films focused on the role of women in wartime including *Millions Like Us* (1943), set in a munitions factory, and *Two Thousand Women* (1944). This superb melodrama, written and directed by Frank Launder, is set in a women's internment camp in France. The women held prisoner by the Nazis are mostly English and come from a wide range of backgrounds and occupations, including nuns, nurses and stripteasers. Says chain-smoking, mannish Maud Wright (Renée Houston): 'That's the trouble here, we're not all out of the same drawer. Not that it worries me much.' However, the most unconventional of the group are two middle-aged spinsters, kind but bossy Muriel Manningford (Flora Robson) and her sweet, gentle friend Claire Meredith (Muriel Aked). On arriving at the camp, they refuse to be parted. Says Muriel to the German guard: 'If we must sleep two in a room I shall share with my friend Miss Meredith.' Throughout the film, the two women are shown having a close, intimate relationship. They are always seen together, and bravely hide an RAF pilot from the Nazis in their room. At first, Claire is worried: 'Muriel, you're not suggesting we should have a man in our room all night?' Replies Muriel: 'My dear Claire, it's our duty. The young man shall sleep in your bed. You shall share mine.' Tragically, the two women are taken away by the Nazis to a 'punishment' camp in Germany for uncovering the blackout, and signalling to a British plane. As Muriel and Claire are escorted from the camp by German guards, one of the women starts playing on the piano 'For he's a jolly good fellow', and all the women prisoners join in, singing 'For they are jolly good fellows.' It is a profoundly moving moment in British wartime cinema.

A more explicit reference to lesbianism is made by Freda Thompson

(Phyllis Calvert) who has assumed the role of leader of the group. In one brief scene she says to Rosemary Brown (Patricia Roc): 'To think that I once had a crush on a girl like that at school.' She is referring to Teresa King (Betty Jardine), a strident, mannish, butch gym instructress who turns out to be a Nazi informer, planted in the camp.

At the end of the film, Maud Wright dons a top hat and cane to sing (in a deep voice) at the camp concert: 'Too many women and not enough love to go round/Too many women and never a man to be found.'

A Canterbury Tale

Lesbianism also surfaces in home-front films, such as Powell and Pressburger's *A Canterbury Tale*. Land Army girl Allison Smith (Sheila Sim) goes to work for Miss Prudence Honeywood (Freda Jackson) on the farm she runs with her sister. Mannish Prudence wears a tie, smokes a cigarette as she talks, wears wellies, and heaves muck. 'Call me Pru, you might as well,' she tells Allison. 'I don't like Prudence. Name or quality.' When Allison describes her home in London, Prudence asks if it is in 'a long street with every house a different sort of sadness in it?' She then explains why she never married: 'The only man who ever asked me to marry him wanted me to live in a house like that. I'm still a maid.'

Fiddlers Three

Fiddlers Three is arguably the silliest film musical produced in Britain during the Second World War. Daft but still lots of fun, the script is peppered with terrible music-hall jokes and *double entendres*, and heading the cast is comedian Tommy Trinder who performs such unforgettable songs as 'Sweet Fanny Adams'. Trinder and his co-star Sonnie Hale play a couple of sailors who are transported back to Ancient Rome where they find themselves caught up in the rites and wrongs of Nero's court. Also featured is the great Ernest Milton (from *It's Love Again*) as Titus, a gay clothes designer, and gay favourite Elisabeth Welch as Poppaea's attendant who sings and shares a few lines of comedy dialogue with Trinder. In the funniest sequence in the film, Trinder drags up as Señorita Alvarez (a creation inspired by Carmen

Miranda) who has arrived from Brazil to entertain the bejewelled, camp Nero (Francis L. Sullivan). 'Oh, yes,' Nero says. 'Where those delicious nuts come from!' The dialogue between Señorita Alvarez and Nero are full of hilarious *double entendres*, and one can only speculate how far gays working on the film had some input into the script and the lyrics to the Señorita's song. Trinder is splendid as Señorita Alvarez, and though he seems a little uncomfortable in his tight-fitting Carmen Miranda outfit, he is clearly having a gay old time as he parades around and sings: 'My mad bolero from Uruguay/Made Emperor Nero feel very gay/He wants to go my South American way/iy iy iy iy!' Afterwards a delighted Nero says: 'We are vastly impressed. We create you a Dame of the Roman Empire!' Finally, as Sonnie Hale (also in drag) leaves, Nero stops him and enquires: 'Surely we have seen your face before?' Replies Sonnie: 'Oh, no, imperial Caesar (coughing and raising his voice) excuse me, I'm a little hoarse.' Says Nero: 'Of course. The Imperial Hunt Cup! We did you both ways!'

Fanny by Gaslight

In Anthony Asquith's Victorian melodrama *Fanny by Gaslight* there are shades of Oscar Wilde when Fanny (Phyllis Calvert) discovers her 'respectable' father, who has been killed, has been running a brothel. Afterwards, on her deathbed, Fanny's mother sends her away, telling her to change her name (like Constance Wilde and her sons). At the end of the film, Cathleen Nesbitt gives a superb performance as Harry's (Stewart Granger) sexually repressed sister, Miss Kate Summerford. Possessive, vindictive, and feeling threatened by Harry's fiancée, Fanny, she stiffens when Fanny touches her arm and says: 'You're jealous because no man will ever need you as Harry needs me.'

1945

Blithe Spirit

Witty, light-hearted and whimsical, Noel Coward's comedy *Blithe Spirit* stars Rex Harrison as Charles Condomine (!), a celebrated novelist who lives in Kent with his socialite wife, Ruth (Constance Cummings). Writing a thriller about mediums, he invites to dinner the local authority on the subject, Madame Arcati (Margaret Rutherford). During an after-dinner seance, Charles is upset by the return of Elvira (Kay Hammond), his first wife's ghost. Arcati is responsible for this unwanted visitation. Coward's original text describes Arcati as 'a striking woman, dressed not too extravagantly but with a decided bias towards the barbaric'. Played by Rutherford, the quintessential eccentric of British films, she is uncomfortable as a woman, preferring to behave like an overgrown schoolgirl. Outrageous, fey, distracted and gauche, she sports a scruffy haircut and wears a striped tweed cape. Madame Arcati is a woman who doesn't care about her appearance. She's not a typical Englishwoman. Unselfconcious and natural, she has 'liberated' herself long before it became acceptable for women to do so. With her masculine walk and big arms, beer-drinking and smoking, there is just a hint of lesbian about her. Coward even refers to it in the script. Says Elvira, looking at Arcati and describing her behaviour: 'I don't approve of these masculine, deviant carryings on.'

Whenever Elvira is in her presence, Arcati is sexually excited. For example, there is a memorable sequence which includes a sapphic *frisson* when Arcati, looking decidedly butch with her specs and tweeds, is teased by the invisible Elvira. First, when Elvira blows into her ear, Arcati's face is a picture of joy and bliss. Elvira is clearly turning her on, and Arcati responds by crying: 'Again! Again!' Sexually aroused, Arcati's wrinkles suddenly disappear, giving her a radiant, youthful appearance. Next, Elvira blows up her arm and Arcati cries in ecstasy: 'You darling! You little darling!'

Rutherford steals the film from the under the noses of Harrison, Cummings and, especially, Hammond. This should have been Hammond's film, but she is miscast and gives an irritating performance, whining instead of being witty. Everytime she appears, this lively film dies. Why would sexy Rexy have married such a blowsy tart? The role cries out for Vivien Leigh.

I Know Where I'm Going!

Michael Powell and Emeric Pressburger's *I Know Where I'm Going!*, a wonderful romantic drama, set in the Hebrides, should be more widely recognized as one of the classic films of our time. Lacking sentimentality, it is an *intelligent* film and not in the least bit whimsical. It tells the story of Joan Webster (Wendy Hiller), the sophisticated daughter of a bank manager, who travels to Scotland to marry 'one of the richest men in the country', the chairman of Consolidated Chemical Industries. While stranded on the mainland in a storm, she falls in love with Torquil McNeil (Roger Livesey), a naval officer on leave, whom she later discovers to be the Laird of Killoran. During the storm she stays with Torquil's friends, Colonel Barnstaple (Captain C.W.R. Knight) and Catriona (Pamela Brown).

This film, about a woman who *thinks* she knows where she is going but doesn't, could be telling us something about lesbians. Sometimes they are women who think they know where they are going (a husband, home, 2 point 4 children and heterosexual domesticity), but discover that life has something else to offer. In this film, Joan Webster is not allowed to go where she wants to. She doesn't even meet the man she has been planning to marry. Instead she encounters Torquil and Catriona.

Long-haired, wild Catriona is a lover of big dogs, and who assertively calls herself an 'old bag'. Torquil describes her as a 'queer girl'. After Joan has almost killed herself trying to get to the island in the middle of the storm, Catriona orders her to *her* bedroom: 'There's a fire in my room and that's where you'll sleep.' The following 'bedroom scene' between the two women is ambiguous. Does Catriona actually leave the bedroom? We don't *see* her leave and, when morning comes, her dogs are *still* sitting at the foot of the bed. In the next scene we see Joan, who has always looked so perfect, looking very relaxed and carefree, sitting on a table and swinging her legs. Looking rather butch, she says wistfully 'I can't do anything with my hair'. Has Catriona liberated her? Has she opened new doors for Joan? Says Joan to Catriona at the end of the film, before she is united with Torquil: 'Goodbye, Catriona. Thank you for everything.' We can only speculate about what she means.

The subtext to this extraordinary film is a fear of sexuality. For example, on the train to Scotland, we see Joan's wedding dress wrapped in cellophane, and later superstition prevents Torquil from entering the Castle of Moy. Finally, there is Catriona, who reveals that, during the war, she was surrounded by RAF pilots stationed in Killoran, but she had her big dogs to protect her.

Off-screen, Pamela Brown was as sexually ambivalent as Catriona. In *Million-Dollar Movie*, the second volume of his autobiography, Michael Powell recalled a conversation he had with his wife, Frankie, in 1950 when he was considering Brown for the role of the boy–girl, girl–boy Nicklaus in *Tales of Hoffman*. Frankie had said to Powell: 'I always thought there was a touch of the lesbian in Pamela.' Says Powell:

> In this she was right. All actors are continually experimenting and inventing with their hormones, their male and female genes, and a few have the luck to be evenly balanced between their sexual drives. Pamela was one of these. She was a witch. Women adored her, men feared her, and for the same reason – she fascinated them . . . . Pamela was 'the ugliest woman in the world' (Emeric Pressburger) or 'the most beautiful' (John Gielgud and Laurence Olivier). . . . The great Continental actresses were her models: Rachel, Bernhardt, Duse. She was blessed with a big voice, and a magnificent chest and lungs upon which she could strike organ notes. Her eyes were like two flames, lighting up every corner of the theatre, and above all she had intelligence, which burned upon her brow and illuminated every move she made and every word she said.[1]

Dead of Night

Ealing's *Dead of Night* is made up of five supernatural tales, and justly famous for two of its segments: *The Haunted Mirror* and *The*

Ventriloquist's Dummy. Fifty years later they can still make audiences feel uncomfortable. But *The Golfing Story* is an enjoyable caper about an inseparable pair of golfers, George and Larry. They're played by the popular comedy team of Basil Radford and Naunton Wayne. With a watchful eye, however, it is possible to glean a much queerer picture of the two men, their love for the same woman, the death of one, and his reappearance in a *menage à trois*. A small pleasure in an otherwise trivial story, but with interesting reverberations all the same.

In the powerful and chilling *Ventriloquist's Dummy* segment, the troubled bisexual Michael Redgrave gives a remarkable performance as Maxwell Frere, an unhappy, tortured ventriloquist. There is an interesting parallel to be drawn here between the actor and the character he plays. Though not as psychologically disturbed as Maxwell, Redgrave was also a complex man whose off-screen unhappiness with his bisexual nature gives the performance a fascinating dimension.

Frere and his dummy Hugo Fitch are the star attractions at Chez Beulah, a smart nightclub in pre-war Paris, owned by a glamorous and friendly black American expatriate (Elisabeth Welch). Maxwell and Hugo have an intense, violent relationship, and Frere expresses strong emotions of fear, jealousy and misogyny throughout the story. He has a sad, haunted look of despair on his face, and the true nature of Maxwell's relationship with Hugo is questionable. If Maxwell is a repressed gay, then one has only to look for the small indications of this. Maxwell's gay sexuality is revealed by the framed photograph he keeps of Hugo on the dressing table of his hotel room, and his hatred of anyone coming too close to Hugo. 'I can't bear anyone touching him,' he says. When another ventriloquist, Sylvester Kee, arrives in Paris and visits the nightclub, Hugo threatens to leave Maxwell and team up with him. 'We two could make beautiful music together,' says Hugo to Kee. Hugo then taunts and insults Maxwell in front of Kee. 'I'm just about through with that cheap ham,' he says, and this results in an unexpected and disturbing act of violence when Maxwell slaps Hugo across the face. Hugo responds: 'You'll be sorry for this later.' Maxwell's emotions finally get out of hand when the fear of losing Hugo overpowers him and he shoots and wounds Kee in a hotel room. They are the emotions of an obsessive and jealous lover. Towards the end of the story, after Maxwell has been imprisoned for wounding Kee, he is reunited with

Hugo in his prison cell. 'I knew you wouldn't leave me,' he says to Hugo. 'I knew you'd come back.' But cruel Hugo taunts him again. 'Not for long, my boy, not for long,' he says. Maxwell then destroys Hugo. But the dummy hasn't really been destroyed for he lives on inside Maxwell and, at the end of the story, he has completely taken over the insane ventriloquist.

In her 1986 autobiography, *A Family and its Fortunes*, Rachel Kempson revealed her husband Michael as a troubled bisexual. He described his bisexuality as his 'difficulties':

> Although I came from a sheltered background, I knew what Michael meant by 'difficulties'. During my seasons at Stratford, I had fallen in love with my Romeo, John Wyse, who was bisexual. And there were many like him in the company. The fact that I loved Michael so much meant that I was sure I could overcome his difficulties. I would have done anything for him. And indeed it was probably this sensitivity in his nature that made me love him so, as I was very scared of the macho type. It was partly his beauty that entranced me. . . . He was a deeply troubled man, and could have benefited from help. But I think it was easier for him to stay as he was.[2]

More recently Redgrave's son, Corin, published a biography of his father which offers a more in-depth analysis of his reluctance to be open about his sexuality. He says:

> I suggested to him that he might wish to 'come out' and write about his bisexuality. I'm sure I never used that phrase, and probably didn't even know it at the time. But I know that my suggestion, however clumsy and formal it must have sounded, was unambiguous. Michael's reply was equally unequivocal. 'I shall certainly write about that,' he said. But months passed and he never broached the subject.[3]

Nearly all the characters in *Dead of Night* are slightly off-centre. Apart from Maxwell Frere, there's Esmé Percy's antique dealer who sells the haunted mirror to Googie Withers, as well as her too-dapper husband, played by Ralph Michael. Then there's the strange sobbing boy in *The Christmas Story*, also directed by Alberto Cavalcanti. And what about Eliot Foley (Roland Culver), the confirmed bachelor who lives with his dear old mum, who sets Mervyn Johns off on on his nightmare ride in *The Linking Story*?

The Way to the Stars

Towards the end of the war, Anthony Asquith and Terence Rattigan collaborated again on one of their most popular films, *The Way to the Stars*. Though set in and around a wartime RAF station, shared by English and American airman, it is not a war film, for there are no battle scenes. Instead Asquith and Rattigan movingly explore the emotional impact of the war on the men and women who live through it. Because the film was released a few weeks after the war ended in Europe, it opened in 1945 on the deserted RAF station with a voice-over saying 'This was the nerve centre of an airfield, and it is now derelict. No more happy landings. . . . Now sheep are returning to this field, which is inscribed in the Doomsday Book.' Going back to 1940, the time of the Battle of Britain, we are introduced to a new RAF pilot, Peter Penrose (John Mills) arriving at the station. He is assigned to a room with quiet, sensitive David Archdale (Michael Redgrave), a lover of poetry and the recipient of the Distinguished Flying Cross. Archdale marries Toddy (Rosamund John) who manages the local inn but, shortly after their son is born, David is killed returning from a mission. After the Americans arrive, Toddy is befriended by Johnny (Douglass Montgomery), but he is also killed.

Unlike his gay American contemporaries, George Cukor and Edmund Goulding, who had reputations for directing women stars, Anthony Asquith directed men with great sensitivity and success. In *The Way to the Stars* he has Redgrave and Mills, two of Britain's finest, and most understated actors, to work with. Together they create a fascinating study of the frailty of masculinity. For example, after Archdale is killed, Penrose grieves for his friend and rejects his girlfriend, fearing that he could also be killed. 'He'd got no right to marry and have a kid. None of us have,' he says.

Sadly, once Redgrave has departed, the film fails to hold together and loses its poetry and elegiac quality. The introduction of loud, abrasive American flyers takes the film in a different direction. It becomes a comedy with only hints of tragedy. Although Asquith and Rattigan try to 'replace' Redgrave with another 'sensitive' actor, the gay Canadian

Douglass Montgomery, he lacks Redgrave's good looks and acting ability.

The popularity of *The Way to the Stars* was so great that in a readers' poll in the *Daily Mail* it was voted the Best British Film of 1939–45.

Brief Encounter

The opening title to this classic film drama says it all: 'Noel Coward's *Brief Encounter*'. Though directed by David Lean, from a gay point of view, it is Coward, the film's producer and scenarist, who is the true *auteur* of this extraordinary film. In his excellent study of *Brief Encounter*, published in the British Film Institute's 'Film Classics' series, gay writer Richard Dyer describes it as a product of gay culture, specifically through the input of Coward. He says: 'If *Brief Encounter* feels gay to me and many other gay people that I know, it is because it was made with gay feeling.'[4]

It is a simple story, nothing more than a low-key romance between Laura Jesson (Celia Johnson) and Dr Alec Harvey (Trevor Howard), a pair of decent, middle-class people both comfortably married to other partners. But in Coward's writing, the film offers meanings and resonances to a gay audience. Says another gay writer, Andy Medhurst:

> *Brief Encounter* is not simply the tearful tale of heterosexual romance that it appears to be: beneath, or alongside, or overlapping this narrative is another, quite specifically related to the homosexuality of its author. Employing the naively biographical paradigm of gay authorship, *Brief Encounter* shows Noel Coward displacing his own fears, anxieties and pessimism about the possibility of a fulfilled sexual relationship within an oppressively homophobic culture by transposing them into a heterosexual context. The furtiveness and fear of discovery that end Laura's and Alec's relationship comprise a set of emotions that Coward would have felt with particular force and poignancy, and which gay men ever since have responded to with recognition and admiration.[5]

Laura is married to Fred (Cyril Raymond), a solid, dependable but boringly predictable gentleman who loves her unconditionally. But Laura's sexual attraction to Alec brings to the surface hidden emotions,

1 Leslie 'Hutch'
Hutchinson in *Cock
O' the North* (1935).
National Film
Archive London

2 Anthony Asquith

3 Ernest Thesiger. BFI
Stills, Posters and Designs

4 Dorothy Hyson and Cicely
Courtneidge in *Soldiers of the King*
(1933). BFI Stills, Posters and Designs

5 Margaret Lockwood
and Jane Millican in *Jury's
Evidence* (1936). BFI Stills,
Posters and Designs

6 Emlyn
Williams in
I, Claudius
(1937). BFI
Stills,
Posters and
Designs

7 Peter
Haddon in
Over the Moon
(1937). BFI
Stills, Posters
and Designs

8 Mary Morris. BFI Stills, Posters and Designs

9 Pamela Brown in *I Know Where I'm Going* (1945). BFI Stills, Posters and Designs

10 Sylvester Kee (Harley Power), Hugo Fitch and Maxwell Frere (Michael Redgrave) in *Dead of Night* (1945). BFI Stills, Posters and Designs

and she finds herself drawn away from Fred by her love (and lust) for Alec. Though Alec is also a gentleman, he is 'rougher' in appearance than Fred, and sexier. Raffish and adventurous, unlike 'safe' Fred, he is willing to take risks. This appeals to Laura, who is the personification of genteel middle-class decency. Even when they meet for the first time, there is immediate intimacy, but she knows she is playing with fire. Even though they are at ease with each other, they know they are playing a very dangerous game. What *Brief Encounter* tells us is that Laura has not married the man of her dreams, and when she finds him, she cannot keep him. Interestingly it is a 'gay' man, Dr Stephen Lynn (Valentine Dyall), Alec's queeny bachelor friend and colleague, who interrupts Alec entertaining Laura in his flat one afternoon. The dialogue is brief, but it is very Cowardian, and ambiguous. Is Stephen jealous of Laura? Were Stephen and Alec lovers?

Throughout the film, *Brief Encounter* has a gay subtext which comes from Coward's own gay sexuality. In 1990 gay film director Richard Kwietniowski re-worked *Brief Encounter* as a short gay romantic drama called *Flames of Passion*. He says:

I love film melodramas, all those with Joan Crawford and Bette Davis where the woman suffers. These films are very gay because they are about true love and sexual passion transcending the mundaneness of the every day. What particularly fascinates me about these films is that, on the one hand, they acknowledge female desire and sexuality, and say 'yes, it exists', but it exists as something that eventually has to be repressed or subordinated or denied. So in nearly all those films, like *Now, Voyager, Mildred Pierce* and *Brief Encounter*, the woman does not get the man. In *Brief Encounter* the housewife does not get the dishy doctor and she returns to the home, to the kitchen sink. But what these films deal with along the way is true romance and desire as fantasy. The cinema is better than any other medium for staging fantasy, and that is the agony and ecstasy of these kinds of films.

The other point of interest in *Brief Encounter* is the fact that Noel Coward wrote and produced it, and it seems to me that what that film is doing with female sexuality could be paralleled with the way homosexuality is seen institutionally in Britain. Which is to say it is reluctantly acknowledged as existing, but we are actively encouraged not to do anything about it, not to corrupt young people, not to frighten the horses by allowing it to actively inform our way of life, our thinking, our commitments, our way of relating to other people.

I feel that there is an enormous subtext in *Brief Encounter* which is Noel Coward's homosexuality. All those things Laura and Alec say like 'We want to, but we can't, we shouldn't, we mustn't'. This is very much to do with Coward's sublimation of his homosexuality. So Noel Coward being gay is incredibly important to the film.[6]

Love is ultimately the basis of *Brief Encounter*. Noel Coward and David Lean encapsulate its suddeness, delights, terrors and responsibilities. It's all here, true and touching, reaching depths other films before and since (most recently the *Brief Encounter*-esque *Bridges of Madison County*) do not.

When it was released, *Brief Encounter* was not popular with working-class audiences in Britain. Said critic Gavin Lambert in the Channel 4 television documentary *Typically British*, shown in September 1995: 'It was sneak-previewed in Rochester in the docklands to a predominantly working-class audience who got extremely impatient and somebody called out in the middle of the film – "*When's he gonna 'av 'er orf!*" It was successful with the middle classes. . . but it is a remarkable document of middle-class repression. . . . It was a rule in British films that sex or passion was a crime.'

In spite of its unpopularity with working-class audiences, *Brief Encounter* was an international success, and one of the most celebrated films of 1945–46. In 1946 it was included in the Best Films list at the Cannes Film Festival. In America it was named one of the year's 'Ten Best' by the National Board of Review, and nominated for three Oscars: Best Actress (Celia Johnson), Best Director (David Lean) and Best Screenplay (Anthony Havelock-Allan, David Lean, Ronald Neame). In addition to her Oscar nomination (rarely given to a British actress for a British film), Celia Johnson received the New York Film Critics Circle Best Actress award.

Notes

1. Michael Powell, *Million-Dollar Movie* (Heinemann, 1992), pp. 95, 533–4.
2. Rachel Kempson, Lady Redgrave, *A Family and its Fortunes* (Duckworth, 1986), pp. 95, 159.
3. Corin Redgrave, *Michael Redgrave: My Father* (Richard Cohen, 1995), p. 17.
4. Richard Dyer, *Brief Encounter*, BFI Film Classics (British Film Institute, 1993) p. 11.
5. Andy Medhurst, 'That special thrill: *Brief Encounter*, homosexuality and authorship'. *Screen,* vol. 32, no. 2, Summer 1991, p. 198.
6. Richard Kwietniowski, interviewed by Stephen Bourne in *Gay Times*, June 1990.

1946

I See a Dark Stranger

In *I See a Dark Stranger* there is a brief but memorable reference to the gay Irish patriot Sir Roger Casement (1864–1916) who was shot as a traitor to Britain. A young Irish girl, Bridie Quilty (Deborah Kerr), dreams of joining the IRA. Leaving her village to go to Dublin, where she plans to contact a member of the IRA, Bridie visits the Redmond Porter art gallery. Wandering into the portrait section, she encounters a patriotic Irish guide showing a group of school girls some of the portraits. He describes this as 'the gallery of the famous'. As the girls gather round one of the portraits, the guide explains 'Here's our old friend Sir Roger Casement. A lovely man. Knighted by the British for his fight against Belgian tyranny over there in Africa. Hung by the British for his fight against British tyranny here in Ireland. It's a mad world me darlings, a mad world!'

London Town

After the war the Rank Organization made an ambitious attempt to impress American audiences with *London Town*, Britain's first Technicolor musical. Starring popular music hall comedian Sid Field, with Greta Gynt, Kay Kendall, Tessie O'Shea and Petula Clark in support, it was a colossal, expensive failure. Dull and disappointing, *London Town* has often been cited as proof that success in the musical genre is impossible outside Hollywood. However, the film does preserve several famous sketches by Sid Field including one in which he plays Mr Sidney Boothroyd, an effeminate gay photographer. Jerry Desmonde co-stars as Mayor Whittaker who visits Sidney to have his photograph taken, and between them the two create a most outrageous pair of woopsies. When he isn't clasping his hands together, Sidney cannot keep them off the Mayor, forever touching and grabbing him. When they take tea, there is an hilarious exchange. Says Sidney, pouring the tea: 'I love a nice strong cup, don't you? Forgive me for pouring that way – I used to work on the railway.' Sidney's camp persona clearly made an impression on another comedian, Larry Grayson, especially when he talks about the operation he had on his leg: 'It's a big house to clean and I can't get up the stairs like I used to. I've never been the same since my last operation. Fourteen weeks on me back with me leg up!' Asks the Mayor: 'Were you stitched?' Replies Sidney: 'Well, I certainly wasn't crocheted!' Throughout the film, it is apparent that Field is not relaxed when he is in the company of his leading ladies, Greta Gynt and Kay Kendall. However, when he strikes out on his own and recreates his sketches, he is outstanding.

A Matter of Life and Death

In Michael Powell and Emeric Pressburger's beautiful fantasy *A Matter of Life and Death*, David Niven stars as Peter, an RAF pilot who claims he has been accidently chosen to die, and pleads for his life in a heavenly court. But the film's most interesting character is Conductor 71, an effeminate French aristocrat, played by Marius Goring. Conductor 71 was guillotined during the French Revolution and has been sent from 'above' to convince Peter to accompany him to 'heaven'. Conductor 71 is a gay man with style and flair. In his 'seduction' of Peter he is flirtatious, but always keeps his dignity. 'Do you play chess?', he asks. When Peter replies yes, Conductor 71 responds wistfully and eagerly: 'We could play every day.' Goring plays the scene in a suggestive manner, as though he is sexually excited by Peter. Clearly Powell and Pressburger are sympathetic with gays, for example, Conductor 71 is a 'fairy godmother' with total authority. He is not demeaned in any way. Says Dr Reeves (Roger Livesey): 'The rights of the uncommon man must always be respected.'

Other films of interest released in 1946

In the thriller *Appointment With Crime* a gay couple exist in the underworld. Herbert Lom plays Gregory, an art dealer who is also the leader of a gang of criminals. It is taken for granted that camp Noel (Alan Wheatley) is his boyfriend. Needless to say it is Noel who betrays Gregory; Gainsborough camp can be found in *Caravan*, especially in the performances of Dennis Price and Robert Helpmann; Michael Redgrave starred in the film version of Daphne du Maurier's *The Years Between*.

1947

Judith Furse

Today Judith Furse is remembered for playing over-bearing battleaxes, and the menacing, leather-clad, freak Dr Crow in *Carry On Spying* (1964). However, when she commenced her film career she was often cast in kind and gentle roles, and in 1947 gave a memorable performance as the sympathetic and understanding nun, Sister Briony, in *Black Narcissus*. The film's director, Michael Powell, later recalled that Furse came from a 'talented and attractive family' that had been 'associated with the Old Vic and the avant-garde theatre for some years'. He also described Judith as a lesbian who was 'unforgettable with her huge body, commanding height and masculine voice'.[1]

Judith Furse came from a military family. The daughter of Lieutenant-General Sir William Furse, she was born at Deepcut Camp, Camberley, Surrey in 1912. Her brother, Roger, became a celebrated stage designer and painter who occasionally worked in films. In 1948 he won an Oscar for his Art Direction and Set Decoration of Olivier's *Hamlet*. Their sister, actress Jill, died tragically young at the age of 28 in childbirth in 1944.

Judith was educated at St Paul's Girls' School and was a student at the Old Vic in 1931–32. By the end of the decade she had become a respected stage actress and director, and in 1939 Judith made her screen debut as Flora, Greer Garson's companion in *Goodbye Mr Chips*. Underneath Judith's gruffness was this softness and in most of her early films, such as *Johnny Frenchman* (1944) and *Helter Skelter* (1949), she gave convincing performances as gentle young wives and mothers. In the comedy *Quiet Weekend* (1946) Judith appears as the warm, friendly, maternal Mrs Ella Spender who arranges village concerts. 'I must have arranged more frightful concerts than anyone now living!'

she says. Derek Farr describes her as 'Our famous producer, a sort of C. B. Cochran of Throppleton.'

Sadly, by the 1950s, Judith found herself being cast for her physical type than for her emotional qualities and, apart from *Black Narcissus*, she was never given a film role which allowed her scope. She was cast for her immediate physical impact and, after a while, it became boring, for Judith's voice and manner did not go with this stentorian female. After *Black Narcissus* her roles, and her acting, lacked energy. For example, in the 1949 comedy *Dear Mr Prohack* Judith has one scene as the doyenne of the avant-garde socialist theatre. It's rather a nice part but she doesn't throw herself into it with the gusto of someone like Margaret Rutherford. Judith's holding back.

One of Judith's most overtly lesbian appearances occured on television in 1960 when she appeared in W. Somerset Maugham's *The Three Fat Women of Antibes* with Anne Shelton and Joan Young. Judith played the mannish member of the trio, a wonderful character called Frank who dresses in collar and tie and plays golf! What a pity she didn't play Sister George!

In 1966 Judith made one of her last film appearances as a villager in *Sky West and Crooked* but by that time she was just going through the motions. Her heart wasn't in it. In 1972 she made her last film appearance in *The Adventures of Barry McKenzie* as Edna Everage's 'minder', a shocking waste of talent. For 1970s audiences she was nothing more than a freak. In reality Judith probably didn't want to play big ladies. Like her contemporary, Hattie Jacques, maybe there was a little lady, a charming, romantic heroine, dying to get out. Instead she was cast for her bulk. In British films she was a gentle giant, and an interesting talent was wasted.

Very little is known about Judith Furse's private life. Interestingly when her brother-in-law published an autobiography, he didn't mention her at all. When he talks about Jill Furse's illness and death there is one mention of 'her sister'. Judith Furse died in 1974 at the age of 62.

Black Narcissus

In her entire film career, Judith Furse never really had a memorable part except, of course, as Sister Briony in *Black Narcissus*, and the depth and sincerity she managed to give that role is astonishing. At the beginning of the film, when the Reverend Mother sends Sister Clodagh (Deborah Kerr) to a deserted palace in the Himalayas to open a school/hospital, she says: 'I will give you Sister Briony. You will need her strength.' In the cold, remote world of the Himalayas, Sister Briony proves to be the 'rock' of the group of nuns, always loyal and dependable. There is intimacy and warmth in her scenes with Sister Clodagh (always beautifully lit by cameraman Jack Cardiff), but in these scenes we never see Sister Briony's face. We are not permitted to observe *how* she looks at Sister Clodagh in these brief encounters.

Strikingly handsome David Farrar is cast as rough, macho Mr Dean, the cool, cynical British agent who lives nearby. He is presented as a sex object, rare for a British film at this time. Eroticized by the constant display of his legs and bare chest, Mr Dean is one of the most virile and sexiest men ever seen in the movies. Former child star Sabu plays Dilip Rai, the young 'General', sent to the nuns to be educated. Exotic-looking, but not ridiculed, he tells Sister Clodagh: 'You don't need to count me as a man. I'm only interested in studious things.' He is the opposite of Mr Dean: soft-spoken, sensitive and effeminate. Exquisitely dressed in turban and jewels, he is a camp creation as great as Maria Montez in one of her Hollywood Arabian Nights adventures. We see him do 'unmanly' things, such as typing, and pulling out a scented peacock blue handkerchief. He describes the scent to Sister Ruth (Kathleen Byron) as: 'Black Narcissus. It comes from the Army and Navy Stores in London.' Sister Ruth is not impressed with Dilip Rai. She describes him as 'Vain. Like a peacock.'

Unsurprisingly, Dilip Rai is in love with Mr Dean. 'Oh I do like his voice. It's so nice and loud,' he tells Sister Clodagh. ' I think he's lovely, don't you?' It is an innocent attraction to an older, stronger man, but old Ayah (May Hallatt), the outspoken, bawdy guardian of the palace, does not approve. She conditions him to become heterosexual by forcing him to beat the native girl Kanchi (Jean Simmons). 'You're going to be a great man,' says Ayah. 'Finish the beating and begin to be a man!' In this scene Dilip Rai loses his innocence. He is no longer a boy, or treated like one. After Ayah leaves, Dilip Rai gives Kanchi his jewels, and her head falls seductively on his shoulder. Afterwards the young couple run away. Heterosexuality has won the day!

Or has it? Later, in a very emotional scene between Sister Clodagh and Mr Dean, she breaks down and tells him: 'You can't hold back nature and what is natural. You can't stop it interfering with you.' She goes on to explain that she *had* to take Dilip Rai into the school, and *couldn't* evict the Holy Man, two disruptive influences. 'I couldn't stop the wind from blowing in the air, from being as clear as crystal,' she continues. 'I couldn't hide the mountains.' This is sheer poetry and central to the film, for *Black Narcisuss* is telling us what is natural cannot be contained, or restrained. It has to flow. This is a film of extraordinary power and resonance for minority groups, especially lesbians and gays.

They Made Me a Fugitive

In the crime thriller *They Made Me a Fugitive*, directed by Cavalcanti, Trevor Howard stars as Clem, a demobbed ex-RAF officer, who finds civilian life unsettling. Taking to drinking in nightclubs, a woman comments: 'What he needs is another war.' Instead of finding another war, he meet a queer black marketeer with the rather obviously gay-sounding name of Narcy Narcissus. He's 'cheap, rotten, after-the-war trash', and superbly played by Griffith Jones. Looking to recruit a bit of 'class', he invites Clem to join his gang, but when the two men fall out, Narcy has Clem framed for murder. Later, Clem escapes from prison to avenge himself on Narcy and the Soho drug pushers. Narcy is a reprehensible character, and his embodiment of sinister brutality with hints of perversity and kinky sexuality, anticipates the 1960s London underworld of the Kray twins.

Other films of interest released in 1947

Gay actor Dennis Price had leading roles in Brian Desmond Hurst's melodrama *Hungry Hill*, based on the novel by Daphne du Maurier, *Dear Murderer*, as the murder victim of Eric Portman, and *Holiday Camp*, as the homicidal squadron leader; Terence Rattigan co-authored (with Graham Greene) the screenplay for *Brighton Rock*; Alexander Korda produced and directed a lavish, Technicolor version of Oscar Wilde's *An Ideal Husband* with gorgeous costumes by Cecil Beaton; Robert Newton played the effeminate, alcoholic painter 'Lukey' in Carol Reed's *Odd Man Out*. After 'rescuing' the wounded Irish revolutionary leader Johnny McQueen (James Mason), he hugs him in

the back of a carriage, takes him home, and is determined to capture the
dying man's face on canvas.

Notes

1. Michael Powell, *A Life in Movies: An
   Autobiography* (Methuen, 1987),
   p. 577.

1948

The Red Shoes

In Powell and Pressburger's dazzling *The Red Shoes*, Victoria Page (Moira Shearer), a young ballerina, dances to international stardom with a celebrated European ballet company. But her successful career is complicated by her love for – and marriage to – Julian Craster (Marius Goring), a struggling composer, and her divided allegiance to Boris Lermontov (Anton Walbrook), a martinet impresario. He tells her 'The dancer who relies on the comforts of human love will never be a *great* dancer. *Never!*' However, though *The Red Shoes* has been celebrated for nearly half a century as one of the screen's great heterosexual love stories, the central relationship in the film is essentially a gay one. Yet it doesn't exist on the screen. Why the paradox?

It is a well-known fact that Walbrook plays a renowned ballet impresario who was based on Diaghilev. His extraordinary gay relationship with the ill-fated Nijinsky evolves into two chaste, heterosexual professional associations in *The Red Shoes*. One is with Craster, the young composer. His first appearance is very queeny with heavy makeup under his blond locks, but this was probably an attempt to make Goring look younger (he was thirty-six at the time). The other – and more central to the story – is with the beautiful, red-haired dancer Victoria. However, even a superficial reading of the film reveals that no such 'love' exists between Victoria and Lermontov, nor was it meant to. Victoria is a slave to the dance; Lermontov has no personal feelings for her whatsoever. She wishes to be a star of the ballet; he has the means to make her one of the greatest. The bargain is struck. Her fate is sealed. She dances – and dies. He will carry on, searching for another Victoria, and then another.

The evidence is there. Just look again at their first meeting. Disturbing (not romantic) music plays on the soundtrack, and this cleverly works against, and disrupts, the 'heterosexual romance'. He looks radiant, but not because of her. It is the dance he loves, *not* the woman. 'I know nothing of her charms, and I care less,' he says. Also, Lermontov's appearance says it all. He wears a 'dress'. He's decadent (he eats grapes). In short, he's a magnificent queen, with flowers in his room and a love of opera. He knows exactly what he wants. Boronskaja (Ludmilla Tcherina) says 'he has no heart', but she is wrong, he has a heart of fire. He is cool in the middle of chaos, always in control, never rude, never abuses his power. He's the gay man as perfect leader. He doesn't have children, so he has to create. When he says 'it's about time I sat down with my family', he is referring to his dance company, his constructed family.

Walbrook's performance is magnificent. He is not Clark Gable, Burt Lancaster or Charlton Heston, nor is he meant to be. Neither is he overtly camp, or effeminate. His performance is subtle, and the actor seems totally at ease with his role. Perhaps Walbrook was comfortable with Lermontov because he was not playing a heterosexual, or love scenes with Moira Shearer. Said Michael Powell: 'Anton conceals his humility and his warm heart behind perfect manners that shield him like a suit of armour . . . . He goes underneath every line of dialogue, every emotion.'[1]

Lermontov's dealings with Julian Craster (who loves – and is loved by – Victoria), are curt and business-like. This inhibits the dramatic richness of the film more than somewhat, and it is regrettable that censorship prevented Walbrook and Goring having the love affair that would have created exciting tensions. Goring's part is essentially bland and underdeveloped. When they appear together, Walbrook's repressed feelings and tunnel vision are very much in evidence. The depth and colouring this actor gave to his role as the 'eternal beloved' friend of Candy in *Colonel Blimp* (see 1943) are missing from his role as Lermontov. Lermontov becomes nasty towards Craster only when he realizes he is going to take Victoria, and all those wonderful ballet roles she is going to play, away from him. Says Craster: 'You're jealous of her.' Replies Lermontov: 'Yes, but not in the way you're thinking.'

Apart from Walbrook and Lermontov, *The Red Shoes* is also important for the way it portrays other gay characters. Gay ballet dancer and actor Robert Helpmann is cast as Ivan Boleslawsky, Lermontov's principal male dancer. He has a moderately important role in the backstage story. Wearing what we now recognize as gay apparel (for example, the safari jacket he chooses for a dinner party scene must have been *de rigeur* casual wear for certain gay men in the 1940s and beyond), Helpmann acts in a restrained, but still markedly gay manner. It is a pity that the core of the film's drama couldn't have been similarly authentic. Throughout the film, Ivan and the other gay men are seen as equals and professionals. For a change, they are not caricatured. They integrate, work together, and in this respect *The Red Shoes* is a progressive film.

In one of the most famous screen debuts, Moira Shearer almost obliterates her male co-stars with her bewitching charm and intensity. *The Red Shoes* is much loved for Moira's performance, and highly regarded for its astonishingly rich decor, and Hans Christian Andersen ballet. The film remains one of the most loved in British cinema, fitting in perfectly with the sado-masochistic underpinnings of other popular camp melodramas of the era like *Madonna of the Seven Moons* and *The Seventh Veil* (and Asquith's earlier *Pygmalion*). That the relationship between master and slave betrays none of the erotic charge of those films, is something which most audiences and many critics have chosen to ignore. That *The Red Shoes* is only a beautiful shadow of what it could have been is a source of regret. On the evidence of *Colonel Blimp*, Powell and Pressburger could have handled the subject with much greater insight.

In Britain *The Red Shoes* was nominated for a British Academy Award as Best British Film (it lost to Carol Reed's *The Fallen Idol*). In America it received an Oscar nomination for Best Film, rare for a British film, but lost to another home-grown success, Laurence Olivier's *Hamlet*. It received Oscars for its art direction/set decoration and music score, as well as nominations for Pressburger's screenplay, and editing. In his 1993 book *Alternate Oscars*, Danny Peary named Walbrook his Best Actor of 1948. He noted Walbrook's elegance, charm and wry wit, and said he gave a 'sad, disturbing portrait of a complex, frustrated man who is so dedicated to his art – he calls ballet his religion – that he suppresses his human qualities'.

The Winslow Boy

Adapted from the play by Terence Rattigan, *The Winslow Boy* is a disturbing study of the isolation experienced by an innocent public school boy who is falsely accused of stealing. Rattigan and director Anthony Asquith sensitively explore the emotional impact on the boy Ronnie who is well-played by Neil North. The scenes in which Ronnie hides his embarrassing secret from his family has great resonance for gays. Frightened of what his father might say and do to him, Ronnie hides in the garden in the pouring rain. Later, after his father has declared his support for Ronnie, he says: 'In future I trust a son of mine will have the sense to come in out of the rain.' The film includes many superb performances, and Margaret Leighton is particularly memorable as Ronnie's sister who wants to know why they 'have to torture a child of that age?' There is also a wonderfully camp turn by dancer and light comedian Cyril Ritchard who performs 'Who Were You With Last Night?' in a sequence set in a music hall. 'I met Bertie Harkaway in the House of Lords today/Lilac waistcoat, grey top hat/Oh, he looked extremely gay!' he sings.

The Mark of Cain

Brian Desmond Hurst's costume drama *The Mark of Cain* is a compelling, though somewhat hysterical study of two brothers who destroy each other's lives. It is based on the novel by Joseph Shearing, a pseudonym for a female writer. Eric Portman gives a very queer performance as Richard Howard, a wine connoisseur who plays the piano and enjoys amateur dramatics. Prissy, flamboyant and sadistic, he constantly clashes with his younger brother, John (Patrick Holt), who prefers to take care of the family business. When John confronts Richard he reveals his older brother's cruel nature: 'We've never liked each other. Once when we were kids, you tied me to the bed post and beat me, remember?' When Sarah (Sally Gray), John's fiancée, interrupts and tries to make peace, Richard dismisses her with the following explanation: 'We weren't quarrelling – this is just English family life!'

After Sarah marries John, she discovers that he is *also* something of a brute: 'You don't want a wife. You want a sleeping partner in your business,' she screams. But just after John apologizes for his behaviour, and is reconciled with Sarah, Richard kills his younger brother in a fit of jealousy, and frames Sarah. She stands trial for murder, but at the last minute Richard admits he is responsible for his brother's death.

The Fool and the Princess

Based on a story by Stephen Spender, *The Fool and the Princess* is a fascinating low-budget melodrama concerning the problems faced by a middle-class couple trying to settle down after the war. The pre-war suburban domestic bliss of Harry and Kate Granville (Bruce Lester and Lesley Brook) has been disrupted by the war. After returning from Germany, Harry is troubled and unsettled, and Kate finds it impossible to bridge the gulf between them. At the beginning of the film Kate explains that she and her husband Harry have been 'pulled apart' by the war. 'Since then he seems to have lost all peace of mind,' she says. But she also reveals that it is not only the war that is distracting her husband from her and their young son: 'If only he were not so easily influenced by other people,' she says. 'Graham Ballard, for instance, with his big ideas on books, art and what not.' Kate expresses hostility and jealousy towards Graham (Murray Matheson), though it is obvious he has been a friend of Harry's for many years. The couple have even named their son after him, and Ballard is the boy's godfather. Interestingly, the hostility expressed by Kate towards Ballard is reminiscent of that later shown by Laura Farr (Sylvia Syms) towards Phil Stainer in the better-known *Victim* (see 1961).

Graham lives in Chelsea and when Harry visits him he is revealed as a camp aesthete, forever preoccupied with changing the paintings on his walls. 'In the soft light, and sacrifice its colour value,' he asks Harry, 'or over here in the strong light. . . (stands back, shakes his head). . . hopeless. Loses all its delicacy. The wall's wrong. I shall have to use it with a different colour scheme.' When Graham shows Harry a photograph he has found of the two men together in the war, he describes it as: 'an interesting example of how the uniform of war reduces us all to a common factor – the theme of my next book which I shall dedicate to little Graham.' In this scene Graham clearly finds Harry attractive, revealed by the way he looks at him. After this exchange, the two men drink gin and listen to Beethoven. Needless to say, at the end of the film, Kate and Harry are united in post-war domestic bliss and heterosexuality, perfect propaganda for its time.

Other films of interest released in 1948

In *Quartet*, W. Somerset Maugham made the first of three film appearances as himself, introducing omnibus versions of some of his short stories. *Trio* (1950) and *Encore* (1951) followed. Maugham is a camp delight, a cross between Dame Edith Evans and headmistress Miss Millicent Fritton (Alistair Sim in *The Belles of St Trinians*).

Notes

1. Michael Powell, *A Life in Movies: An Autobiography* (Methuen, 1987), pp. 635–6.

1949

Kind Hearts and Coronets

Ealing's *Kind Hearts and Coronets* is an unusual film for it is one of the first British comedies about murder. Its director, Robert Hamer, was attracted to the subject because he wanted to make a film 'which paid no regard whatever to established, although not practised, moral convention,' as well as, 'of making a film not noticeably similar to any previously made in the English language'.[1] The film stars Dennis Price in one of his most memorable performances. He plays Louis Mazzini, the decadent son of an aristocratic lady who was dispossessed by her family, the d'Ascoynes, for marrying a penniless Italian street singer. In a brief prologue, Price camps it up as Mazzini's Italian father. After the death of his mother, Mazzini, whose existence is denied by the d'Ascoynes, swears to take revenge on eight members of the family, inventing appropriate murders for each of them. In doing so, Mazzini hopes to inherit the title to a dukedom.

Robert Hamer co-scripted the film with John Dighton, basing their screenplay on Roy Horniman's turn-of-the-century novel *Israel Rank*. Horniman was a great admirer of Oscar Wilde and there are parallels to be drawn between Wilde and Mazzini. For example, Mazzini's aristocratic heritage versus his low social standing and ostracism. Mazzini's (amoral) relationship with Mrs Holland, a sparkling performance by Joan Greenwood, ends with her blackmailing him. Mrs Holland is the name Wilde's wife Constance took for herself and their children after Wilde's disgrace.

Audiences are not given an easy time with *Kind Hearts and Coronets*. It is absolutely different from any other Ealing production, except perhaps *Half-Way House* (1944) and *Dead of Night* (1945). Though it is a comedy, and a highly sophisticated one at that, it contains a dark, disturbing and hard-hitting critique of race and class. Racism has alienated Mazzini from his family but, though he is a victim, and should win audience sympathy, he fails to do so. He is not a likeable young rogue, but a very unpleasant snob. He lacks warmth, and the film gives him several 'queer' characteristics in an attempt to alienate audiences even further. He looks a bit of a poof with his long permed hair and quilted smoking jacket, and when he goes to work as a draper's assistant, a profession usually associated with gays, he is seen attached to 'women's things' (lingerie, etc). Mazzini, who also has a queenly 'air' about him, is portrayed as an unhappy, remote man. By committing murder, he recalls the gay killers in Patrick Hamilton's play *Rope*, which was made into a Hollywood film one year earlier by Alfred Hitchcock. In a remarkable *tour de force*, each of the d'Ascoynes is played by Alec Guinness. They include the formidable Lady Agatha, a suffragette, but in an article in *Gay Times*, drag artist Regina Fong said: 'I wasn't very impressed. . . the make-up was very clever, but everything was done for him; he just had to put the voice on and do an Edith Evans.'[2]

Cardboard Cavalier

Cardboard Cavalier is a failed attempt to capture on film the considerable talents of music hall comic Sid Field. He plays a barrow-boy who gets involved in a plot against Oliver Cromwell in seventeenth-century England. But there is an hilarious party sequence. Field, in drag as 'cousin Matilda', is introduced to Cromwell by the Doverhouse family. Getting very drunk and forgetting he is impersonating a woman, there is a lesbian *frisson* when he kisses 'sweet cousin Mary Ann' on her cheeks. 'Mary Ann, how you've grown!' he exclaims in front of the the surprised guests. Cromwell looks on in horror as 'cousin Matilda' approaches Milady Doverhouse and kisses her on the lips! Walking over to Cromwell, who is now very confused, he almost becomes the subject of a gay encounter when 'cousin Matilda' asks: 'Would you like to be my cousin too?'

Other films of interest released in 1949

Dennis Price starred as the poet Lord Byron in *The Bad Lord Byron*; Anton Walbrook starred in the film version of Pushkin's *The Queen of*

Spades with a screenplay co-authored by Rodney Ackland; Emlyn Williams wrote, directed and starred, as the 'gay' brother of Richard Burton, in *The Last Days of Dolwyn*. Burton went on to play a gay thug in the crime drama *Now Barabbas Was a Robber*.

Notes

1. Jerry Vermilye, *The Great British Films* (Citadel Press, 1978), p. 132.
2. Regina Fong, 'Having a Ball: Drag in the Movies', in *Gay Times*, November 1994.

1950

The Wooden Horse

The Wooden Horse was one of the most popular prisoner of war films to be made in Britain in the post-war years. It stars the breathtakingly handsome – but as wooden as the horse – Anthony Steel as John who urges the men to 'carry on jumping' while others tunnel out of Stalag Luft III. Although its plot and clipped, middle-class accents have been ridiculed in a score of British television comedies in subsequent decades, *The Wooden Horse* retains its power and conviction. The film also contains a languid, sensual atmosphere in the camp which is both homoerotic and fascinating.

There are no below-the-ranks 'cor blimey' types here. All the men are RAF officers and gentlemen. With so many attractive hunks draped across the screen, there are times when the film resembles a health and efficiency magazine. No opportunity is lost in the first half to show Anthony Steel naked, except for his skimpy shorts and boots. There is even one glorious shot where Steel casually scratches his nipple! There is not one, but two shower scenes. The second shows Bryan Forbes and David Tomlinson almost chest to chest, with Tomlinson playfully washing Forbes's hair. Quiet conversations, mainly between Steel and his co-conspirator, Leo Genn, are filmed in intense close-up. There's also a hospital scene in which Genn and Peter Finch (in a tiny role) appear to be in the process of devouring each other! Genn and Steel are shown very much as a faithful couple both before, and after, their escape. While Tomlinson, though married, is effete and scatty.

The wooden horse of the title is not the monster used outside the walls of Troy, rather it is a vaulting horse upon which the men practise all day while a tunnel is being dug beneath it. The Trojan analogy is valid in a homoerotic sense. Chest, navels, legs and body holds are focused upon at regular intervals. Steel is photographed like a Greek god, always serious and pensive. There are few mentions of home, for this is a film about male bonding. There is romance in the air rather than machismo, especially in the relationship between Steel and Genn. There is not a hint of ambiguity in Steel's screen persona. He strides manfully around, and his limitations as an actor are used to create a consistent aura of grim determination.

Pool of London

After collaborating on scripts for George Formby, and co-directing Will Hay comedies, Basil Dearden began to direct a much wider range of films. In collaboration with his partner, Michael Relph, Dearden would be responsible for a number of ground-breaking films, and the first to include realistic gay characters (see *The League of Gentlemen,* 1960 and *Victim,* 1961). With *Pool of London* he took a semi-documentary approach for a 'slice-of-dockland-life' story. It follows the adventures of a crew from a merchant ship who come ashore for a weekend. The film was praised for its extensive use of real London locations (it is one of the last films to feature a London tram-ride).

Among the crew is American seaman Dan (Bonar Colleano) who becomes involved in a jewel robbery with Vernon, the 'gentleman acrobat'. He is played by the gay actor and revue artiste Max Adrian who was memorable as the Dauphin in Olivier's *Henry V* and would later appear in Ken Russell's *The Devils* and *The Boy Friend.* Dan and Vernon meet for the first time at the Queen's Theatre, a run-down music hall where the acrobat is appearing in a third-rate revue called *Lipstick and Lace.* We first see Vernon performing his act on-stage, in top hat and tails, but he has no grace or charm. He's just a second-rate Fred Astaire. Dan enters the bar where he meets Mike (Christopher Hewitt) and asks: 'What's the idea of meeting in this place?' Replies Mike: 'Someone wants to meet a nice obliging sailor.' Dan, thinking he is going to meet a woman, becomes excited: 'That's me! Where is she?' Enter Vernon, an effeminate, queer-looking chap, the big close-up of his face revealing that he doesn't take off his make-up when he leaves the stage. Mike's reference to someone wanting to meet a 'nice obliging sailor' indicates that Vernon is gay, and his appearance confirms it. Vernon hates his job in the seedy music hall and he is desperate to get out. He assists Dan and the gang of crooks with the robbery, but turns nasty and viciously murders the elderly watchman. An unhappy, reprehensible gay man, Vernon is killed at the end of the film while being pursued by the police.

There is a brief, but interesting scene in the film when the police are looking for the murderer of the watchman. When they are 'checking all the likely ones' (gay suspects?), they are seen approaching at least two effeminate men including Edward, a speaker at Hyde Park Corner, and a pianist in a public house, played by Michael Ward. This actor later became a popular sissy-type in films, mostly Norman Wisdom comedies (see 1956).

Basil Dearden's real name was Basil Dear, but when he joined the film industry in the late 1930s, he changed it to Dearden. Apparently this was not because of its gay overtones, but to avoid confusion with film director Basil Dean, with whom he worked as a production assistant.

Other films of interest released in 1950

Noel Coward adapted *The Astonished Heart* for the screen, based on a short play from *Tonight at 8.30*. When Michael Redgrave had difficulty with the role of the tortured psychiatrist, Coward took over. Coward's friend and companion Graham Payn had a supporting role but the film was a flop. Coward described himself in it as 'that splendid old Chinese character actress'; Ivor Novello's stage musical *The Dancing Years* starred Dennis Price in the role created by Novello at Drury Lane in 1939.

1951

The Browning Version

Michael Redgrave's portrayal of public schoolmaster Andrew Crocker-Harris, known as 'the Himmler of the Lower Fifth', in *The Browning Version*, is a lesson in great screen acting. Inspired by Terence Rattigan's screenplay, based on his own stage play, and Anthony Asquith's direction, this film has something to offer the gay spectator. It is interesting to note that the role of Crocker-Harris has had special appeal to other gay actors. Eric Portman created the role of Crocker-Harris on the London stage in 1948, Maurice Evans played the part on Broadway in 1949, and John Gielgud made his American television debut in the play in 1959. But Michael Redgrave made the role his own. In an extraordinary, understated performance he uses the camera to draw out the deep-felt emotions and mannerisms of this repressed, frustrated martinet. *The Browning Version* isn't *Goodbye, Mr Chips*. It's cruel, unsentimental and full of unsympathetic characters, including the headmaster who tactlessly asks Crocker-Harris to make his leaving speech to the boys before the popular sports master. The story also resembles Edward Albee's *Who's Afraid of Virginia Woolf?* in its painful study of Crocker-Harris's loveless, torturous marriage to the selfish, callous and adulterous Millie (Jean Kent).

There is only one character in the film who shows warmth and compassion and it is the boy Taplow, superbly played by Brian Smith. He's a soft-spoken, gentle lad who defends Crocker-Harris when some of the boys describe him as 'barely human'. Says Taplow: 'I feel sorry for him.' This nice young chap is keen to please the master, and he is completely unselfconscious in his outspoken defence of him. Unlike Crocker-Harris, and other characters in the film, Taplow shows his feelings. He is the only person who shows an interest in Crocker-Harris, and expresses affection for him. It is possible that Taplow is in love with the older man. When he gives him a present of a copy of Robert Browning's translation of the *Agamemnon* of Aeschylus, it is a very touching and revealing gesture. His thoughtfulness moves the older man to tears, a rare moment when Crocker-Harris shows his feelings. Taplow is also the only boy in the school who goes to say goodbye to the master and applauds enthusiastically for him when he takes the stage to make his farewell speech.

In some ways Taplow 'liberates' Crocker-Harris from his repression, and in doing so it is possible that his repression is sexual. Though the story appears to be preoccupied with Crocker-Harris's heterosexual impotence, it seems that Taplow's desire to be 'friends' with the master hints at another side to the man. Finally, Crocker-Harris's farewell speech at the end of the film unexpectedly becomes a memorable and moving 'coming-out' statement. He admits he has been a failure as a teacher, and apologizes to the surprised congregation. When he asks for their forgiveness, all the boys applaud wildly. For his performance as Crocker-Harris, Redgrave received the Best Actor Prize at the Cannes Film Festival.

Other films of interest released in 1951

In *Emergency Call* camp actor Michael Ward made a brief but memorable appearance as Roberto, a weedy-looking 'strong man' in a variety act, wearing a loin-cloth and carrying dumb-bells. As he is about to make his entrance on the stage, he squeezes past Inspector Lane (Jack Warner). 'Not much *room*, is there?' he says haughtily; set in Ireland, and starring Orson Welles, *Return to Glennascaul* was a short supernatural drama written and directed by Hilton Edwards, the lover–partner of Micheal MacLiammoir, who produced the film. Edwards later played the blind conman in *Victim*, while MacLiammoir was memorable as Iago in Welles's *Othello* (1952). He also narrated Tony Richardson's *Tom Jones* (1963). *Return to Glennascaul* was nominated for a 1953 Oscar for Best Short Subject.

1952

The Importance of Being Earnest

Oscar Wilde's *The Importance of Being Earnest*, produced seven weeks before his arrest in 1895, is a masterpiece of English comic theatre. With its vocabulary, characters, subversion of the theatrical conventions of the 1880s and 1890s, and its coincidences, mistaken identities and skeletons in cupboards, poet W. H. Auden called it: 'the only pure verbal opera in English [subordinating] every other dramatic element to dialogue for its own sake to create a verbal universe in which the characters are determined by the things they say.'

Anthony Asquith's film version of *The Importance of Being Earnest* has been a popular success with audiences for more than forty years. When it was shown on television – for the eighth or ninth time since 1965 – on 1 November 1988 at 2.15pm on BBC1 – it attracted an audience of 2.5 million. This screening coincided with the British Film Institute's *One Day in the Life of Television* national survey in which viewers compiled a diary for just one day. For many, the screening of Asquith's film was the highlight of their day's viewing. Alison Fell was moved to describe it as 'this brilliant, polished gem of a work' while Dorothy Miles said 'it's lovely to see these superb actors in their prime again. That's one inestimable gift of television, to bring back the past by showing old films. Margaret Rutherford, a joy! Because I know the story I watch longer than I should. Anthony Asquith was a director who knew his medium.'[1]

In his stylish film version, Anthony Asquith made a comedy classic. It's a really fine piece of direction. His casting of camp British theatricals, such as Joan Greenwood, Michael Redgrave, Margaret Rutherford and, best of all, Edith Evans as Lady Bracknell, is perfect. And Asquith keeps the viewer interested by the simplest of means.

Michael Denison (who played Algernon) later recalled:

> I loved Asquith as a director. He was an interpreter and that is
> how I like my directors to be. I like them to know the script and
> the subject. He obviously loved the play, loved the wit and the
> shape of it, and loved the characters. He was completely in tune
> with the subject and, indeed, with the players.[2]

In many ways this is a better film than the more highly praised *Kind
Hearts and Coronets*, which never becomes as witty as it thinks it is.
However, the stars of that film might have been perfect for *Earnest*.
Dennis Price would have been gorgeous as Worthing, or possibly Alec
Guinness (with Price as Algy). Dorothy Tutin's performance ranks as
one of the most charming screen debuts ever (it earned her a British
Academy Award nomination as Most Promising Newcomer, but she lost
to Claire Bloom in Charlie Chaplin's *Limelight*), and Asquith even tones
down Margaret Rutherford's mannerisms.

At every turn Asquith – and Wilde – ridicule heterosexual romantic
fantasies while keeping the sugar coating that allows the bitter pill to be
swallowed. In the last shot, Redgrave and Greenwood appear to be
kissing but they are not. Instead they are adopting an absurd pose which
is typical of the mischief this film makes. We have all been conned into
thinking that Wilde's sparkling, witty production is a romantic,
heterosexual comedy but, says Jack Babuscio:

> Algernon and Jack are the two dandies living out double lives in
> *The Importance of Being Earnest*, a play whose homoerotic
> undertones lie closer to the surface than in any other Wilde work,
> excepting *The Portrait of Dorian Gray*. There is little doubt why,
> when asked on opening night if the critics were likely to
> understand the play's real meaning, Wilde quickly replied: 'I hope
> not!'
>
> The author was alluding not to the play's surface intentions,
> which are plain enough to polite audiences; but, rather, to the gay
> insinuations lurking behind the cunningly contrived charades and
> chiselled chatter of the two central characters – all of which
> would be totally unacceptable to the conventional middle-class
> audiences of Wilde's day.
>
> For *The Importance of Being Earnest* is essentially the story of

two men who engage in dandyish dating of females as a convenient cover-up for the pursuit of 'Bunburying', i.e. illicit and, it is strenuously suggested, *homosexual* pleasures. Thus, for Jack and Algernon lying becomes second nature, and, in the course of long practice, a delight as well, for the well-made or ingenious lie gives pleasure, and also indicates defiance of conventional morality.

Though doubtless unintentional, the faithful rendering of Wilde's play by director Anthony Asquith tactfully sustains suggestions of uranian love's aesthetic supremacy. Fidelity, for Asquith, also means making an unashamed slice of filmed theatre with little attempt at creating visual metaphors to frame Wilde's visual wit.[3]

Top Secret

In the comedy *Top Secret* a group of Russian spies kidnap Mr Potts (George Cole), an innocent sanitary engineer, who they mistake for an atom scientist. On his arrival in Moscow, Mr Potts enters a hotel and spots Cecilia (Eleanor Summerfield), a mannish lesbian dressed in tie and tweeds, and Aubrey (Ronnie Stevens), a woopsie. They are defectors to Russia, but when Mr Potts asks Rakov (Frederick Valk): 'Are they happy workers too?', the Russian replies: 'Certainly not. They're just a delegation of British intelligentsia on a goodwill mission.'

When Mr Potts shouts across to them: 'I say, hello. Good old England. Up the Empire!', Cecilia is not impressed: 'What's the fellow doing here with his bourgeois slogans?' she asks. Replies Aubrey: 'Goodness knows. But he'd better mind his ps and qs.' Later, Mr Potts tries to talk to Cecilia and Aubrey, but the Russians prevent him. Says Aubrey: 'Don't look now, but there's that dreadful man who shouted "good old England".' When Mr Potts calls to the couple: 'I say, you're English aren't you? How about a pint before you go?', a horrified Aubrey clasps his hands to his chest and exclaims: 'Saucebox! I don't trust him an inch!' Afterwards, when Cecilia complains: 'Oh, bother. I've lost a button,' Aubrey quickly responds: 'Don't worry. I've packed my needle and thread.'

The background to this film is important. *Top Secret* was made at the time of the Cold War when Russians were seen as a major threat. The year before this film was released, Guy Burgess and Donald Maclean, two gay spies, had escaped from Britain to Russia, leaving behind a link in the minds of the British public between gay sexuality, communism and 'traitors'. Queers, like Cecilia and Aubrey, undermined the British way of life, and it is hardly surprising to find them played by Eleanor Summerfield and Ronnie Stevens. Summerfield was often cast in unconventional roles, such as the umarried girl friend of the heroine (e.g. Phyllis Calvert in *Mandy*), and Stevens made a career out of playing all sorts of camp roles.

Other films of interest released in 1952

In the emotional melodrama, *Mandy*, Mrs Garland (Phyllis Calvert) sends her deaf daughter to an oral education school where she meets a kind, sympathetic teacher called Dr Jane Ellis (Nancy Price). There is fascinating ambiguity in the brief scene when mannish-looking Dr Ellis tells the mother 'Yes. I'm one of *them*' (deaf).

Notes

1. Sean Day-Lewis, (ed.), *One Day in the Life of Television* (Grafton Books, 1989), p. 186.
2. Brian McFarlane, (ed.), *Sixty Voices: Celebrities Recall the Golden Age of British Cinema* (British Film Institute, 1992), p. 77.
3. Jack Babuscio, 'Screen Gays No. 19 – Shooting Wilde: Oscar on the Screen' in *Gay News*, no. 89.

1953

Personal Affair

In the emotional melodrama *Personal Affair*, Leo Genn stars as a schoolteacher who is accused of having an affair with one of his pupils, Barbara Vining, played by Glynis Johns. She disappears but eventually returns home to her kind, sympathetic and understanding parents, Harry and Vi (Walter Fitzgerald and Megs Jenkins). Also at home is Harry's spinster sister Evelyn (Pamela Brown, see *I Know Where I'm Going*, 1945), a repressed lesbian. In one brief, but memorable scene Evelyn consoles the distressed teenager. 'You need me Barbara,' she says. 'My whole life has been directed towards this moment. I'm the only one who can understand and guide you.' Barbara turns towards her aunt and the two women hug each other. The camera concentrates for a moment on Evelyn's arm clasping Barbara around the waist, then shows her looking down at Barbara. Cupping the young girl's face in her hands, she moves to kiss her on the lips, but changes her mind and kisses her on the left cheek instead, and then twice on the neck. But this embrace is interrupted by Harry who has been observing the incident. Clearly, this is not the first time Evelyn's lesbianism has surfaced. After asking his daughter to leave the room, Harry says to his sister, tactfully and not unsympathetically: 'Evelyn, my dear, you must find yourself somewhere to live immediately. We're going to have a difficult time with that child. I'd prefer to handle it myself. I hate to seem harsh, but I must insist on this.' Upset, Evelyn replies: 'I'll go now. Tonight. I have friends, lots of friends.'

Marilyn

The low-budget crime melodrama *Marilyn* stars blonde, glamorous Sandra Dorne, a rival to Diana Dors in British films of the 1950s. Many years later, in 1982, Sandra resurfaced on the opening night of Channel 4 as the randy and defiantly blowsy Aunt Fanny, married to gay Uncle Quentin, in the Comic Strip's *Five Go Mad in Dorset*. *Marilyn* was based on Peter Jones's play *Marian*, and the film's alternative title had been *Road House Girl*. Interestingly, until the 1960s, the name Marian was often used for quasi-lesbian fictional characters in Britain. As Marilyn, Sandra Dorne's 'heterosexual' glamour is contrasted with the dark-haired, plain lesbian Vida Hope as Rosie. As directed and played it's fairly obvious that the two women share an intimate relationship with each other, especially in the hair-brushing scene when Rosie sensuously combs and teases Marilyn's blonde hair. Later, Rosie expresses jealousy when she discovers her friend is planning to run away with her (male) lover. After he departs without her, Marilyn turns to Rosie in desperation. 'Oh, Rosie,' she says, 'he's gone. There's only you and me left now. Just you and me together.' Rosie glares at Marilyn, and the selfish blonde realizes it is too late. Says Rosie: 'It would have been better if I'd gone before. I would have done anything for you. I would have died for you. I don't know why, but I would.' Marilyn pleads with Rosie: 'You can't leave me now because you're all I've got in the world.' When she asks Rosie why she is deserting her, Rosie replies: 'Because tonight you were ready to leave me without even a thought. You promised but you didn't mean it.' Rosie walks out on Marilyn, just before the police arrive to arrest her.

It is important to note that the director of *Marilyn* was Wolf Rilla, who also adapted the screenplay. Ten years later he returned to this theme in a slightly more adventurous way when he made *The World Ten Times Over* (see 1963) with June Ritchie and Sylvia Syms.

The Cruel Sea

Ealing's *The Cruel Sea*, based on the novel by Nicholas Monsarrat, enacts the Battle of the Atlantic from the points of view of the men aboard the HMS *Compass Rose*. It's an overlong, gritty and grim drama, shot in a semi-documentary style. Of the numerous male-dominated war films to be produced in the 1950s, such as *The Wooden Horse*, *The Colditz Story*, *The Dam Busters*, and *Reach for the Sky*, this was one of the most critically and commercially successful. It also generates a degree of homoeroticism which cannot be fully repressed.

This sometimes happened in Hollywood productions, especially genre films like the Western. Howard Hawks's *Red River* (1948) is the best example with young Montgomery Clift expressing an attraction for John Wayne. Perhaps the closest the British film industry came to producing anything similar are the war films of the 1950s with their emphasis on male bonding. Occasionally deeper feelings in the relationships between the men come to the surface.

Men and women are separated throughout *The Cruel Sea*, beginning with the opening credits when the four lead actresses are billed separately from the male actors. Then Jack Hawkins, the star of the film, is heard narrating off-camera. 'The men are the heroes. The heroines are the ships,' he tells us. Later, relationships between men and women are either unsatisfactory or end in tragedy. Morell (Denholm Elliott) is married to a selfish show girl who ignores him when he comes home on leave. Though he mentions her briefly, we never see the wife of Captain Ericson (Jack Hawkins). When he has leave, he remains on the ship. 'My wife is working,' he explains. Bachelor Bob Tallow (Bruce Seton), who says he *might* marry one day, takes his mate, widower Jim Watts (Liam Redmond), home on leave and introduces him to his sister, a widow. A little while later Jim tells Bob he intends to marry her, but she is killed in an air raid. The exception to this rule appears to be Lockhart (Donald Sinden) and Julie (Virginia McKenna), a WREN, until she tells him the Navy is moving her away and 'it might be some time before we see each other again'. There is some tension in their relationship anyway for Lockhart confesses to Julie that he will not consider marrying her in wartime. Julie accepts his decision without question.

At the beginning of the film, the 'sensitivity' of the three newcomers to HMS *Compass Rose,* Lockhart, Morell and Ferraby (John Stratton), is contrasted with Bennett, the First Lieutenant (Stanley Baker). A hard, insensitive disciplinarian, he drinks too much and is rude to the new men. They, in turn, are patronizing to him behind his back ('four months ago he was a car salesman') and predict he will get an ulcer. When their prediction comes true, Bennett is rushed to hospital and never seen again, leaving it possible for the 'sensitive' men to take centre stage. It's a pity, for Bennett was the most interesting of the four men, anticipating some class conflict between the characters.

The most interesting relationship in the film is developed between Captain Ericson and his second-in-command, Lockhart. Both men cry, and they are very intimate and tender towards each other, on-duty and off. Lockhart responds to Ericson's decency and kindness and it's almost as if he is hero-worshipping him. When he finds Ericson after a drinking binge, Lockhart settles him down for the night in his cabin. 'That's the best I can do for you. I wish it could be more,' he tells him. Their homoemotional bonding comes to a climax towards the end of the film when Lockhart chooses to remain with Ericson as his lieutenant-commander, passing up the opportunity of being captain of his own ship. He tells Julie that he 'loves' Captain Ericson: 'I feel I want to finish the war with him and with no one else. David and Jonathan. Does it sound silly?' Julie replies: 'No'. Says Andy Medhurst:

> The fiancée doesn't bat an eyelid; any modern audience is likely to erupt with amazed laughter. Such an apparently glaring reference to homosexuality could be made then because the idea of such 'real men' being homosexual was inconceivable to a general audience. . . . Only mischievous homosexual audiences would dream of taking Sinden's remark literally. Of course, Hawkins and Sinden were not 'really' sleeping together, but the codes of comradeship and camaraderie (such words having been military euphemisms for homosexuality from the Spartans to the Eighth Army) that Sinden's remark mobilizes are shown as so much more emotionally deep and rewarding than any heterosexual relationships seen. Similarly, in *Reach for the Sky* (1956), the anaemic attractions of Muriel Pavlow are so much less binding, despite the heterosexual drive of the narrative, than the togetherness of the 'chaps' in the Squadron.[1]

Street Corner

Various adventures of several policewomen are depicted in the London-based crime drama *Street Corner*. In one amusing scene in the police canteen the 'dramatic society' needs three more men to complete the male chorus for their forthcoming Christmas pantomime. But when WPC Lucy (Barbara Murray) approaches Constable Ross (James Gilbert), a pretty policeman with long eyelashes, sitting alone by himself, she is met with a hostile reception. Asking him if he will consider volunteering, he refuses in a slightly effeminate Scottish accent, glaring at the WPC. 'Oh, go on,' she says. 'I said no,' he rudely replies. 'Got any reason?' she asks. 'Aye. Several,' he says. 'In the first place I've got to study for my examination, and in the second I don't sing and I canna dance. And in the third I wouldn't if I could on account that I don't crave for the company of women!' Could Constable Ross be the first gay policeman to appear in a British film?

Tom Gill

Tom Gill was a comedy actor who, like his camp contemporary Michael Ward (see 1956), never achieved star status but gave many memorable performances in supporting roles in British films. Born in Newcastle upon Tyne in 1916, he first appeared on the stage as a small child in 1924. His London stage debut followed in 1935, the same year in which he made his first film appearance, with Hughie Green in *Midshipman Easy*. A long and successful West End career followed.

A typical Gill performance can be seen in the low-budget comedy *The Wedding of Lili Marlene* (1953). Here he makes a brief but hilarious appearance as Willy, a mincing, fluttery, wrist-flapping queen, a set designer working on the stage musical *Dancing on Air* at the Imperial Theatre. This is being produced by short-tempered Finnemore Hunt, played by a pre-*Carry On* Sidney James in one of his numerous impersonations of an American. Willy swishes into Hunt's office with some curtain material for the set, but Hunt rudely rejects it. Disappointed, Willy exclaims: 'Oh, well, it will just have to make a nice dressing-gown for poor little me!' Stumbling out of the office, Gill is not seen again, though he is given a screen credit at the end.

The asexual, sissy stereotypes played by Gill were popular in Hollywood films of the 1930s. In British comedies of the 1950s they're still the butt of the joke, and politically incorrect. But in spite of this, Gill's Willy in *The Wedding of Lili Marlene* is in keeping with the silliness of the film. It's a priceless example of a gay man making a tiny impression with an overtly camp performance, and he is clearly having fun. Tom Gill died on 22 July 1971, aged 54.

Off-screen, Gill's life took a dramatic turn during the war when he took part in a 'cover-up' for a famous gay man. During the war a famous actor was touring with ENSA through the West Country and was invited to a private party in the Bristol area. A party of guardsmen from a local barracks were also in attendance. The police raided the party and arrested the actor and a couple of the guardsmen for 'acts of gross indecency'. Hugh 'Binkie' Beaumont, the powerful and influential gay managing director of the production company H. M. Tennent, intervened on the actor's behalf in an attempt to save him from scandal. Beaumont made a series of telephone calls to contacts in Parliament, the Royal Household, the Home Office and finally the police. It was not only the actor's career that faced ruin, but Beaumont's organization.

A deal was suggested. The actor of fame and distinction would be released at once, no charges would be preferred, his name would be erased from the charge book and other official documents and nothing would be said to the press or anybody. In exchange, Binkie offered two scapegoats who had been at the party; they would be arrested, charged and imprisoned. He pointed out that this was a form of justice very popular in the Middle and Far East where it is believed that if a crime has been committed then *somebody* must be punished but it doesn't have to be the guilty party. It doesn't matter who because justice will have been done and *seen* to be done.

Binkie's delicate and persuasive argument was convincing and the authorities agreed. One of the two scapegoats was a young actor named Tom Gill, well known for playing breezy service and establishment types. He declared himself willing to go to prison for a year in exchange for £2,000 cash, £1,000 before and the other £1,000 afterwards, and the promise of permanent employment for the rest of his life. He wasn't newsworthy and with small newspapers as a result of wartime newsprint control, the matter was not reported. Binkie was as good as his word: the money was paid and the work flowed in whenever he wanted it. He had only to call at the office or telephone. 'I took Binkie up on his promise and he always gave me a part: nothing very big or important but something,' said Gill later. 'But there was always such an air of embarrassment when I called on his office or met him in the street or at first nights that I eventually stopped. So I never again worked for Binkie after the war. But that was *my* decision, not his.'

Gill had been sworn to secrecy but, like Binkie, he was a born gossip and chatterbox. He would tell the story to anybody in earshot while he propped up the bar at the Salisbury in St Martin's Lane, his favourite watering hole and second home. Inevitably, the news leaked out since a secret which is known to a dozen people has a limited lease of life, but it was common knowledge only within the narrow circle of the profession. It was never mentioned in the press and the identity of the famous actor (and the second scapegoat) has remained a secret. . . . The account of his sexual misdemeanours and his willingness to act as a scapegoat was told to me by Tom Gill at the MGM studios at Elstree when we were both appearing in *The Yellow Rolls-Royce*. The name of the second scapegoat cannot yet be revealed as he is still alive and I do not wish to cause him any distress.[2]

Jacqueline Mackenzie (Jackie Forster)

The Wedding of Lili Marlene is also of interest for an appearance by Jacqueline Mackenzie, eighteenth billed on the cast list as 'theatre barmaid'. In the 1950s this Scottish-born actress became a popular television celebrity and *TV Mirror* put her on their cover in 1958. Later she became the much-loved and respected activist Jackie Forster. While editing *Sappho* magazine from 1972–82, she was one of the few lesbians to speak out on British television. She is particularly memorable in *Speak for Yourself* (1974) and the discussion programme *Gays: Speaking Up* (1978). In 1994 the Sisters of Perpetual Indulgence ordained her St Jacqueline of the Eternal Mission to Lay Sisters, and in 1995 she made another impressive television appearance in the Channel 4 documentary *We Recruit*, about the Lesbian Avengers. Her other film appearances from this period include *Lilacs in the Spring* (1954) and *The Dam Busters* (1955), but if you blink, you'll miss her! She also made stage appearances, including the original production of Philip King's *Serious Charge* (see 1959) produced by the Repertory Players at the Adelphi in London's West End in 1953.

Gilbert Harding

Gilbert Harding was an outspoken English panellist, quiz-master and broadcaster, known as 'the rudest man in Britain'. A former teacher, police constable and journalist, from 1951 he became part of the post-war British way of life with his appearances as a panellist in the long-running television panel game show *What's My Line?* Every week he entertained and shocked viewers with his intellect, sharp wit and rudeness. He often bullied innocent guests if they gave evasive answers, or didn't speak perfect English. After one clash between Harding and chairman Eamonn Andrews, the BBC received over 175 phone calls and six telegrams from viewers complaining about Harding's appalling behaviour! For over a decade *What's My Line?* was an institution on British television, and Harding became a national celebrity. The possibility of marriage between this 'confirmed bachelor' and his close friend, lesbian writer and broadcaster Nancy Spain, fascinated the British public.

Such was the television celebrity status of Harding that he quickly found himself in demand for guest appearances in films (he did not have the performing experience to carry a whole film). Most of these were comedies and included *The Oracle* (1953), as the voice that makes predictions from the bottom of a well, *Meet Mr Lucifer* (1953), *An Alligator Named Daisy* (1955), *As Long As They're Happy* (1955), *Simon and Laura* (1955) and *Expresso Bongo* (1959).

In 1960 Harding agreed to be interrogated by journalist John Freeman on a famous live television interview programme called *Face to Face*. But Harding was reduced to tears in front of millions of viewers when Freeman asked about the recent death of his mother. This was, in fact, a deliberate attempt to try and 'out' him as gay at a time when homosexuality was still illegal in Britain. Harding didn't admit anything, but clearly the interview was a distressing experience for him, though he confessed on-screen that 'my bad manners and bad temper are quite indefensible. . . I'm almost unfit to live with. . . I'm profoundly lonely. . . I should be very glad to be dead.' John Freeman later admitted his lack of sensitivity but Harding died on 16 November 1960 shortly after the programme's transmission on 18 September. He was 53.

Owen Spencer Thomas described him on BBC Radio London's *Gilbert Harding* in 1979 as 'That enigmatic man. . . bad-tempered and rude, yet his friends counted him as one of the kindest, and most generous.'

Other films of interest released in 1953

Robin Maugham collaborated on the screenplay of the crime thriller *The Intruder*, based on his novel *Line on Ginger*. Dennis Price starred.

Notes

1. Andy Medhurst, *Homosexuality and British Cinema: Representations and Readings*, unpublished MA Film Studies Dissertation, University of East Anglia, 1982.

2. R. Huggett, *Binkie Beaumont* (Hodder & Stoughton, 1989), pp. 350–51, 548.

1954

The Young Lovers

Anthony Asquith's exquisite *The Young Lovers* is a variation on *Romeo and Juliet*, a love story set during the Cold War. Asquith's Ted/Romeo (David Knight) works in intelligence in the American Embassy in London, while his Anna/Juliet (Odile Versois) is the daughter of a Russian diplomat. The couple meet and fall in love at a performance of the ballet *Swan Lake* in Covent Garden, and thereafter Tchaikovsky's haunting music beautifully underscores the plight of the young couple. Surveyed and hounded by representatives of their paranoid governments, each believing that the other is spying for their respective countries, Ted and Anna are eventually separated. Neither of them wants to renounce their country, there is no 'third place' for them, but when Anna becomes pregnant, they run away together. Anna leaves a note for her father telling him: 'We are running away, not because we are guilty, but because you will not believe we are innocent. You say that the world is divided in two. We cannot escape that fact. We are going to try. You who live in separate worlds cannot believe in innocence because you no longer believe in love. But without love you will destroy, not as you think, each other, but yourselves.'

Shot in an effective semi-documentary style, this emotional film of forbidden love is the closest Asquith came to making a gay love story. He gently explores the desperation felt by two people who love each other but are kept apart by sinister forces. One critic, C. A. Lejeune in the *Observer*, even described it as 'the most moving British film since *Brief Encounter*'. In having Ted and Anna 'stand in' for a gay couple, Asquith invites comparison to the Noel Coward classic, and there are similarities between the two films. While Tchaikovsky stands in for Rachmaninov, Ted and Anna meet in secret in shadows and darkness, in cafés, in Foyles bookshop. Smoky train stations are also dominant. Though David Knight and Odile Versois are believeable as the young lovers, Asquith makes one blunder. In the scene when the couple are about to have sex, the music of *Swan Lake* swells on the soundtrack and he cuts away to a shot of waves breaking on rocks. By 1954 this had become a well-used cliché. But only nine years after *Brief Encounter* it's still quite daring of Asquith to even suggest an unmarried couple having sex, and then have it confirmed when she gets pregnant. Though *The Young Lovers* doesn't have the overall emotional impact of *Brief Encounter*, it remains a glorious, passionate plea for the understanding of forbidden love.

The Weak and the Wicked

The Weak and the Wicked is a women's prison drama based on Joan Henry's novel *Those Who Lie in Gaol*, based on her own experiences. Glynis Johns stars as Jean Raymond who is framed and incarcerated in HM Prison Blackdown, with Betty Brown, played by Diana Dors. One of the prison officers at Blackdown is P. O. Arnold, played by Joyce Heron, a tough, tight-lipped disciplinarian. Arnold is also a repressed and predatory lesbian who gazes silently and longingly at Miriam Lane (Josephine Griffin), a young, pretty, nervous and soft-spoken inmate. Miriam is frightened of Arnold. Later, in the prison yard, Miriam is seen walking along, talking to another inmate, Tina (Simone Silva), when Arnold approaches her, touches her arm, and warns: 'Don't get so close together.' Could she be jealous? Hisses Tina angrily to Miriam: 'Do you know that screw? Keep out of her way. She got me three days in the punishment cell, and I won't ever forget it!' Later, Arnold warns Miriam to stay away from Tina: 'She's a born mischief-maker. Get yourself another friend.' Arnold appears again when she discovers the two women trying to communicate with each other through their cell walls. She shows signs of jealousy and warns Tina: 'If I catch you trying to communicate with Lane just once more, you'll regret it.'

In the sewing-machine room, Arnold is supervising, dressed in masculine attire: white shirt, black tie, black cardigan and black skirt. She approaches Miriam and picks up a piece of material from her table. She moves on to Tina's table where she picks up a shirt. Everyone looks at her, expecting something to happen. Arnold then rips the shirt in front of the women, who immediately stop working, and stare at her. Arnold stares back but there is no confrontation. Instead they all put their heads down and continue working. Arnold, determined to provoke Tina, says: 'Well, this won't do. I thought you were supposed to be a dressmaker.' Arnold threatens Tina, telling her if she doesn't meet her quota: 'No pay. No pay, no cigarettes.' Tina grabs a pair of scissors and tries to attack Arnold but Jean Raymond intervenes and restrains her. This is Arnold's final appearance in the film and, though her role is short, we are left with a clear impression of a lamentable, vindictive lesbian unable to hide her feelings of jealousy. She is stereotypically portrayed as predatory and 'unnatural'.

The Belles of St Trinian's

A decade before she appeared on the stage and screen in *The Killing of Sister George*, Beryl Reid made a brief but memorable appearance as lesbian school mistress, Miss Sybil Wilson, in *The Belles of St Trinian's*. This hilarious comedy stars Alistair Sim in drag as Miss Millicent Fritton, the genteel but corrupt headmistress of a girl's school. At the beginning of the film she tells her equally corrupt brother, Clarence (also played by Sim): 'When poor Freda and I started this school during the General Strike of 1926 we vowed to make it the happiest, most carefree establishment in the whole of Britain, and what a gay arcadia of happy girls it was then – until the war broke out.' 'Poor Freda' is clearly Millicent's deceased 'other half', but we can only speculate what kind of relationship the women shared. In the 1950s the school has become a haven for anarchic young women who do everything they can to disrupt the lives of their mistresses.

Miss Fritton drives everyone mad too, including Miss Holland (Jane Henderson), her frustrated, lean-faced, mannish secretary. 'We need *cash*!' she screams at Miss Fritton.

Lilacs in the Spring

Producer–director Herbert Wilcox created a series of highly profitable, and much-loved vehicles for his wife, Anna Neagle. For seven years she was Britain's most popular female star. From *Goodnight Vienna* in 1932, to *The Lady is a Square* in 1959, this durable team collaborated on numerous box office hits including *Nell Gwyn*, *Victoria the Great*, *Sixty Glorious Years*, *Spring in Park Lane* and *Odette*. However, few critics took them seriously. Reviewing *Nurse Edith Cavell* in 1939, Graham Greene said in the *Spectator*:

> We get from his films almost everything except life, character, truth. Instead we have flags, anthems, leading articles, a tombstone reticence. It would be unfair to call his Way of a Neagle vulgar showmanship. . . for there is seldom anything vital enough to be called vulgar in the successive patriotic appearances of this rather inexpressive actress. Miss Neagle looked nice as Queen Victoria, she looks just as nice as Nurse Cavell: she moves rigidly on to the set, as if wheels were concealed under the stately skirt: she says her piece with flat dignity and trolleys out again – rather like a mechanical marvel from the World's Fair.

However, by the mid-1950s, Neagle was no longer a major box office attraction, so in 1953 she returned to the stage in *The Glorious Days*, recreating some of her most famous screen roles (Nell Gwyn, Queen Victoria, etc). Its success inspired a screen version, *Lilacs in the Spring*, in which Wilcox starred her opposite Hollywood's legendary swashbuckler Errol Flynn.

Lilacs in the Spring is a camp classic, with mature Anna still entrancing, and songs by Noel Coward ('Dance Little Lady') and Ivor Novello ('We'll Gather Lilacs'). Anna plays Carol Beaumont, the song-and-dance girl 'from the Coward revue just before the war' working with ENSA during the Second World War. Describing show business, Carol says: 'I adore it. But then I've never known anything else. I don't think I could get along without it.'

Opening in 1944 with a rehearsal for an ENSA show at the Theatre Royal, Drury Lane, Carol is seen dancing with a mincing queen who looks young enough to be her son. Their dance routine, all swaying bodies and waving arms, is pure pre-war Ivor Novello kitsch. As Charles King, Carol's producer, handsome, rugged David Farrar, once memorable as the bare-chested sex object of Powell and Pressburger's *Black Narcissus*, looks embarrassed and tired. When the mincing queen fails to impress him, he interrupts the dance and orders him off the stage: 'You're not playing to a West End audience,' he complains. 'You're playing to a lot of chaps who haven't seen their wives or sweethearts for months, maybe years.' Macho King then proceeds to demonstrate to the queen how to dance 'like a man' for the 'chaps'.

An even more bizarre sequence follows when a V1 bomb lands near Carol during an air raid and she is knocked unconcious. Reminiscent of *The Wizard of Oz*, the black-and-white photography suddenly turns into colour, and Anna becomes Nell Gwyn! Throughout the rest of the film, Carol dreams of living in the past. For instance, falling asleep, she becomes Queen Victoria, singing to Albert at the piano. It's an embarrassing scene, for Anna cannot sing. However, Anna shows us what a marvellous dancer she is by giving a terrific version of the charleston to Noel Coward's 'Dance Little Lady'.

By 1954 the movie career of Errol Flynn was in decline. Washed-up in Hollywood, and an alcoholic, he was desperate to earn money and complete his ill-fated and one-time homoerotic version of *William Tell*. Wilcox and Anna came to his assistance, but for Errol it must have been a humiliating experience playing Anna's father briefly at the end of the film. Off-screen, he was five years *younger* than her!

Other films of interest released in 1954

In Anthony Asquith's *Carrington VC* Michael Bates played the campish Major Broke-Smith, holding a cigarette holder in one hand, and dabbing his face with a handkerchief in the other; comedian Frankie Howerd made his screen debut in *The Runaway Bus*.

1955

I am a Camera

Laurence Harvey plays gay writer Christopher Isherwood in *I am a Camera*, the screen version of John Van Druten's play based on Isherwood's short stories *Berlin Stories* and *Goodbye to Berlin*. In John Collier's screenplay, the overt gay sexuality of Isherwood's stories is toned down but, though submerged, it does not become completely invisible. For instance, Harvey as Isherwood introduces himself as 'a novelist. Comfortably off. Set in my ways. A confirmed bachelor', and this is enough to *imply* that he is gay. Also, Isherwood describes himself as a 'camera', a man who observes others, and throughout the film he remains a detached, somewhat remote figure, both sexually and emotionally.

At the beginning of the film he attends a literary cocktail party given by his publisher for the author of a new book. When he arrives, he approaches Richard Wattis, appearing as one of the partygoers, who is sitting majestically in a chair, flanked by a couple of queens. Wattis gives him a book by the author, who turns out to be Sally Bowles (Julie Harris), the nightclub singer whom Isherwood befriended in Berlin in 1931. Recounting his friendship with Sally to Wattis and the two gays, in flashback the film tells the story of their unconventional relationship. It is important to note that Isherwood and Sally do not have a sexual relationship. Instead they become 'buddies', free spirits who are determined to have fun, though they have no money. They meet in a seedy nightclub where she performs a cabaret act but, after she is robbed, and left homeless, Isherwood insists that she stay the night in his boarding-house room. Naturally she's suspicious, but he assures her: 'You needn't be afraid of me. There's no room for that sort of thing in my life. You see, there's work to do. Very important work.' Taken aback, the sexually uninhibited Sally replies 'Must be!' Later, their mutual friend Fritz (Anton Diffring) finds it difficult to believe that the couple share a room, but are not sexually involved. 'Fritz, there is *nothing* between Sally and me,' Isherwood insists, and Sally confirms this, saying 'Strange, but true.'

However, an uncomfortable undercurrent surfaces in the initial portrayal of this 'odd couple'. When it is revealed that Isherwood is a hypochondriac, fond of 'vitamins and things' (he owns a vast collection of pill bottles), we begin to notice that he is also a bit fey, and prissy. In spite of her 'unconventionality', Sally doesn't approve of this. When she moves into the boarding-house, she says to Isherwood: 'I'm awfully glad we're going to be friends. I don't think I ever had a real friend before. One or two girls, maybe, but girls are so effeminate.' This is said almost like a warning to Isherwood. After all, women are not usually described as 'effeminate'. In spite of being 'divinely decadent' in Weimar Germany, Sally appears to be just an old-fashioned homophobe at heart, intolerant of gays. To her, men are there for sex, *not* platonic friendships. And if they don't give her what she wants, then they'd better behave like *real* men, and not like pansies who are fond of vitamins.

But, in spite of this, the friendship between the 'odd couple' does grow, and Sally cannot help but warm to Isherwood, who is a strong, sensible, likeable man. Determined to seduce him, she fails because there is no sexual charge between them. He tries to kiss her, but his attempt is clumsy, and she doesn't respond because she knows it is a waste of time. But she does begin to care about him, and tries to be a supportive friend.

Unfortunately, in spite of their enthusiasm and obvious commitment to the story, the excellent performances of Laurence Harvey and Julie Harris are almost buried by weak direction, censorship, too many script compromises, and a low budget.

Confidential Report

Ten years after playing the tortured ventriloquist in *Dead of Night*, Michael Redgrave played another gay role in *Confidential Report*, an unusual, compelling mystery thriller written and directed by Orson Welles. Redgrave is Burgomil Trebitsch, a scruffy, effeminate, hairnetted

Polish antique dealer whose shop is overrun by cats. By using the term 'my dear', and shuffling about the shop, he seems to be impersonating Alec Guinness as Fagin in David Lean's *Oliver Twist*. Grotesque and frightening, it's not Redgrave at his best.

Gordon Heath

An actor who also appeared in *Confidential Report* was the African-American Gordon Heath. He appears briefly as an elegantly dressed pianist in a restaurant. Heath was born in New York in 1918 and enjoyed early success on the Broadway stage in 1945 in *Deep Are the Roots*, a powerful drama about racism in post-war America. In 1947 the production transferred to London's West End where Heath received more critical acclaim. Heath's arrival in London coincided with the emergence of a new generation of black actors and actresses, mostly from the Caribbean, and it is important to acknowledge that their talents were not always wasted in stereotyped roles. For instance, in 1954 Heath provided the narration for Halas and Batchelor's award-winning animation film of George Orwell's *Animal Farm*. The following year he acted with Elisabeth Welch in a BBC radio version of Alan Paton's *Cry, the Beloved Country*; and for BBC television and director Tony Richardson he gave a memorable performance as Shakespeare's *Othello* in 1955. In 1956 he took part in a reading of black poetry at the Royal Court with Cleo Laine. However, unlike their white contemporaries, actors like Heath were denied a proper career structure. For example, in Britain in the 1950s, talented and attractive black actors like Heath, Cy Grant and Errol John were not put under contract and promoted like some of their white contemporaries. Opportunities to work in British films at this time were rare, though Heath did give impressive performances in small roles as the 'queerish' coroner in *Passionate Summer* (1958), the arrogant lawyer in *Sapphire* (1959) and as Emile in *The Nun's Story* (1959) with Audrey Hepburn, though most of this role ended up on the cutting-room floor.

From the early 1950s Heath lived in Paris with his lover, Lee Payant, and ran a popular Left Bank café called L'Abbaye for many years. Says Paul Breman in his moving obituary of Heath in the *Independent* (13 September 1991):

The proud, haughty, temperamental, extrovert New Yorker found in Lee Payant a partner to make all of life possible and most of it enjoyable. For nearly thirty years they appeared every evening, seven days a week, in their crowded little folksong 'club' L'Abbaye, behind the abbey church of St Germain. When Lee died (in 1976) Gordon could not face continuing the club, no longer enjoyed the Paris they had taken to heart so unreservedly, and went back to the States for five long and bitter years of what to him was exile. He went back home to Paris where he was fortunate enough to find a new partner, Alain – as different, as gentle and as devoted as Lee had been.

Gordon Heath died in Paris on 28 August 1991 from an AIDS-related illness. He was undoubtedly one of the most talented and respected actors to emerge in Britain in the early post-war years.

Other films of interest released in 1955

Terence Rattigan adapted his stage play *The Deep Blue Sea* for the screen with a supporting cast that included Eric Portman, Emlyn Williams and Alec McCowen; gay writer Alan Melville supposedly based his satirical comedy *Simon and Laura* (about a bickering show business couple forced to pretend to be madly in love with each other in a television sit-com) on Vivien Leigh and Laurence Olivier. In the film, Peter Finch – Lady Olivier's former lover – sent up Larry as a vain, marginally camp drama queen who is always threatening to 'go home to mother'. This film also included an appearance by Alan Wheatley as a very swishy, over-the-top television art director; Powell and Pressburger camped it up with *Oh. . . Rosalinda!*, based on *Die Fledermaus* by Johann Strauss. It featured Michael Redgrave, Anton Walbrook, Dennis Price and, in a minor role, John Schlesinger (before he became a director); Herbert Wilcox teamed Anna Neagle and Errol Flynn again for Ivor Novello's musical *King's Rhapsody*. The script required Flynn, as Prince Richard, to say: 'Hardly desirable. A horrible necessity.'

1956

The Spanish Gardener

In *The Spanish Gardener*, based on the novel by A. J. Cronin, Jon Whiteley plays Nicholas, the 'delicate' young son of Harrington Brande (Michael Hordern), the British consul in Madrid. Nicholas's mother has deserted the family, an unusual theme for a British film, and Brande has become very protective of his son. Hordern's performance is the most interesting in the film. He plays Brande as a neurotic, fussy, bad-tempered old queen, looking and behaving remarkably like Noel Coward. He even speaks like the 'Master'. However, Brande clearly cares about his son, and is very affectionate towards him, brushing his hair, hugging him. No explanation is given for his wife's desertion and so, with the absence of a woman in his life, it could be suggested that, in spite of their son, the Brandes had a sterile marriage, and that Brande is a repressed gay.

Nicholas is a polite, kind, well-mannered and innocent child who is also sad and lonely, until he befriends the new gardener, José, played by Dirk Bogarde. This is Bogarde at his most sensual, erotic and handsome. With a calm and gentle nature, José forms a close attachment to Nicholas, and 'liberates' him from his stifling and overbearing father. José encourages the boy to take his shirt off and enjoy the sunshine. They work happily together in the garden. José chases him into the sea and takes him trout fishing. But inevitably Brande becomes envious, although there is ambiguity in his jealousy. Is he jealous of José's close friendship with his son, or is Brande attracted to the gardener, and repressing his gay feelings? All through the film there is a homoerotic undercurrent, especially when Bogarde appears. He looks absolutely gorgeous with his suntan, bare chest and deep, soulful eyes. But *The Spanish Gardener* is Michael Hordern's film. He gives a fascinating performance, suggesting hidden depths in an underwritten character, and encouraging us to question Brande's true motives. Of course everything ends happily with Brande realizing his mistakes, apologizing to José and, thanks to the gardener, living happily-ever-after with his son.

The Case of the Mukkinese Battlehorn

The Case of the Mukkinese Battlehorn is a short comedy in which an Inspector unmasks a museum curator as head of a horn-smuggling ring. Peter Sellers plays several characters, including a brief appearance as screaming queen Jervis Fruit, Assistant Commissioner of Police. Complete with wavy blonde hair, a smoking jacket, frilly shirt and cigarette holder, Fruit reclines on a chaise-longue and discusses the case with the inspector on his white telephone. He's as camp as Christmas, and Sellers is having a ball! But this is not sophisticated comedy, it's blatantly homophobic. In the 1950s Sellers enjoyed telling anti-gay jokes while touring in his variety shows, and at least one gay member of the audience at one of his performances is known to have stood up and asked him to stop.

Michael Ward

Tall, thin comedy actor Michael Ward, sounding a little like Quentin Crisp, acted in numerous British films, and created a niche for himself as photographers, salesmen, dress designers and bank clerks, all of them sissies. Like many other gifted British character actors, he was a scene-stealer, though his roles were often very small (if you blinked you missed him). But nothing could prevent him from drawing attention away from the likes of Frankie Howerd and, later, the *Carry On* team. With perfect timing, Michael always made an immediate impact, forcing cinema audiences to take notice of him, however small his role. He is, perhaps, best known for his appearances in five Norman Wisdom comedies of the 1950s. Though mostly 'bit' parts, he provides brief, but welcome diversions from Wisdom whose antics can be extremely irritating. In 1956 Michael played a rare featured role, memorably cast as mincing Uncle Maurice in a Wisdom comedy called *Up in the World*. Though he's playing a gay stereotype, he's still the best thing in the film.

The son of a country clergyman, Michael was born in Cornwall in 1909 and at an early age often pretended to be someone else. He once recalled in an early press release: 'As a small boy I enjoyed dressing up and pretending to be other people. Once I visited several villagers dressed up as a very old woman. I wore a dress, a hat and a fur stole round my neck and I took everybody in.' Determined to become an actor, Michael won a scholarship and trained at the Central School of Acting in London. Approaching several agents for representation, one of them told him: 'I don't think you will ever become a successful actor. You have an odd voice and your nose is quite large.' Michael replied: 'Well, sir, one day you'll be very sorry because I will be quite famous and you'll be watching me from the back row of a cinema, a poverty-stricken agent, wearing a threadbare coat!' Michael worked in repertory before appearing in the lavish revue *The Night and the Music* with Vic Oliver at the London Coliseum in 1945. Another early stage role was Beverley Carlton, a caricature of Noel Coward, in *The Man Who Came to Dinner*.

In 1947 Michael made his screen debut with a bit part in Alexander Korda's version of Oscar Wilde's *An Ideal Husband*. Desperate to continue working in films, Michael was advised to write to directors asking them for work. This paid off when the director John Paddy Carstairs screen tested him and gave him a good role as Mr Elvin Sullivan, a snooty ornithologist, in the crime drama *Sleeping Car to Trieste* (1948). Set on board the Orient Express, Mr Sullivan shares a train compartment with a handsome, horny American GI (Bonar Colleano). But Mr Sullivan bores him silly with his lecture on birds. The GI is thrilled when they are interrupted by a couple of young French women. When the GI suggests that he and Mr Sullivan pair up with them, the latter scowls. He is not interested in the opposite sex! Says the GI: 'Maybe I'll have to handle both of you myself.' Afterwards, Carstairs often cast Michael in his films, including several 1950s comedy hits such as *Trouble in Store*, *Man of the Moment*, *Jumping for Joy*, *Up in the World* and *Just My Luck*. When the actor asked him why he helped him so much, the director replied: 'Because you have very nice manners.'

In *Trouble in Store* (1953), comedian Norman Wisdom made a huge impact with his screen debut and walked off with a British Academy Award as Most Promising Newcomer. Set in a department store, he plays a stockroom clerk with an ambition to be a window dresser, but he is constantly hired and fired. However, his wish comes true when he outwits a robber and becomes a hero. Michael is featured briefly as a window dresser called Wilbur who is horrified when Norman introduces himself as a window dresser. 'You?' cried Wilbur. 'How utterly grotesque!' With just one line, Michael Ward stole the scene, and guaranteed himself a future in Norman Wisdom's comedies.

In *Man of the Moment* (1955) Michael plays a smartly-dressed but intolerant gay photographer. He attempts to take a passport photo of Norman Wisdom, but the comedian cannot stop mugging. 'I cannot take you smiling,' Michael says, exasperated. 'Under no circumstances can we allow a passport photograph to look pleasant!'

In *Jumping for Joy* (1956) Frankie Howerd poses as a lord and finds himself fussed over by a trio of gay salesmen in a department store. They are bespectacled Richard Wattis as well-spoken Mr Carruthers, tubby, cherubic, effeminate Reginald Beckwith as Mr Smithers, and Michael Ward, easily the campest of the three, as a mincing tie salesman called Mr Pertwee.

In *Up in the World* (1956), Norman Wisdom stars as a window cleaner who saves Sir Reginald Banderville, the mischievous, spoilt-brat son of an aristocrat, from kidnappers. In this film Michael Ward enjoyed a much larger role than usual as the boy's Uncle Maurice, who is also his tutor. Maurice is one of the screen's most outrageous mincing queens, a harmless, asexual sissy who nevertheless takes pleasure in putting down childlike, irritating Wisdom. 'Monstrous little man,' he says, winning a great deal of audience sympathy. At a family conference Uncle Maurice discusses Sir Reginald's future. Says the boy's mother, Lady Sybil (Ambrosine Philpotts): 'He needs a mother's guiding hand.' Replies Uncle Fletcher (Colin Gordon): 'He needs an uncle's guiding foot! Trouble is,' he adds, looking at Maurice, 'the wrong uncle's got hold of him!' Maurice looks surprised and offended, but Lady Sybil immediately leaps to his defence: 'Maurice is a very *good* tutor.' Says Maurice: 'Thank you, Sybil.'

Later, the same three are seen together in the living-room. Fletcher approaches Maurice who is concentrating on his needlepoint. 'What is that?' asks Fletcher roughly. Replies Maurice: 'As a matter of fact it's a pyjama case for Reginald. It's rather pretty, don't you think?' Fletcher glares at his brother who ignores him and carries on sewing. Yawning,

Maurice says: 'I think I'll turn myself in. I must catch up on my beauty sleep.' Replies Fletcher: 'Yes. You need to.'

Maurice's bedroom is wonderfully camp. He has a large, white double-bed with matching curtains and dressing table. There's also a vase of flowers on the side table. Kidnapped by mistake, terrified Maurice, gagged and still in his pyjamas, finds himself surrounded by mean-looking crooks in the back room of a nightclub. When the kidnappers realize their mistake, one of them says: 'Couldn't we collect a ransom on him?' The tough, brazen blonde ringleader's moll replies, nastily: 'More likely they're glad to get rid of it!'

In *Just My Luck* (1957) Michael plays Cranley, an effeminate, short-tempered jewelry salesman and, once again, he steals the film from its star, Norman Wisdom, with just one line: 'Madam has such *excellent* taste.'

Off-screen, comedy actors like Norman Wisdom and Frankie Howerd were not friendly towards Michael. They felt insecure about his ability to steal scenes from them. In some ways this is a tribute to Michael's artistry. He later said: 'It is most important in acting to be interesting. Whatever you do, don't be a bore.' Michael continued acting until the 1970s. See also the *Carry On* films (1958) and *Doctor in Love* (1960).

Other films of interest released in 1956

In Anthony Asquith's short drama *On Such a Night*, a young American (David Knight from the *The Young Lovers*) visits Glyndebourne and hears excerpts from the *Marriage of Figaro* as well as seeing the beauty of England; gay Hollywood director George Cukor made *Bhowani Junction* for MGM here (and on location in India). It was a passionate melodrama starring Ava Gardner as an Anglo-Indian confused about her racial identity; another Hollywood director, John Huston, brought Herman Melville's *Moby Dick* to the screen with an Anglo-American cast, but the novel's homoeroticism, and passionate love of Queequeg and Ishmael ('You had almost thought I had been his wife. . . . Thus, then, in our heart's honeymoon, lay I and Queequeg – a cosy, loving pair'), is lost in the translation.

1957

Night of the Demon

M. R. James (1862–1936) was the author of numerous macabre and ghostly stories featuring 'bachelors'. These include *Casting the Runes* which was filmed as *Night of the Demon*. Directed by Jacques Tourneur, who was famous for a number of American 'horror' classics of the 1940s (*Cat People, I Walked With a Zombie*), *Night of the Demon* is a genuinely frightening and chilling thriller.

When American psychologist Dr John Holden (Dana Andrews) visits Britain, he finds himself in conflict with the strange Dr Julian Carswell (Niall MacGinnis). He believes he can conjure up a demon from hell but Holden is sceptical. Gradually Carswell begins to sow seeds of doubt in the tough, no-nonsense American.

Carswell is a something of a monster. Unmarried, he lives with his mother in a large mansion in the country. It's a 'feminine' household, he's surrounded by porcelain, but evil Carswell hides behind his kind, gentle mother, and children. Every Hallowe'en he throws a party for the village children and dresses up as a clown to entertain them with 'magic'. At the party we are given a few more 'clues' to Carswell's true nature. He owns a pet cat and his mother (Athene Seyler) says to Holden: 'He really ought to be married, but he's so fussy.' Says Julian to Holden while the two men are watching children play snakes and ladders: 'Funny thing, I always preferred sliding down the snakes to climbing up the ladders.' But, in spite of the party, Carswell's no Santa Claus. He has a menacing authority which takes over the film.

Night of the Demon includes several shocking moments, but nothing can surpass its creepy, terrifying seance. This sequence even takes the unusual step (for a film) of having a male medium. However, *Night of the Demon* is more interesting – and frightening – for its superb portrait of an overtly macho, rational, 'heterosexual' man (Holden) being terrorized and slowly broken down by a powerful, 'feminine' but evil 'gay' (Carswell). Needless to say, it is Carswell who ends up being destroyed by his 'demon'.

No Road Back

In the excellent 'B' picture No Road Back, strong, tense, sharp Mrs Railton (Margaret Rawlings), a blind-and-deaf nightclub owner, saves her medical student son, John (Skip Homier), from being framed by jewel thieves. Clearly there is a lesbian feeling between Mrs Railton and her companion, sweet young feminine Beth (Patricia Dainton), who is engaged to John. Mrs Railton looks mannish, dressed in black with her short, cropped dark hair. In one scene Mrs Railton is sculpting a bust of pretty blonde Beth who is dressed in white. The women touch a great deal, not only when Mrs Railton feels all over Beth's face while sculpting her, but all through the film, for Beth is Mrs Railton's ears and speech. The older woman communicates through Beth by using sign language on the young woman's hand. Consequently the film includes numerous scenes of the two women grabbing each other's hands.

When John discovers his mother is really a crook, he asks Beth to leave with him. Beth replies: 'I can't leave her. Do you think I wouldn't have gone a long time ago if I could? It takes two of us to make one person.' At the end of the film, when Mrs Railton is shot and dies, it is not her son's hand she grabs, but Beth's, squeezing it tight as life drains from her.

Other films of interest released in 1957

The cast of the screen version of George Bernard Shaw's Saint Joan included Anton Walbrook and John Gielgud. In his 1977 autobiography, the film's director, Otto Preminger, recalled: 'On the first day of filming, after I had finished a scene with him [John Gielgud] and Anton Walbrook, he took me aside and asked cheerfully: "Well, how does it feel to direct two old aunties?"'; the Children's Film Foundation serialized Enid Blyton's popular children's novel Five on Treasure Island. Rel Grainer played the fiery Georgina Kirrin. She hates being a girl: 'I don't like doing the things that girls do. I like doing the things that boys do. I can climb better than any boy, and swim faster too. I can sail a boat as well as any fisher-boy on this coast. You're to call me George.'[1]

Notes

1. Enid Blyton, *Five on Treasure Island*
   (Hodder & Stoughton, 1942), p. 19.

1958

Charles Hawtrey and the *Carry On's*

When producer Peter Rogers and director Gerald Thomas made *Carry On Sergeant* in 1958, little did they realize they had launched what was to become the most popular comedy series in British cinema. For more than two decades these films depended on smut, innuendo and the talents of comic actors like Charles Hawtrey (1914–88) and Kenneth Williams (1926–88), to poke fun at British institutions. These included the army, hospitals, teaching profession, police force and, in 1964, James Bond! Snooty intellectual Kenneth Williams, though his origins were working class, with his unmistakable high nasal English twang, was 'a master of snobbery and sexual innuendo'.[1] He was an invaluable member of the team. But it was Charles Hawtrey who enjoyed the most public affection of the two.

Hawtrey stole scenes in numerous (he appeared in twenty-three) *Carry On* films from *Sergeant* to, his last, *Matron* (1972). He was a weedy-looking fairy who entered with a ladylike 'Hello', and this was always guaranteed to raise laughs. He was once described as 'Resembling a mischievous stick insect, with a face curiously reminiscent of an elderly maiden aunt topped by an incongruous toupee, and with a distinctive high-pitched voice verging on the hysterical.'[2] Sometimes he played rampant heterosexuals (*Cleo*, *Camping*), hilariously mocking masculinity. But were his characters gay? Says Richard Dyer:

> the [*Carry On*] films are oddly ambiguous – he is both 'obvious' and yet not explicit. Even in his private life, though his sexuality is hardly in doubt, he was not what we would now call 'out'. . . . He certainly had a queer sensibility before the *Carry On's*. . . . The films sometimes come on quite strong about his sexuality. In *Spying*, he is asked why he was given the odd number 000, when

all the other spies have been given a final digit greater than zero. He recalls that the people assigning the numbers looked at him and said 'oh-oh' (as in 'What have we got here?') and then 'oh' (dragged out, as in 'dear me!'). It's clear here that everyone has his number. . . . I have always loved him, yet he does embody one of the things that the Gay Liberation movement tended to disapprove of – the stereotype of the effeminate gay man. And no doubt much of the straight laughter at him is oppressive laughter. He confirms that gay men are ineffectual, trivial and, worst of all, like women. Yet for all the hatred that is expressed through the stereotype, it is also the case that Hawtrey was much loved – and anyway, I'll take the comparison with women as a compliment, thank you. Besides, who cares what people think? The most attractive thing about the turn to 'queer' in recent years is that it implies a rejection of worrying about what people will think. In his way, Charlie was like that too. What I relish most about him is his utter disregard for what anyone else may think. He just gets on with being himself.[3]

There are at least two early *Carry On* films which bear this out. *Carry On Nurse* was the second film in the series, and the highest grossing film in Britain in 1959. But it is one of the least memorable in the series. Turgid and heavy going, the only member of the cast who is animated, and funny, is Hawtrey. He plays Mr Hinton, a patient in a men's surgical ward. Popping up from time to time, he's seen listening to the radio, laughing hysterically at a comedy programme, crying at the soap opera *Mrs Dale's Diary*, pretending to conduct an orchestra, and passing on recipes he's heard. He even drags up as a nurse! In other words, he's a screaming queen. Desexualized, of course, and sadly marginalized from the rest of the men in the film. But, as Richard Dyer says, Hawtrey couldn't care less what people think about him, and the film is his triumph. His brief appearances are easily the best.

This is also the case with *Carry On Constable* (1960) in which he plays – wait for it – PC Timothy Gorse, perhaps British cinema's first 'out' policeman! With dainty, mincing steps, Hawtrey makes one of the screen's greatest entrances. Into the police station he goes, wearing his uniform, carrying a bunch of chrysanthemums in his right hand, and Bobby, his budgie, in a birdcage in his left ('I just couldn't leave him behind,' he explains). Gorse has been asked to come to work to 'cover' for some sick constables who have caught the flu. To his exasperated Sergeant (Sidney James), PC Gorse says: 'Hello,' in that wonderful ladylike way, and explains why he has brought some flowers to the station: 'Sorry I'm late, Sergeant, but I just couldn't leave home without bringing something bright and gay for the poor indisposed constables. So, it was off to my greenhouse and, with a little snip here, and a little snip there, snip, snip, and here we are with my love.' (Gives flowers to the Sergeant.) 'Ooooh! What have I said! With my very best floral greetings!' PC Gorse's slip of the tongue ('with my love') is a 'coming out' statement which is as significant and memorable as Melville Farr's in *Victim*, made the following year (see 1961). The fact that the gruff Sergeant (superbly played by Sidney James) doesn't insult him for being gay is also important. PC Gorse is tolerated along with the rest of the outrageously behaved constables who have been sent to the station to 'cover' for the sick PCs.

Carry On Constable is also one of the most memorable in the series because it includes the classic sequence in which Hawtrey and his gay co-star Kenneth Williams (as PC Stanley Benson) drag up. They dress up as a couple of middle-class, middle-aged ladies, and work undercover in a department store. Says Hawtrey, who calls himself 'Agatha', to Williams: 'Do you know, I haven't done this since I was in the army at a camp concert.' Williams calls himself 'Ethel', his grandmother's name. Hawtrey responds: 'If grandmama could see you now, she'd be so proud!' Hawtrey and Williams are clearly loving every minute of it, and drag artist Regina Fong has described this as:

> The nearest British cinema ever got to drag. . . . They just put on women's hats and coats and swish around unashamedly – so over the top they nearly vanish up their own finales. It's pure pantomime; they have no make up on at all. It's just two men with funny hats on, walking around the store and pretending, calling each other Gladys or Mavis or whatever it was. It's hysterical. That's drag. You can see they're having the time of their life, these two queens flying around this shop – there's a joy about it. It's not embarrassed, it's not self-conscious, it's open and it's honest. When a gay man does drag, it's not self-conscious and there's no feeling of 'I'm just acting this part.'[4]

Apart from Hawtrey and Williams, there was at least one other member of the *Carry On* team who camped it up. Michael Ward (see 1956) had already enjoyed fame with his appearances in several Norman Wisdom comedies before he made his *Carry On* debut in *Regardless* (1961). Later appearances include *Spying* (1964), *Cleo* (1964), *Screaming* (1966) and *Don't Lose Your Head* (1967), but it is his appearance in *Cabby* (1963) which is his most memorable. It's a brief – easily missed – role as a smartly dressed gay passenger in Kenneth Connor's taxi cab. After paying Connor, he minces off down the street, but stops when Connor calls him back and asks him if he has left a pearl earring in the back seat. 'What?', Ward replies in great surprise, as if Connor should have known better. 'With tweeds?' The knowing look on Connor's face says it all. This scene may only last for a few seconds, but it is one of the gayest, funniest and most beautifully played in the entire series.

Gay liberationists and the politically correct brigade would probably argue the *Carry On's* are guilty of every 'ism' in the book. But Andy Medhurst argues that such criticisms are unwarranted. He says:

> I would not want to condemn these stereotypes because in *Carry On* films heterosexuality is subject to just as much ridicule. . . . No matter who you do it with – girls, boys, yourself – it comes in for stick. It's all there to get laughed at. But really, the big joke is that no one ever does it. It's all nudge, nudge, wink, wink. Along came the *Confessions of* films in the 1970s, where people actually did it, and the *Carry On's* appeal, which was based on old-fashioned innocence about sex, was suddenly out of touch.[5]

Notes

1. *Variety*, 20 April 1988.
2. *Daily Telegraph*, 28 October 1988.
3. Richard Dyer, 'Idols: Charles Hawtrey' in *Attitude*, May 1994. Also, Richard Dyer, 'Carry on Regardless: The Genius of Charles Hawtrey' in *Dangerous to Know*, a talk given at the fourth London Lesbian and Gay Film Festival, 24 October 1989.
4. Regina Fong, 'Having a Ball: Drag in the Movies' in *Gay Times*, November 1994.
5. Andy Medhurst interviewed by Matthew Linfoot in the *Gay Gazette*, 9 August 1995. See also Andy Medhurst, 'Carry On Camp', in *Sight and Sound*, August 1992.

1959

Serious Charge

Serious Charge, adapted for the screen from the play by Philip King, was first produced by the Repertory Players at the Adelphi in London's West End in 1953. Alec McCowen appeared as the juvenile delinquent Larry Thompson who falsely accuses a vicar of sexually assaulting him. In 1955 it was presented at the Garrick with Patrick McGoohan playing the vicar (the day before *Serious Charge* opened, one of Philip King's biggest West End successes, the comedy *Sailor, Beware!* starring Peggy Mount as the battleaxe Emma Hornett, opened at the Strand). Says Nicholas de Jongh in *Not in Front of the Audience*:

> [*Serious Charge*] deals with a man displaying some character-istics that are regarded as signs of homosexuality. And here too a man is threatened with ruin on the basis of a trumped-up charge . . . . King suggested that the malign and blackmailing accuser is unhesitatingly believed, because the accuser confirms what stereotypically signs of homosexuality suggest. Yet the play. . . never mentions the word 'homosexual'. As soon as it comes to matters of sexuality, people speak in innuendo and circum-locution.[1]

Originally intended for filming in the mid-1950s with Laurence Harvey, *Serious Charge* posed a censorship problem for the British Board of Film Censors (BBFC). At that time censorship prevented any whisper of homosexuality in a British film, even though in *Serious Charge* no 'indecent act' takes place. But in 1958 John Trevelyan, Secretary of the BBFC, relaxed the rules. This was one year after the publication of the Wolfenden Report which proposed the de-criminalization of homo-sexuality. The BBFC passed the script, but only on the grounds that homosexuality was used as a device to further the plot and, like the stage play, any mention of the word homosexual was strictly forbidden. Yet, in spite of the restrictions imposed by the BBFC, *Serious Charge* can lay claim to be a landmark in British cinema. It was the first British film with a contemporary setting to even touch upon the theme of homosexuality, albeit timidly.

Set in a small English town, and featuring a mildly disruptive group of 'juvenile delinquents', *Serious Charge* is a British attempt at joining the series of Hollywood films which explored the 'problems' of teenagers. Released in 1959, it came rather late to have any real impact. Its American counterparts, such as *The Wild One* (1954) with Marlon Brando, *Rebel Without a Cause* (1955) with James Dean, *The Blackboard Jungle* (1955) and the launch of Elvis Presley into films in 1956, had long since come and gone. From a 1990s perspective some of the dialogue in the film is very dated and cringe-making. The film-makers impression of 'hip' and 'with-it' 1950s teenagers is patronizing and way off-centre. 'They're a bunch of squares from Squaresville, England!' says Larry Thompson (Andrew Ray), one of the little monsters. He is an unemployed tearaway who is also the leader of the unruly gang of teenagers. Ray's attempt at being sinister and sexy is laughable. His younger brother Curly is played by the inexperienced Cliff Richard, sporting a brylcream quiff, puppy fat and a pout. At the beginning of the film he is up before the law for a crime Larry instigated. Curly is supported by a butch probation officer (Judith Furse), and the new vicar, Howard Phillips. He is played by Anthony Quayle in the role created by Patrick McGoohan in the stage version.

While Larry does everything he can to cause trouble at the church youth club run by Howard, the new vicar becomes something of an idol because of his caring approach, his boxing skills and the fact that he gives permission for rock 'n' roll to be played in the club. His unconventional approach to his work, and success at keeping the local youths on the straight and narrow, does not meet with the approval of Hester (Sarah Churchill). She is the local do-gooder and daughter of the former vicar who finds herself sexually attracted to Howard. But Hester is upset when she finds that the only woman Howard is interested in is his acerbic mother (Irene Browne). Naturally she is disappointed when Howard fails to respond to her advances. Although Howard is presented as a big strong chap, and a soccer star to boot, he is probably unconsciously gay. For example, we see him going shopping and having a rather matey relationship with the lesbian probation officer. The knowing, teasing presence of his mother would seem to suggest that he has not had girlfriends in the past, nor had she encouraged any.

A tragedy occurs after Larry rejects a young girl he has made pregnant and she commits suicide. Howard is determined to confront the youth but, after smashing up Howard's living room, Larry claims that the vicar has tried to molest him. It is a scenario Larry has concocted knowing that Hester will witness part of it. When Larry tells his strict father, Bill (Percy Herbert) 'he tried to interfere with me', and Hester backs up Larry's accusation, the persecution of the 'gay' man begins. Bricks are thrown through his window, the butcher refuses to send his boy to the vicarage: 'I'll drop 'em in myself, Sir' he says; his tyres are slashed by youths and he begins to receive 'filthy, obscene' hate mail. No one comes to his church services, a little boy throws mud at him in the street, and the youth club empties. When Howard visits the local pub to talk to Bill, he is laughed at, and ends up being thumped by the angry father.

As Howard becomes an outcast in the town, Terence Young's direction is increasingly gripping as the central dilemma comes into sharper focus. *Serious Charge* movingly acknowledges the existence of homophobia and how wrong and unfair it is. It also shows that lesbians and gays are not necessarily the only victims of homophobia. Howard prepares to give up the parish, but luckily his mother has a few well-chosen words with Hester, who then traps Larry into molesting her and admitting his accusations against Howard were untrue. In the film's awful 'happy' ending, Howard decides he has a vocation as a priest after all, and is persuaded to stay in the parish. However, when his mother hopes that Hester will provide him with the love of a 'good' woman, Howard still fails to respond.

Cliff Richard's role and his acting are negligible, though he does perform three songs by Lionel Bart including 'Livin' Doll'. This topped the British charts in July, 1959. Perhaps the film might have been more honest if Cliff had played the vicar's would-be nemesis, as the young pop singer does occasionally smoulder with loose-limbed, pouting eroticism. And it is worth noting that *Serious Charge* ends with an extraordinary climax: Judith Furse roaring off with Anthony Quayle and Cliff squashed into her old banger!

Danger Within

In the superb war drama *Danger Within*, set in 1943, a group of British prisoners who are planning to escape from a prisoner-of-war camp in North Italy are threatened by a traitor in the midst. Bryan Forbes and Frank Harvey's excellent screenplay is based on Michael Gilbert's novel, and the cast includes such 'reliable' British actors as Richard Todd, Bernard Lee, Michael Wilding, Richard Attenborough and Donald Houston as some of the prisoners. Dennis Price is also on hand to play the camp Captain Rupert Callender, determined to stage his version of *Hamlet* with the Rupert Callender Players. The Players consist of a group of prisoners who lack talent, much to Callender's frustration.

In one very funny scene he is rehearsing the cast in the grounds of the prison camp when he is interrupted by Captain Tony Long (William Franklyn). Their conversation reveals Callender's disapproval of other prisoners' attempts to escape (clearly he'd much rather work on his production), as well as his gay sexuality. Asks Callender sarcastically: 'To what do we owe this honour, gentle knight? More trouble in the precious tunnel perchance?' Replies Long: 'Trouble? No.' Says Callender bitchily: 'Oh, how nice. Then I suggest you go and play in the bloody thing. . . swaggering about the place playing cops and robbers. The rest of the camp's heartily sick of you. You'd be kicked out of any decent regiment.' Long responds: 'What's your regiment? Catering Corps or ENSA?'

Also making (brief) appearances throughout the film are four wonderfully camp and bitchy card players, echoing Callender's indifference to their fellow prisoners and attempts to escape. They act as a 'Greek chorus', detached from the rest of the men, either silent in the background, or occasionally on-screen commenting on the escape attempts. The most vocal is Second Lieutenant Betts-Hanger (Ian Whittaker), who bitches with his 'partner' about their card game, and sarcastically observes: 'I know these escaping types – everything's sacrificed to the cause.' Naturally the tunnel diggers are portrayed as tough 'real' men, like Todd, Attenborough and Donald Houston. Callender, Betts-Hanger and the card players are never seen dirtying their hands. In fact, Betts-Hanger even bemoans the fact that they are included in the mass escape at the end of the film. When the card players play their final game he complains: 'Our last evening of bridge here. A pity really, don't you think?'

Make Mine a Million

In the comedy *Make Mine a Million*, a weak attempt to satirize commercial television, Arthur Askey and Sidney James play a make-up man and salesman who use a mobile television transmitter to advertise a detergent. Two stereotypes are included in the story. Early in the film Tom Gill makes a brief appearance as Mr Langtry, a camp but temperamental and interfering 'production supervisor' on a television programme. He's described by Askey as 'a pain in the neck'. Later, a lesbian is included on an otherwise all-male board of directors of a commercial television company. The director general has summoned Askey to meet the Board but when he enters the boardroom, the man accompanying him addresses all the Directors as 'gentlemen'. The mannish-looking lesbian has her hair pulled-back into a bun, wears glasses, a tweed jacket, a white shirt and a tie. She looks fearsomely at the nervous Askey, but she is not being singled out for the entire Board of Directors are all frightening to look at.

Notes

1. Nicholas de Jongh, *Not in Front of the Audience: Homosexuality on Stage* (Routledge, 1992) p. 64.

1960

Oscar Wilde/The Trials of Oscar Wilde

In 1958 John Trevelyan, Secretary of the Board of British Film Censors, declared: 'In our circles we can talk about homosexuality, but the general public is embarrassed by the subject, so until it becomes a subject that can be mentioned without offence it will be banned.' Says Tom Dewe Mathews in *Censored*:

> Two weeks later, however, in a decision which probably marks the high point of moral courage in Britain's film censorship, the Secretary announced that he had changed his mind. From now on films with homosexual themes would not be banned provided the subject was treated 'responsibly'. 'Responsibly' was a codeword for 'consultation', which in turn meant that the producers of such films would be advised to submit their scripts to the BBFC. Within two years three British screenplays – *Serious Charge* (1959), *Oscar Wilde* (1960) and *The Trials of Oscar Wilde* (1960) – had been submitted; but none of them posed a censorship problem for the Board, either because sex between men was only referred to within the clinical confines of a court-room or, in the case of *Serious Charge*, because homosexuality was merely employed as a device to further a plot concerning a vicar (Anthony Quayle) falsely accused of abusing a teenage boy.[1]

In 1960 not one but two films about literary giant Oscar Wilde were produced in Britain, though neither mentioned the word homosexuality in their scripts. *Oscar Wilde* was the weaker of the two, filmed on a low budget in black and white, and starring Robert Morley. Fortunately it did not harm the success of *The Trials of Oscar Wilde*, a beautifully crafted film shot in glorious Technicolor and widescreen, and containing a magnificent performance by Peter Finch. Physically, portly Robert Morley may have been more appropriate casting as Wilde than handsome, rugged Australian Finch. Years earlier Morley had triumphed in London (1936) and New York (1938) in the stage play of *Oscar Wilde*, and no doubt he expected great things from a film about Wilde. But he must have been very disappointed. Morley's film, which was still being edited up to a couple of hours before the press show, does look as if it were thrown together, and Morley doesn't help matters with a poor performance. He plays Wilde as a blustering, foolish old duffer. He lacks Finch's sensitivity and passion, and Micheal MacLiammoir's dazzling flamboyance and tragic mask in Granada television's *On Trial: Oscar Wilde*, first broadcast in August, 1960. The supporting cast includes Dennis Price as Robbie, and one can only speculate what magic the film would have contained if *he* had been cast as Wilde! John Neville is inappropriately cast as Bosie. He's far too old for the role, and his scenes with Morley are amateurish. Phyllis Calvert plays Constance Wilde as a silly, passive Victorian wife, lacking the intelligence of Yvonne Mitchell's characterization in the Finch version. The courtroom scenes are played to the gallery, like an hysterical Victorian melodrama, instead of the intimacy of the camera, and cinema auditorium. However, the prison sequence is much grimmer and realistic than that shown in *Trials*. Finally, there is a grotesque, disturbing climax to *Oscar Wilde*. Robert Morley sits drinking outside a Parisian café, looking untidy and weary. He asks the accordionist: 'Will you play something gay?' and then, like a madman, roars with laughter.

Oscar Wilde reached the screen five days before *The Trials of Oscar Wilde*, to disappointing reviews. Said *Monthly Film Bulletin*: 'Unfortunately the hasty circumstances of its arrival can neither excuse nor account for the funereal pace of the film itself, which has the extraordinarily stiff and stagy look of some tea-cup screen drama of the very early Thirties. . . . Like the entire film, Robert Morley's performance is external, cautious and afraid.'

In 1977, when Keith Howes interviewed Morley for *Gay News*, the actor admitted:

> When I did the play I was ten years too young and when the play was filmed I was ten years too old, so I didn't exactly hit it. They

did another film version at the same time called *The Trials of Oscar Wilde*. I think Finch's did a bit better than ours but the public didn't want to see either of them. I sort of squinted at his once on television and I thought it was more elaborate but I was much better as Oscar Wilde. I remember we did a scene with a rather nervous young extra and I said: 'Do you realize,' I said, 'that in the next scene I'm going to kiss you?' He said: 'What!' and began to move away. I said 'Yes, it's really a blue film, essentially a blue film and I don't think it will do you much good at the beginning of your career.' He fled, left the set and the director, Gregory Ratoff, who was the last of the old screamers – not in the *Gay News* sense but in the sense of temperament, throwing fits – went crazy because the extra was in some other shots and the continuity was ruined. I never dared own up and say: 'Well, actually he ran away because he thought he was going to have to kiss me'.[2]

The lavish, tasteful though somewhat artificial opening credits of *The Trials of Oscar Wilde* whet our appetite for what is to come. Director Ken Hughes also wrote the screenplay which he based on the book by Montgomery Hyde, and the play *The Stringed Lute* by John Furnell. Advisors included the Marquis of Queensberry, Lord Cecil Douglas and Vyvyan Holland, son of Oscar Wilde.

In the opening sequence, two men leave the St James's Theatre after the première of *Lady Windermere's Fan*. Says one: 'I wish I could approve of the playwright as much as I approve of the play.' His companion replies: 'Who cares about him as long as he continues to give us plays like this?' But, of course, people *do* care about Wilde's sexuality, especially the Marquis of Queensberry, played with tremendous energy and menace by Lionel Jeffries. As he screams abuse at Wilde for having a relationship with his son, Bosie, they are interrupted by the Prince of Wales, the future King Edward VII, and his mistress, Lillie Langtry. This is an interesting acknowledgement by the film of the double standards and hypocrisy of Victorian society.

Peter Finch, in a beautifully restrained, understated and seductive performance plays Wilde as a warm, witty but ultimately self-destructive man with, he says, a 'strange fascination' for the younger Bosie. Constance warns her husband that Bosie will destroy him, but

Wilde cannot help himself. He is in love. Each actor in the film gives a thoughtful, believable performance. Apart from Finch, handsome John Fraser superbly conveys the selfish, impulsive nature of the precocious Bosie. Together, Finch and Fraser are believable as the doomed, ill-matched lovers.

For his performance in *The Trials of Oscar Wilde*, Peter Finch deservedly received his second British Academy Award for Best British Actor (he won his first in 1956 for *A Town Like Alice*). Finch won against tough competition from six other nominees: his co-star, John Fraser, Richard Attenborough (*The Angry Silence*), Albert Finney (*Saturday Night and Sunday Morning*), Alec Guinness (*Tunes of Glory*), John Mills (*Tunes of Glory*) and Laurence Olivier (*The Entertainer*). Finch also received the 1961 Moscow Film Festival Award for Best Actor and, in the USA – where it was released as *The Man with the Green Carnation* – the film won the 1960 Hollywood Foreign Press Association's Golden Globe for Best English-Language Foreign Film. There were no American Oscar nominations.

The League of Gentlemen

One year before they made the ground-breaking *Victim*, producer Michael Relph and director Basil Dearden collaborated on *The League of Gentlemen* with a screenplay by Bryan Forbes. In this clever, entertaining comedy-thriller, Jack Hawkins plays ex-Lieutenent Colonel Hyde who, embittered by his enforced retirement after twenty-five years army service, conceives a daring plan to rob a bank of one million pounds. After consulting army records he enlists the help of seven other 'single-minded men', ex-officers whose post-war careers have become as dodgy as their service records. They include former army captain Frank Stevens (Kieron Moore), a ruggedly handsome, athletic, curly-haired gym instructor who has been thrown out of the army for being gay. Hyde describes him as a 'one-time fascist back-room boy. Mosley speaks and all that. Saw the light just in time and was made an officer and a gentleman. Unfortunately he couldn't quite behave like one. The Sunday newspapers had a field day. There's nothing the British public like better than catching the odd men out.'

With his rugged, masculine appearance, and quiet, thoughtful persona, Stevens is an unexpected departure from the limp-wristed stereotype. He is also the victim of a seedy, raincoat-wearing blackmailer who says: 'They say girls are expensive enough, but... well, it takes all sorts to make a world.' After the blackmailer has departed, Stevens massages one of the lads who has just finished reading a book Stevens has loaned him. Confused about its contents, he asks: 'What are them two blokes up to?' Replies Stevens: 'Well, there are thrills and thrills.'

Unfortunately *The League of Gentlemen* contains an outrageous screaming queen stereotype. When the men meet in a rehearsal room at the New Gate Theatre Club to plan their robbery, they are interrupted by a swishy, wrist-flapping chorus boy. He's played by Oliver Reed in an early, minor role, but the young actor hasn't got a clue. Taking his cue from Hollywood movies of the 1930s, with one hand firmly clutching a hip, he lisps: 'Isn't this *Babes in the Wood*?' 'No,' replies Hyde. 'We're rehearsing *Journey's End*.'

When the men stay together at a country retreat, Hyde allocates them rooms but Lexy (Richard Attenborough) is nervous about sharing with Stevens who turns to him and says 'It's a bit like being back at school.' Replies Lexy: 'I sincerely hope not.' Later on he tells the men: 'I don't know about you lot, but I'm gonna keep my lights on all night.'

The League of Gentlemen is an interesting film in that it is the first British production about an all-male group to include an explicitly gay member. Unlike the numerous post-war British films which focused on heroic heterosexual men at war, and safe 'buddy' relationships, Stevens is a fully integrated member of the group. He is accepted by the men because they know he is competent. Even if they do not approve of his sexuality, though Lexy is the only one to voice his disapproval, they need him. The film also anticipates two other major British films of the 1960s. The following year the blackmailing of gay men is explored more fully in Dearden and Relph's *Victim*, and in *The L-Shaped Room* (1962) writer Forbes echoes one of his lines from *The League of Gentlemen*: 'It takes all sorts to make a world.'

Doctor in Love

When censorship rules gradually began to relax in the late 1950s, the popular *Doctor* comedies became increasingly daring. And longer. And duller. Such was the case with *Doctor in Love*, the fourth entry in the series. Both Dirk Bogarde and Donald Sinden declined to appear, giving opportunities to 'silly ass' Leslie Phillips as Dr Tony Burke, and gorgeous, handsome but wooden Michael Craig as Dr Richard Hare. *Doctor in Love*, which is neither funny or entertaining, is also one of the most blatantly homophobic films ever made in this country. To add insult to injury, nothing could stop it from becoming the highest-grossing film in Britain in 1960.

In an early sequence in the film, Burke and Hare volunteer to become guinea pigs with the Foulness Anti-Cold Research Unit. But research is far from their minds when they pair off with a couple of strippers (Liz Fraser and Joan Sims). The unit is run by Professor MacRitchie (Irene Handl), a strident lesbian who wears brown tweeds, sensible brown shoes and smooth, straight hair. Resembling a Nazi officer in a German concentration camp, the Professor is described by one of the strippers as 'an Aberdeen Angus'. To drive home the point of this character's unnatural being she is played by the otherwise wonderful character actress Handl at full throttle. The professor is accompanied on her rounds by a truly pathetic fairy called Dr Flower (Michael Ward). When the professor and Dr Flower catch the strippers in a drunken state in their room (Burke and Hare are hiding in the next room), she booms in horror: 'It's disgraceful. Monstrous. I've never known such crass infringement of the rules. It's an orgy!' The drunken strippers collapse into a fit of giggles, and then attempt to 'rape' Dr Flower who shrieks and squeals like a stuck pig. Offensive in any context, this deeply disturbing sequence achieves a greater degree of nastiness by being drenched in the gloss and glamour of director Ralph Thomas and his producer, Betty Box.

The *Doctor* series staggered on. Dirk Bogarde returned, with obvious disdain, in *Doctor in Distress* (1963), followed by Leslie Phillips again in *Doctor in Clover* (1966) and *Doctor in Trouble* (1970). This final outing included the unpleasant spectacle of Graham Chapman as a swishy photographer. After *Doctor in Love*, Ralph Thomas and Betty Box continued to waste talented actors in a succession of unimaginatively used foreign locations, trite romantic situations and a particularly nasty strain of homophobia. Not only did Chapman play a camp photographer in *Doctor in Trouble*, but the great Robert Morley (who should have known better) appeared as 'Miss Mary' in a spy comedy called *Some Girls Do* (1969). A banal view of the world, easy laughs, unquestioning sexism, and a determination not to rock any boats made Thomas and Box the ideal cohorts for the Rank Organization's crowd-pulling (though decreasingly so), lightweight comedies of the 1950s, 1960s and early 1970s.

Other films of interest released in 1960

In the comedy *The Battle of the Sexes* Robert Morley appeared as an upper-class gentleman searching for his manservant on a train. Tapping a porter on the shoulder he asks: 'I say, aren't you my chap?' The burly cockney turns to him and, with an amused look on his face, replies: 'No, not me, mate. I'm promised to another!'; in *Circus of Horrors* spectators are being guided around several motionless groups of people representing scenes from history. Following on from a tableau showing Adam and Eve the guide announces: 'and now ladies and gentlemen, in all her beauty, surrounded by her gorgeous handmaidens, the incomparable Sappho.' This is a rare inclusion in mainstream entertainment of the celebrated lesbian Greek poet.

Notes

1. Tom Dewe Mathews, *Censored: What They Didn't Allow You to See, And Why: The Story of Film Censorship in Britain* (Chatto & Windus, 1994).

2. Robert Morley interviewed by Keith Howes in *Gay News*, no. 129, 1977 reprinted in *Outspoken: Keith Howes' Gay News Interviews 1976–83* (Cassell, 1995).

1961

A Taste of Honey

When director Tony Richardson was planning his film version of Shelagh Delaney's play *A Taste of Honey*, a Hollywood producer made him an offer he flatly refused. 'I have just one suggestion to make,' said the producer. 'This girl who's been made pregnant by the Negro – now don't worry, I don't wanna change that, that's good off-beat drama. But let's give the film an up-beat ending. Let her have a miscarriage.' One Hollywood studio even agreed to back the film if Audrey Hepburn played the lead, and she was offered the role, but Richardson was having none of this. Social realism had reached its peak in British cinema, and Richardson was not interested in compromising Delaney's text. He intended to retain her 'controversial' themes, which included interracial sex, teenage pregnancy and homosexuality. The result is a poetic, moving and often funny observation of 'real' life, which contains some of the most outstanding performances ever seen in a British film.

A Taste of Honey is an unsentimental story of a working-class Salford schoolgirl called Jo (Rita Tushingham), a slum Cinderella who finds happiness with a black Prince. In reality he's a young sailor called Jimmy (Paul Danquah). Finding herself pregnant with his child after he has returned to the sea, her irresponsible, selfish and vulgar mother Helen (Dora Bryan) abandons her to live with her wide-boy lover Peter (Robert Stephens). Though independent and resourceful, Jo agrees to set up home with the shy, but equally capable Geoffrey Ingham (Murray Melvin), a lonely gay art student she has befriended. Geoffrey even offers to marry Jo and raise the child as his own, as much for his convenience as hers. The 'odd', childlike couple have fun living together, and planning their future, but it isn't long before Helen returns and evicts poor Geoffrey. Our final view of him is heartbreaking. He stands alone in the freezing cold, hiding in the shadows outside the safety and warmth of the home he has shared with Jo. With a duffle-bag slung over his shoulder, Geoffrey disappears into the night, leaving us with a profound sense of loss and disappointment, for we know he is better equipped at taking care of Jo than her mother. Though we are spared seeing him commit suicide, which is usually the fate of such characters, at the end of the film we do not know what will happen to this rather sad, pathetic gay youth, and this is very upsetting.

A Taste of Honey is a story full of misfits, people who don't 'fit in'. Though Jimmy enjoys his brief encounter with Jo, he is clearly more at home on his ship. Helen cannot settle, flitting from one boyfriend to another, and climbing out of a succession of boarding-house windows with her suitcase to avoid paying overdue rent. Jo leaves school with dreams of becoming an artist, but she barely reaches the age of sixteen before pregnancy (and adulthood) intervenes. Gentle Geoffrey has been thrown out on to the streets by his landlady for having a man in his room, but his friendship with Jo temporarily saves him. They need each other for friendship and support. 'You're just like a big sister to me,' she tells him. But Geoffrey is not a fully-rounded character. He embodies sexual repression which manifests itself in self-pity. The scene in which he kisses Jo, a pathetic attempt at demonstrating heterosexuality, is also disturbing for a gay audience to experience because it reveals the fear he has of his gay sexuality. Says Andy Medhurst:

> Big sister is no threat because she has no sexual desire. . . . 'You're unique, Geoffrey,' Jo tells him, and as far as the film is concerned he might as well be the only homosexual in the world. Thus any heterosexual audience is bound to read him not just as another homosexual, but as homosexuality, which is why, given his self-pity and sexlessness, I see A Taste of Honey as a deeply reactionary film. Geoffrey's unhappiness could, perhaps, be seen as another example of the harm done by repressing desire, but by allowing that desire no space, the film renders Geoffrey's plight as inevitable and immutable. He has one moment of vague defiance, when Jo asks him about his sex life, he replies 'I don't go in for sensational confessions.' One can't help wishing that he did, as they can lead to a crucial self-awareness – as shown by Victim.[1]

Vanessa Redgrave once described her ex-husband Tony Richardson as having 'an absolute scorn of playing safe'. She added that he can be 'very provocative'. But, ironically, though Richardson was a non-conformist and rebel in British film and theatre at a time when 'angry young men' were all the rage, he only took it so far. This was a man with a secret. After Richardson died of AIDS in 1991, his daughter Natasha discovered his unpublished autobiography, *Long Distance Runner*, at the back of a dusty cupboard. Published in 1993, director Lindsay Anderson (who wrote the introduction to the book) said Richardson 'wrote only of the things he wanted his girls – and us – to know.' The 'secret' life of Richardson, his bisexuality, was hidden from readers, but after the book was published a revealing article by Gavin Lambert appeared in *Sight and Sound*. He said:

> There is no mention of the bisexuality that was surely a key factor in his life. This part of himself he left hidden, like the typescript, in a closet. I dislike the premise of 'outing', with its implication of revealing a guilty secret, but to ignore this aspect of Tony's life not only falsifies him, but slurs his memory by lining oneself up with those who regard the secret as guilty.
>
> Even though he introduced me to several of his male lovers, Tony's ground rule forbade us to discuss his sexual identity. It was part of the game that I should take it for granted. He was far too intelligent to feel ashamed of being bisexual, but obviously it made him uncomfortable. . . . Tony's whole life was a high-wire act, and he seems to have handled his sexual identity as one of the trickier parts of the act.[2]

In 1961 *A Taste of Honey* won four British Academy Awards for Best British Film, Best British Actress (Dora Bryan), Most Promising Newcomer (Rita Tushingham) and Best Screenplay of a British Film (Shelagh Delaney and Tony Richardson). Murray Melvin was nominated for Most Promising Newcomer. At the 1962 Cannes Film Festival, Murray Melvin and Rita Tushingham both won a prize for Best Acting.

The Greengage Summer

In *The Greengage Summer* director Lewis Gilbert gently explores the sexual awakenings of two teenage girls from England, stranded in

France with their younger brother and sister when their mother is unexpectedly hospitalized. Gilbert is assisted by Freddie Young's ravishing photography, a lovely music score by gay Richard Addinsell, and an excellent script by Howard Koch which is based on Rumer (*Black Narcissus*) Godden's novel. The cast, headed by Kenneth More and Susannah York, are equally superb.

When Joss (Susannah York), Hester (Jane Asher), Willmouse (Richard Williams) and Vicky (Elizabeth Dear) arrive at the hotel owned by the beautiful Zizi (Danielle Darrieux), they meet her mysterious companion, Claudette Corbet (Claude Nollier). Cold and abrupt, Claudette is dressed in black and worried about Zizi because she has gone out for the evening with her lover, a debonair Englishman called Eliot (Kenneth More). When Zizi arrives home, an agitated Claudette shows signs of jealousy and says: 'You know I cannot sleep until you are home safe.' Eliot, who has followed Zizi into the hotel, says to Claudette: 'Still up, Claudette?' As he joins Zizi they giggle cruelly, and go upstairs. Afterwards, when Hester asks Paul (David Saire), a hotel worker, why Zizi and Claudette are always arguing, he replies: 'Because Madame Corbet loves Mademoiselle Zizi.' At first it appears that Claudette's love for Zizi is unrequited, and she is going to be just another lonely, embittered lesbian stereotype. But when Claudette apologizes to Zizi and asks her to give up Eliot, Zizi refuses. 'You're asking me to do the impossible,' she says. Claudette responds: 'We were so happy before he came. So happy.' Clearly the two women have had a relationship, but now Zizi is interested in Eliot. This lesbian love affair really happened, it is not just hinted at.

From a gay point of view the most interesting character in the film is the sisters' brother, Willmouse, who behaves more like their sister. Intelligent, articulate, unselfconscious and effeminate, he has a poncy hairstyle, and respects Eliot because 'he's the only one besides mother who doesn't laugh at me because I make clothes.' In one sequence Willmouse is seen sketching a beautiful picture of a woman, and in another he happily dresses two female dolls – one in blue, one in red – and calls them Miss Dawn and Dolores. When Hester interrupts him, he shoos her away: 'Oh, don't bother me.' he says, 'I can't get Miss Dawn's dress to hang straight.' Willmouse notices things like Zizi's dyed hair. 'From the first time I saw her it was a little black at the roots,' he says, and when he discusses Zizi's bosoms with Hester, he reveals his knowledge of them too. 'I've made bosoms for Miss Dawn and Dolores,' he says.

Unlike Geoffrey, his slightly older 'artistic' gay counterpart in 1961's *A Taste of Honey*, Willmouse is not an object of ridicule. Perhaps because he is a child, he is allowed to please himself, and be what he wants to be. His sisters and, more importantly, the kindly Eliot, accept his 'feminine' interests. Unfortunately Willmouse exists on the periphery of the film, and we do not see enough of him. The main focus of attention is Joss, who falls in love with Eliot, a jewel thief, and unwittingly causes his arrest.

The Singer Not the Song

The Singer Not the Song should have been called *Simon Sparrow Goes to Mexico* but nevertheless it contains one of Dirk Bogarde's most extraordinary film performances. He plays Anacleto Comachi, a leather-clad Mexican bandit who is fond of cats, especially white ones. He becomes involved in a love–hate relationship with Father Keogh, an Irish Catholic priest, played by John Mills. Almost a homoerotic *Duel in the Sun*, it fails to convince because it lacks the heat and passion of David O. Selznick's grandiose Western classic, made in 1946. Also, Bogarde sleepwalks through his part, and Mills lacks concentration, struggling in vain to master an Irish accent, and desperately needing strong direction from Roy Baker. In some ways Bogarde could be playing his first overtly gay role in this film. With one hand on his hip, a swishy walk, a white shirt, leather trousers and riding a white horse, he's as camp as Christmas. But take away the outfit and we're left with an unconvincing performance. It's Bogarde at his least erotic. He lacks sensuality and dynamism. One can only imagine the tension and excitement that would have been created if Marlon Brando and Montgomery Clift had played the bandit and priest! Bogarde and Mills are simply too polite and well-behaved, and there is an obvious lack of chemistry between the two actors. More interesting is 'Old Uncle', the character played by Laurence Naismith, who appears to be in love with Bogarde.

The colour photography is gorgeous, but black and white would have been more appropriate, and enhanced the drama. At no time does the film have the courage of its convictions, constantly diverting the audience's attention from real issues, such as religion, politics and sexuality, all of which are repressed. This is British film-making at its worst. A subject full of potential thrown on the scrap heap.

Dentist on the Job

In the comedy *Dentist on the Job* Bob Monkhouse stars as David Cookson, a dentist who invents a toothpaste and tries to promote it by planting an advertising jingle in a space satellite. At the beginning of the film, Charles Hawtrey makes a memorable appearance as Mr Roper, a chemist selling Dreem toothpaste. He has a Dreem display in his shop, and is taken aback when three bowler-hatted gentlemen enter with a giant tube of Dreem toothpaste for the display. One of them, Mr Fuller (Ian Whittaker), is very camp, but upset when Hawtrey cries in desperation: 'Oh, no! Not the giant economy size!' Asks Mr Fuller, suggestively: 'Where would you like me to put it?'

Later, Monkhouse's assistant Sam Field (Kenneth Connor), is overcome by the pretty young women patients until he calls for Judith Dobbin. Enter a loud, deep-voiced, butch lesbian stereotype played by an uncredited, unknown actress. She is subjected to some very offensive humour in a screenplay co-authored by Hazel Adair (who later created and scripted such popular television soaps as *Compact* and *Crossroads*), Hugh Woodhouse and Bob Monkhouse. Says Connor to Judith: 'Stable number . . . (pause). . . chair number three, Madam.' Says Judith to dentist Bob Monkhouse in a rough, demanding voice: 'I want scaling.' Replies Bob: 'I'm sure you do but I haven't got my climbing boots.' Working on her teeth, Judith complains to Bob: 'Come on, you're not hurting me at all!' Replies Bob: 'But I need a rest. I'm not used to heavy manual work.' Afterwards, Judith asks Bob: 'Now what do you advise? Shall I keep off the sweets?' Bob replies: 'No, but I should lay off the oats for a while!'

Other films of interest released in 1961

No Love for Johnnie was the first film made by the Rank Organization to receive an X certificate. When Labour MP Johnnie Byrne (Peter Finch) overhears a conversation between two gay men, they are probably the first modern gays (outside Michael Ward in Norman Wisdom comedies) to be squeezed past Rank's moral watchdogs. First gay man: 'Of course he's queer. He's not just trying to get on. He's queer.' Second gay man: 'But he's got swarms of children.' First gay man: 'How naive can you get? Of course he's got swarms of children. What's that got to do with it? He's as queer as a coot.' The film was released some months before *Victim* which Rank distributed, but did not actually produce; in the comedy *Petticoat Pirates* Charlie Drake has fun in drag, while Murray (*A Taste of Honey*) Melvin and Angus Lennie play a couple of camp sailors who engage in gayish banter. Melvin criticizes Lennie's spotted dick, telling him it 'tasted very funny'. Replies the offended Lennie: 'My spotted dick *always* tastes funny.'

Notes

1. Andy Medhurst, *Homosexuality and British Cinema: Representations and Readings*, unpublished MA Film Studies Dissertation, University of East Anglia, 1982.

2. Gavin Lambert, 'Tony Richardson: An Adventurer'. *Sight and Sound*, volume 3, no. 11, November 1993, p. 33.

Victim

When *Victim* was released in this country in 1961 it had an enormous impact on the lives of gay men who, for the first time, saw credible representations of themselves and their situations in a commercial British film. Its star, Dirk Bogarde, later said that *Victim* was the first film to treat gay men seriously, and that the film made a lot of difference to a lot of people's lives (see Appendix). Bogarde, the 'heart throb' of British films in the 1950s, described himself as 'the Loretta Young of England'. He said he was tired of playing insipid, one-dimensional romantic heroes, but this is a myth for he played a variety of interesting characters before the 1960s in films like *Hunted*, *The Gentle Gunman* and *The Spanish Gardener*. Even so, in order to make the final break from 'Loretta Young' parts, he readily agreed to be cast as a successful, middle-class barrister who is forced to reveal he is gay. In an interview at the time of the film's release Bogarde said:

> I realized it was a risk. I knew a lot of people would far rather see me kill my wife on the screen than play the barrister. I knew the X certificate would cut off a large slice of my young public. . . . But I decided it was a risk worth taking. Better one film like *Victim* than a dozen of those negative white telephone films full of dashing chaps wearing sporty cravats and driving pretty popsies around in Bentleys. . . . This was a film about a real person with a real problem. . . . This film may shock my nice-young-doctor public, but you can't go on making films just to please your fans. You can't leave *all* the adult, intelligent films to the French, Italians and Swedes.[1]

In 1957 the Report of the Wolfenden Committee on Homosexual Offences and Prostitution was published. This suggested that 'homosexual practices' in private between consenting males over twenty-one should not be considered a criminal offence. At that time, gay men were open to the most vicious forms of blackmail. *Victim* concentrated on the vulnerability to blackmail of anyone suspected of being gay. It highlighted the fact that around 90 per cent of blackmail cases involved gay men. In the early 1960s the publicity surrounding the release of *Victim*, and Bogarde's participation in the film, contributed to the public debate on homosexuality. However, it was not until 1967 that a change in the law finally took place. Michael Relph, the producer of *Victim*, says:

> In those days film directors like Anthony Asquith and Brian Desmond Hurst, as well as Noel Coward and Ivor Novello, were protected by the theatrical world. There wasn't any harrassment of gay people in our profession. Asquith was a very sweet, nice person but he was not open about his homosexuality. In fact, I don't think it was dominant in his life. So he was quite happy and safe working within the protected world of film and theatre. On the other hand, Hurst was quite flamboyant and did venture outside the theatrical world. He walked a very dangerous path by picking up guardsmen, but I don't think he was ever caught!
>
> However, a cat-and-mouse game existed with the police if gays stepped outside their particular world. I remember when John Gielgud was caught cottaging in the early 1950s. Sometimes the police turned a blind eye because the law was transparently ridiculous and hypocritical as far as homosexuality was concerned. From their point of view, provided you didn't overstep the mark, they were quite tolerant. But the law that existed seemed distasteful and out-of-date to me.[2]

In *Victim* Bogarde plays Melville Farr, a respectable, happily married barrister who investigates the suicide of a young gay man, Jack 'Boy' Barrett (Peter McEnery). The plot reveals that Barrett was in love with Farr, and was trying to protect him from blackmailers. During the investigation, Farr risks his career and marriage by helping to expose the blackmailers. By playing this part, Bogarde shattered his bankable screen persona with his sympathetic portrayal of a gay man. 'It is the biggest slap in the eye Dirk Bogarde has dealt his more emotional female fans since the day he objected to a girls' school next door to his house in Buckinghamshire,' said the *Daily Express*. Afterwards, Bogarde was no longer the 'Loretta Young of England', and his screen persona was often associated with gay sexuality. This is particularly true of his subsequent appearances in *The Servant*, *Modesty Blaise* and *Death in Venice*.

In 1978 Bogarde recalled the impact the film had on audiences in the early 1960s in his autobiography *Snakes and Ladders*:

> It is extraordinary, in this over-permissive age, to believe that this modest film could ever have been considered courageous, daring or dangerous to make. It was, in its time, all three. To start with, very few of the actors approached to play in it accepted; most flatly refused. . . . Janet Green's modest, tight, neat little thriller, for that is all it was fundamentally, might not have been Shaw, Ibsen or Strindberg, but it did at least probe and explore a hitherto forbidden Social Problem, simply, clearly, and with great impact for the first time in an English-speaking film. . . . The countless letters of gratitude which flooded in were proof enough of that, and I had achieved what I had longed to do for so long, to be in a film which disturbed, educated, and illuminated as well as merely giving entertainment.[3]

Bogarde's performance is perceptive and honest. When, as Melville Farr, he risks his successful career as a barrister to expose the blackmailers, one can only speculate how Bogarde must have felt when he put his own acting career at risk by agreeing to play the 'controversial' role of a gay man. He said that he agreed to play the role on condition that there would be no compromise in treating the story. 'Otherwise why make it?' he asked.

One of the most powerful and memorable scenes in the film takes place when Farr confesses to his wife that he was sexually attracted to Barrett. 'I *wanted* him!' he cries. This, says Andy Medhurst:

> turns a cautious plea for sexual tolerance into an eroticized melodrama. . . the emotional excess of Bogarde's performance . . . pushes the text beyond its liberal boundaries until it becomes a passionate validation of the homosexual option. Simply watch the 'confession' scene for proof of this.[4]

Victim was produced by Michael Relph in collaboration with his partner, director Basil Dearden. They were a socially conscious team who, since the early 1950s, had been praised for the realism of their films. The duo were responsible for making so-called 'problem pictures' and these included *Sapphire* (1959), winner of the British Academy Award for Best British Film. In their screenplay, Janet Green and her husband John McCormick cleverly explored racial tension in post-war Britain by using a thriller structure. Says Michael Relph:

> Homosexuality was something we accepted completely and it seemed to us absolutely preposterous that the law was the way it was. So when we were thinking of a social problem we could deal with after *Sapphire*, this seemed a natural one because the Wolfenden Report had just been published and it was very much in the news, and topical. Because we were all part of the theatrical world, everybody knew gay men, so the script didn't need a lot of research. I had worked with John McCormick in the theatre when he was a very prominent stage manager and then he married Janet. She was a well-known detective story writer and the three of us always wanted to collaborate, especially on films concerning social problems. We decided to contain them within a thriller structure, for which we were attacked quite a lot because it was felt we belittled the subjects we dealt with. But as far as reaching a wide audience was concerned, I think it was really necessary to use the thriller form. When you make a political film, you don't want to preach to the converted. We were always trying to reach a wider public, which was a very ambitious thing to do at that time.
>
> Though it may look a bit tame today, we were encouraged that gay men all over the country identified with *Victim*, and I am certain it contributed to the debate on homosexuality which eventually led to a change in the law. Certainly it kept the subject before the public.[5]

Dirk Bogarde has said the first actor approached to star in *Victim* turned it down because he was afraid of losing his knighthood, but Michael Relph doesn't agree with this:

> Dirk was always our first choice. He was perfect for *Victim*. It was very courageous of him to play the gay barrister. Until then his career had been built on being an attractive heterosexual matinee idol. From the start he was very sympathetic to the subject, and helpful with the script. However, we expected Dirk

to turn us down, so we had Michael Redgrave as our second choice because we knew about his homosexuality, and felt he would be sympathetic to the subject.[6]

In October 1988 the British Academy of Film and Television Arts presented Dirk Bogarde with its first Lifetime Achievement Award for Outstanding Contribution to World Cinema. At the ceremony, Bogarde paid tribute to Sylvia Syms, who played his wife, Laura, in *Victim*. He told the audience that Syms was the only actress who would consider taking part in a film about homosexuality. Earlier, in *Snakes and Ladders*, Bogarde wrote: 'Every actress asked to play the wife turned it down without reading the script, except Sylvia Syms who who accepted readily and with warm comprehension.'[7]

Syms dared to be different in her choice of film roles at a time when most British leading ladies of her generation, such as Janette Scott, Virginia McKenna and Heather Sears, found difficulty avoiding roles as well-spoken, middle-class 'English Rose' types. One of the few exceptions was Diana Dors. Rarely were these actresses offered strong dramatic roles like their male contemporaries. Says Sylvia:

> I came from a politically aware background, and tried to seek roles that were interesting. I was aware of the Wolfenden Report, and I wanted to do *Victim* very much, partly for the subject, and partly to work with Dirk. The film is of its time and would never have been made if it hadn't had the element of the thriller. I had a short role, which was rather underwritten. I did not have many lines to express her feelings, so I added a subtext. I played her as an innocent middle-class virgin who adored her husband.
>
> Basil Dearden was a meticulous technical director, but he was not very concerned with actors. So Dirk and I developed our characters on our own, though he did support us on the set.
>
> The film was truthful in that homosexuals do get married and have children. The character Dirk played was accurate because homosexuality was not acceptable then. For him, it was a sin, and that was how some gay men felt in those days. The part was very true. In those days gay men had to behave like gentlemen in order to 'pass' as heterosexuals. An exception was Quentin Crisp, but then he did not do any ordinary job so he could get away with being outrageous![8]

The problem of censorship reared its ugly head when a copy of the script was sent to John Trevelyan, Secretary of the British Board of Film Censors. In a letter to Janet Green dated 1 July 1960 he said:

> We have never banned the subject of homosexuality from the screen but we have not until recently had very much censorship trouble with it, because American film producers were prevented from dealing with the subject by the inflexible ruling of the Code and because British film producers knew that the subject was not one of general discussion in this country and was one that would probably not be acceptable to British audiences. . . . As you know, on the subject of homosexuality there is a division of public opinion, and, if this week's debate in the House of Commons is anything to go by, it appears that there is still a majority opposed to any compassionate treatment of it. In these circumstances a film-maker dealing with this subject is treading on dangerous ground and will have to proceed with caution.[9]

However, Michael Relph found a way to please Trevelyan. He says: 'Trevelyan was terribly stagestruck so to get round him we invited him to lunch at the studio and introduced him to a few film stars!' During the filming of *Victim*, Relph did not encounter any problems with the crew, either: 'We didn't have any problems with anyone working on the set, such as technicians, because they'd come into contact with gays all the time in the film world. There was certainly no hostility. But I don't really know what they thought of the subject matter.'[10]

On the whole the film received favourable reviews from film critics in Britain. Said Peter G. Baker, editor of *Films and Filming*:

> *Victim*, for all its faults, is a landmark in British cinema. . . . And when, as inevitably will happen, the law is changed and a man is no longer penalized for expressing his sense and sensibility as he will, *Victim* will have made its contribution to that understanding. And we'll have to find a new name for 'queer'.[11]

However, on its release in America in 1962, the film ran into censorship difficulties and was denied a 'Seal of Approval'. It also received a hostile reception from the critics. *Time* called *Victim* 'a plea for perversion' and described its gay characters as deviates and sodomites, while the respected critic Pauline Kael longed for 'those old-fashioned movie stereotypes – the vicious, bitchy old queen who said mean, funny things'. She also warned her readers that 'homosexuals are going to be treated seriously, with sympathy and respect, like Jews and Negroes'. (See Appendix for extracts from some of the British and American press relating to this film.)

By the 1970s it had become fashionable for some British film critics and historians to dismiss *Victim*, and ignore its historical importance. Alexander Walker, who is one of the most perceptive and illuminating writers on British cinema, was downright patronizing in *Gay News*. He contradicted his favourable review of the film in the *Evening Standard* in 1961 ('I applaud *Victim*. It is a good film. Good as a fast-paced thriller. Overwhelmingly good as an acting triumph for Bogarde.') when he said:

> I never thought *Victim* stood up very well at the time, let alone now. . . . It presented homosexuals as very limp-wristed, arty-crafty people. . . . There was a sense of manipulation about it which showed in its desire to please everybody and offend no one.[12]

However, in recent years, gay writers such as Vito Russo (in *The Celluloid Closet*), Richard Dyer and Andy Medhurst have recognized its importance and relevance. Says Medhurst:

> In the context of 1961, the leading character of a film saying 'I wanted him' is a radical act. And since gay political action cannot exist without the bringing into the open homosexual desire, then *Victim* is performing a vital action.[13]

For his performance in *Victim*, Dirk Bogarde was nominated for a British Academy Award as Best British Actor. The only other nominee that year was Peter Finch. He won the award for *No Love for Johnnie*. In the Channel 4 television documentary *Typically British*, shown in September 1995, Stephen Frears, director of *My Beautiful Laundrette* (1985) and *Prick Up Your Ears* (1987), described his boyhood viewing of Dirk Bogarde's films in the 1950s: 'I remember how sexy Dirk Bogarde was. I mean, he was the sexiest girl in British cinema.'

Notes

1. Interview with Dirk Bogarde, *Daily Mail*, 19 August 1961.
2. Michael Relph, interview with the author, London, 1995.
3. Dirk Bogarde, *Snakes and Ladders* (Chatto & Windus, 1978), p. 201.
4. Andy Medhurst, 'Dirk Bogarde' in Charles Barr (ed.), *All Our Yesterdays: 90 Years of British Cinema* (British Film Institute, 1986), p. 352.
5. Relph, interview with the author.
6. Relph, interview with the author.
7. Bogarde, *Snakes and Ladders*, p. 241.
8. Sylvia Syms, interview with the author, *Gay Times*, June 1989.
9. James C. Robertson, *The Hidden Cinema: British Film Censorship in Action, 1913–1972* (Routledge, 1989), pp. 121–2.
10. Relph, interview with the author.
11. Peter G. Baker, *Films and Filming*, October 1961.
12. Alexander Walker, 'Gays in the Cinema, 1960–1976'. *Gay News*, no. 101, 1976.
13. Andy Medhurst, *Homosexuality and British Cinema: Representations and Readings*, unpublished MA Film Studies Dissertation, University of East Anglia, 1982.

1962

The L-Shaped Room

Bryan Forbes was a successful film actor who became one of our most impressive screenwriters (*The Angry Silence, The League of Gentlemen*) and directors (*Whistle Down the Wind*). In 1962 he combined his writing and directing skills to bring Lynne Reid Banks's novel *The L-Shaped Room*, first published in 1960, to the screen. This was at the height of the vogue for so-called 'kitchen sink' dramas, and this was one of the most popular. However, some critics had grown tired of the genre. Said Derek Hill in *Topic* (17 November 1962): 'Bryan Forbes takes two and a half hours to knock the last nail in the social realist coffin.' But more than thirty years on the film has stood the test of the time, and this is mainly due to Forbes's sensitive writing and direction. He handles the 'difficult' (for 1962) themes of single parenthood, and gay sexuality, with perception and frankness and, like Tony Richardson in *A Taste of Honey*, he inspires memorable performances from a superb cast.

The L-Shaped Room stars Leslie Caron as Jane, insecure, middle class, unmarried and expecting a child. In desperation she takes a room in a run-down boarding-house in Notting Hill and among the residents Jane befriends are Mavis (Cicely Courtneidge), an over-the-hill music-hall performer, Toby (Tom Bell), an aspiring writer, and Johnny (Brock Peters), an African-Caribbean jazz musician. Admittedly the casting of a French actress is something of a compromise (though Caron was a British resident at the time), an obvious attempt to attract an 'international' audience. But this was not the first time a 'foreign' actress had been cast in a pivotal role in a British film to help create a box office success. In 1958 another French star, Simone Signoret, played Alice Aisgill in *Room at the Top* and walked off with numerous awards, including a Best Actress Oscar. Interestingly, among the British actresses who tested for the role of North Country Alice was Patricia Phoenix. She went on to find fame as Elsie Tanner in *Coronation Street* and play a supporting role (as the prostitute Sonia) in *The L-Shaped Room*.

In spite of this, *The L-Shaped Room* works beautifully on an emotional level because, like all the best soap operas, including *Mrs Dale's Diary*, *Coronation Street* and *EastEnders*, once the audience is invited to become 'involved' with the lives of the characters, they want to stay with them until they know how their problems are resolved. This is the secret of success for all soap operas. Audiences enjoy 'looking in' on the lives of other people, and 'sharing' or 'identifying with' their problems.

At the beginning of the film Jane walks past an advertisement for the *News of the World* which claims 'all human life is there' and this is what she finds in the boarding-house. The residents are a mixed group of isolated and displaced people who form a supportive, constructed family. Even Doris, the landlady (Avis Bunnage), is broadminded, unusual for landladies in British films. When Toby helps Jane upstairs with her suitcase, he says: 'I'm just taking a girl up to my room.' Replies Doris: 'That's nice. Don't give the house a bad name.' Apart from Jane, Toby, Johnny and Doris, there are two prostitutes living in the basement (one a refugee from the 1956 Hungarian uprising), and Mavis, an out-of-work music-hall entertainer, who lives alone with her cat Benjy.

We are introduced to Mavis after she has failed an audition for being too old: 'They said I did a very good audition,' she tells Toby, 'but they wanted someone a bit. . . (pause). . . I think they wanted a name.' Lonely and alone (apart from her cat), she lives in the past, surrounded by photographs, records and memorabilia from her long and successful career on the boards. There is a sadness about her, and maybe we should pity her, but Mavis has a heart, and shows genuine concern for her neighbours. In the hands of actress Cicely Courtneidge she has warmth and compassion.

At Christmas, Mavis reminisces to Jane about the happy times she once had during the festive season. 'I love Christmas,' she says. 'I used to love playing in panto on Boxing Day. Lovely audiences. Laughing at all the corny jokes and the cornier they are the louder they laughed! Today's pantos are not much cop. Fancy a man playing the principal boy. It's a disgrace to the profession.' In a tender, subtle scene, Jane enquires about Mavis's family. 'No family,' she replies. 'Only a friend. Never went in for marriage. Not in the sight of God anyway. I did have a friend. We lived together for years. A real love-match it was. Well, I've never wanted anything since.' At this point in the scene Jane looks at the photograph of Mavis's friend. Mavis nods and explains: 'It takes all sorts, dear. And I hope you have a girl. They're less trouble than boys.' It is one of the most touching, beautifully realized 'coming-out' sequences ever put on film. Mavis is not embarrassed to show Jane a photograph of her lesbian partner, or ashamed to reveal she is a lesbian. She behaves naturally, expressing herself as anyone would whose long-term partner has died, regardless of their sexuality. Unlike other lesbians in the movies, Mavis is neither predatory, alien or butch, though we are left wondering about Mavis and her friend. What was her name? How did they meet?

For Bryan Forbes, there was no question that the perfect actress for the role of Mavis was Cicely Courtneidge, the legendary musical comedy star who was created a Dame of the British Empire in 1972. He recalls:

> I never thought of anybody else for the role of Mavis. Cicely Courtneidge was a distinguished musical-comedy star then approaching the twilight of her career and somebody I had long admired and felt had been unfairly neglected by the British cinema once her comedy films with husband Jack Hulbert came to an end. She had no problems with the gentleness of her lesbian character and gave a performance of loving truth and, as her playing triumphantly displayed, was able to bring a sadness to the role. Of course at the time it was considered very 'daring' to put a lesbian on the screen (God knows why, but we still had to contend with the British Board of Film Censors). Mavis, as written by me, did not appear in the novel.[1]

In his autobiography, *A Divided Life*, Bryan Forbes reveals that *The L-Shaped Room* ran into many censorship difficulties with John Trevelyan, Secretary of the British Board of Film Censors. In four closely typed pages he listed numerous items that were unacceptable. Probably the most ridiculous was Leslie Caron having to cover her nipples with Elastoplast for the love scene, even though she kept her back to the camera! As reprinted in Appendix Two of Forbes's autobiography, here is Trevelyan's suggestions for Mavis:

Page 125 Scene 404

When Mavis talks about the love of her life, we learn from the photograph that this love was for another woman. This may well pass especially since Mavis is talking about love and not about sex, and it will be helpful in your casting of Mavis, but I suggest that you shoot the scene in such a way as to make the omission of the photograph, if considered desirable, something which could be done without spoiling the scene.[2]

To his credit, in the margin Forbes has written 'ignore' and the photograph remained in the scene.

The L-Shaped Room was also one of the first British films to include a black gay character. In Lynne Reid Banks's novel, John is presented as a racial caricature and gay stereotype, suggesting that Banks's knowledge of black people had been gleaned from films like *Sanders of the River*, and children's fiction, probably Helen Bannerman's *Little Black Sambo* and Enid Blyton's *Noddy* series. Banks's racism and insensitivity is exposed after Jane has expressed her fear of the black man to Toby. He describes John's 'white eyes rolling' adding that he is 'naturally inquisitive. Like a chimp. . . . He could no more resist having a look at you than a monkey could resist picking up anything new and giving it the once-over.' Jane responds: 'Yes, and then when he's picked it up he'll probably try to eat it.' Later, Toby reveals to Jane other aspects of John's character: 'He wouldn't hurt a fly. . . he's a first-class cook. . . he does needlework too.'[3] However, when Bryan Forbes adapted the novel for the screen, he eliminated the overtly racist and homophobic aspects of Banks's character, and attempted to humanize John.

Changing the character's name to the more informal, friendly Johnny, Forbes was assisted by the tall, muscular American actor Brock Peters who gives a superb performance. In the 1950s, Peters had established himself as one of the most threatening black actors of his generation with brutish roles as the villainous Sergeant Brown in *Carmen Jones* (1954) and the terrifying Crown in *Porgy and Bess* (1959). In 1962 he was cast against type as Tom Robinson, the tragic farmhand falsely accused of rape in *To Kill a Mockingbird*. With this role he proved that, given the chance, he could play warm, gentle giants with intelligence and sensitivity. These were qualities he brought to his role as Johnny in *The L-Shaped Room*.

Brock Peters helped to make Johnny a caring, even sensual character who shares an easy-going, relaxed friendship with Jane and Toby. He is an outsider because of his colour and sexuality, but he is no more isolated from society than his friends. In the boarding-house he is fully accepted as a member of the constructed 'family'.

We first learn that Johnny is gay when Toby describes him to Jane as 'a bit bent'. Adding complexity to Johnny's character, we discover that he is in love with Toby. After Johnny discovers Jane and Toby have slept together, he explodes at her in a jealous rage: 'I had a good friend in Toby. He always talked to *me* before.' Although Johnny is subsequently responsible for terminating the couple's relationship, by revealing Jane's pregnancy to Toby, he apologizes to Jane who forgives him. They remain friends, but Toby stays angry with Jane till the end of the film.

Bryan Forbes fully intended to humanize John, and create a warm, believable character who, like lesbian Mavis, is not a caricature. He says:

> Brock Peters' character was changed – again the gentle approach with a total absence of 'camp' for I have always felt that this is the obvious, easy route to take and much abused. (Although I confess that I did slip in a minor way with the camp chorus boy I wrote for Oliver Reed in *The League of Gentlemen*.) Why did I present Brock as gay? Well, exact memory eludes me as it does most authors, but I guess I wanted a counterpoint – the role played by Tom Bell was somebody who could not face up to the truth of loving somebody who was carrying another man's child. I tried to people that house with a variety of people I knew existed at that time and in those circumstances, but it was never a conscious effort on my part to be 'different' – just, I suspect, an awareness that the public's perception was changing.
>
> At around the same time I was also involved as part of the team responsible for the first truly honest film about homosexuality – *Victim* – written by Janet Green and directed by my partner, the late Basil Dearden. The fact that Dirk Bogarde, an established

matinée idol, agreed to play the role, changed his entire career, as he has frequently admitted.

You have to remember that I began my career (mostly as an actor) at a time when certainly the West End stage was dominated by H. M. Tennents Ltd – masterminded by the late Hugh (Binkie) Beaumont, who along with other notables was homosexual, albeit under wraps as far as the public were concerned. It was known by Fleet Street but largely ignored. Therefore I, along with many others in the profession, were no strangers to the homosexual scene – but there was no prejudice as such – I have always judged people by their talents, not their race, religion or sexual leanings – that is to say I don't care whether somebody is a black, gay, Jewish extrovert – all I care about is whether he or she is a good actor. I think this is largely true of the profession as a whole.

I did write another gay character into *King Rat*, released in 1965, this time being faithful to James Clavell's original – but Columbia Pictures got cold feet when I presented my finished cut of the film and insisted that the entire sequence be deleted – much to my sorrow, for it was a marvellous sequence.

This all sounds as though I have made a career out of portraying such characters! But I can assure you once again that they came about because of a writer's instinct to explore all the facets of human behaviour rather than a determined effort to be daring.[4]

For her performance in *The L-Shaped Room* Leslie Caron received the 1962 British Academy Award as Best British Actress and was nominated for a 1963 Best Actress Oscar. In Danny Peary's *Alternate Oscars* (published in 1993) he names her Best Actress. *The L-Shaped Room* was also nominated for a British Academy Award as Best British Film, thus making it eligible for the award of Best Film from any source. Both awards went to David Lean's *Lawrence of Arabia*.

Lawrence of Arabia

English soldier and folk hero T. E. Lawrence (1888–1935) was once described by Noel Coward as 'strange and elusive, painfully shy, gay and loquacious'. In *The Making of David Lean's Lawrence of Arabia*, Adrian Turner describes Lawrence as a man who 'would never come to terms with his homosexuality and sought ways to suppress it'.[5] Turner adds that, when David Lean's film version was in production, screenwriter Michael Wilson was not paying much attention to Lawrence's sexuality. Wilson was more concerned with the theme of colonialism versus nationalism, and Lawrence's scholastic pursuits.

> This clearly displeased Lean, who wanted to paint more of a controversial character study, albeit on a large canvas, than Wilson had so far achieved. As far as one can judge from Wilson's notes, Lean had two overriding concerns – Lawrence's sexual make-up, and the scene that he would film in Petra. As far as the former is concerned, Wilson noted that Lean had, revealingly, compared the Lawrence–Ali relationship to *Brief Encounter*, his 1945 film about an unconsummated love affair starring Trevor Howard and Celia Johnson.[6]

Years later, after the restored version of the film was released, Lean said that he had addressed Lawrence's sexuality (the credited screenwriter was Robert Bolt, not Wilson): 'The whole story, and certainly Lawrence, was very, if not entirely, gay. We thought we were being very daring at the time, Lawrence and Omar, Lawrence and the Arab boys.'[7] In *Broadcasting It*, Keith Howes agrees that there is a homoemotional relationship between Lawrence (Peter O'Toole) and Sherif Ali (Omar Sharif). He says: 'The restored version begins with Lawrence wearing mascara and behaving for all the world like Noel Coward. The ambiguity of his relationships with King Feisal and with the Omar Sharif character are astonishingly direct, certainly as far as looks, vocal tone, body and camera placement are concerned.'[8] Howes also describes Lean's film as a 'dazzling, churning epic which is satisfying on all levels', but it does have one flaw, the treatment of the sadistic Turkish Bey, played by José Ferrer.

When Lawrence is arrested in Deraa and taken to the Bey's headquarters for interrogation, we have already glimpsed the Bey driving through the city. He's a sinister-looking monster, and his evil appearance warns the audience that Lawrence is going to have an uncomfortable time. When the Bey appears again, with mascara and a horrible little cough, he lusts after Lawrence: 'It's an interesting face,' he says, 'I am surrounded by cattle. . . I have been in Deraa now for three and a half years. If they'd posted me to the dark side of the moon I couldn't be more – isolated.' He adds: 'You haven't the least idea what I'm talking about,' but it is obvious to Lawrence, and the audience, what the Bey wants. He strips Lawrence and touches the young man's body. 'You're skin is very fair,' he says, acknowledging the stark contrast between the two actors playing the scene. Peter O'Toole is blonde and handsome with gorgeous blue eyes. His body is extremely white. There is no question about who the audience is supposed to sympathize with here. José Ferrer is a white actor who has been 'blacked-up'. He bears similarities with the grotesque stereotypes of men of colour who were portrayed as evil villains in silent Hollywood films. In fact, the Bey's animalistic desire for Lawrence recalls the scene in D. W. Griffiths's controversial civil war epic *The Birth of a Nation* (1915) in which the innocent, lily-white heroine, played by Lillian Gish, is attacked and driven to suicide by the menacing mixed-race Silas Lynch (played by a white actor in crude blackface make-up). To add insult to injury, the Bey is gay, too, but a nasty, predatory type. A close-up of O'Toole's eyes, which reveal nothing but sheer terror, is followed by a close-up of Ferrer's lips. The 'rape' is interrupted by O'Toole (and heterosexuality) winning the day when the 'victim' knees the 'rapist' in the groin.

The Bey orders his guards to beat Lawrence, and retires to his office, but he leaves his door open to hear his victim's screams. To emphasize the Bey's sadism, not that Lean needed to, we can hear him coughing in the background, and then observing what happens to Lawrence. Lean lays it on with a trowel. It is a disgusting scene, probably one of the most homophobic and racist ever filmed. It is extraordinary that it exists in the middle of an otherwise great movie.

Lawrence of Arabia was an international success. In America it was the fourth highest-grossing film of 1963 and won seven Oscars including Best Film and Director (Lean). Newcomer O'Toole was nominated for Best Actor and won the British Academy Award for Best British Actor (beating Richard Attenborough, Alan Bates, James Mason, Laurence Olivier and Peter Sellers). The film was named Best Film from any source and Best British Film, and Robert Bolt won for Best Screenplay.

Other films of interest released in 1962

In *The Roman Spring of Mrs Stone,* adapted for the screen by Gavin Lambert and Jan Read from Tennessee Williams's novel, Lotte Lenya played Contessa Gonzales who supplies rich matrons with young male 'escorts'. She has a notebook and is always busy on the 'phone. She comes out of her office and tells the ladies who are waiting what 'arrangements' she has made for their evening. Then she turns to an elderly man sitting in a corner and says 'But for *you*, Count, I need a little more time!' Later he is seen at a café with a young man at his side; in *Billy Budd*, based on Herman Melville's novel, Terence Stamp played the beautiful, innocent sailor who drives the much-despised Master-at-Arms Claggart (Robert Ryan) wild. Says Vito Russo in *The Celluloid Closet*: 'the homoeroticism in the film comes as much from Stamp's angelic embodiment of Melville's Billy as it does from the lechings of the fascinated Claggart'.

Notes

1. Bryan Forbes, letter to the author, 29 August 1995.
2. Bryan Forbes, *A Divided Life* (Heinemann, 1992), pp. 362–3.
3. Lynne Reid Banks, *The L-Shaped Room* (Chatto & Windus, 1960).
4. Bryan Forbes, letter to the author, 29 August 1995.
5. Adrian Turner, *The Making of David Lean's Lawrence of Arabia* (Dragon's World, 1994), p. 16.
6. *Ibid.*, p. 73.
7. David Lean, *Guardian,* 28 April 1991.
8. Keith Howes, *Broadcasting It* (Cassell, 1993).

1963

The Servant

The Servant, directed by Joseph Losey, is an unusual, disturbing study of corruption which focuses on a servant/master relationship. The film opens itself up to a variety of interpretations: roles are reversed, games are played, and class boundaries disintegrate in Harold Pinter's extraordinary screenplay which he based on the 1948 novella by W. Somerset Maugham's gay nephew, Robin (1916–81). Barrett, the main character in *The Servant*, was based on a real-life manservant Robin Maugham's mother had engaged for him after the war. He later recalled:

> When the war ended my mother bought me a little house in Chelsea. I'd been abroad and when I came back she'd installed this manservant and he looked after the house beautifully, cooked terribly well and kept everything very clean. But somehow he gave me the shudders. Something about him frightened me. . . the door to his bedroom was open and, lying naked, face downwards, spreadeagled on the bed was one of the most beautiful boys of about fourteen I've ever seen. . . . While I was staring in wonderment at this beautiful creature a voice behind me said, 'Good evening, sah, I see that you are admiring my nephew. Perhaps you would like him to come up later and say goodnight to you?' At that moment I saw the portals of blackmail and the gates of prison yawning open before my gaze. . . . I pretended I hadn't heard what he said.[1]

In *The Servant* upper-class 'master' Tony (James Fox) thinks he's found the perfect 'manservant' in Hugo Barrett (Dirk Bogarde). However, Tony's cold, unemotional, stony-faced fiancée Susan (Wendy Craig) is on to him. She detects a subtle insolence in everything Barrett says and

11 Anton Walbrook in *The Red Shoes* (1948). BFI Stills, Posters and Designs

12 Joyce Heron in *The Weak and the Wicked* (1954). BFI Stills, Posters and Designs

13 Michael Ward. BFI Stills, Posters and Designs

14 Kenneth Williams and Charles Hawtrey in *Carry on Constable* (1960). BFI Stills, Posters and Designs

15 Murray Melvin in *A Taste of Honey* (1961). National Film Archive London

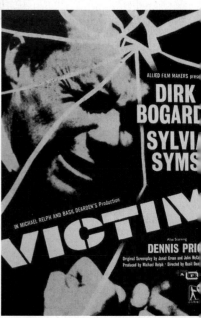

16 *Victim* (1961)

17 Leslie Caron and Cicely Courtneidge in *The L-Shaped Room* (1962). BFI Stills, Posters and Designs

18 BELOW June Ritchie and Sylvia Syms in *The World Ten Times Over* (1963)

19 Susannah York and Beryl Reid in *The Killing of Sister George* (1969). BFI Stills, Posters and Designs

20 Dudley Sutton and Colin Campbell in *The Leather Boys* (1963). National Film Archive London

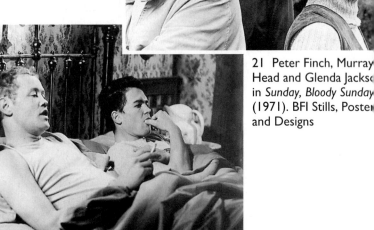

21 Peter Finch, Murray Head and Glenda Jackson in *Sunday, Bloody Sunday* (1971). BFI Stills, Posters and Designs

does, and she probably senses the gay current coming from the servant too. With the arrival of Barrett's gawky 'sister' Vera (Sarah Miles), the trap is set. By the time the true relationship between Barrett and Vera is discovered, it is too late. Tony may have thrown the bounder out of the house, but he cannot rid his home of the memories. He is lost without him and, when Barrett pleads to return, Tony – now adrift in a sea of drugs and alcohol – readily agrees. Susan, disgusted by Tony's affair with Vera, has gone. Barrett takes complete control.

In the original script there is a scene which Joseph Losey filmed but cut from the release print. Pinter's screenplay – his first for the cinema – shows the two men in a slovenly if comfortable domestic relationship. Apparently this made the sexual relationship between Fox and Bogarde slightly more explicit. However, Losey wanted the Barrett/Tony relationship to be ambiguous, but what remains in the film is suggestive enough in its decadent intensity and sado-masochism.

After playing the gay barrister in *Victim*, this was Bogarde's second attempt at losing the Rank glamour-boy image and his role as Barrett is totally unsympathetic. But then so is the character played by James Fox, in his first starring role. Blond, smooth and pretty, Tony is an opportunistic git, first class in accent and manners, but indolent and uncaring. His fiancée, Susan, is hardly more attractive. Giggling, girlish Vera, with her bedraggled looks, is the perfect below-stairs catalyst, plotting to bring down the whole house of cards.

An ex-patriate American from the McCarthy witchhunts of the early 1950s, former communist Joseph Losey revealed the façade and hypocrisy of British society in *The Servant*, and showed how easily it could crumble. Interestingly, *The Servant* was released just a few months after the famous Christine Keeler–John Profumo scandal which precipitated the collapse of Harold Macmillan's Tory government. Like *Victim*, the film was quite successful at the box office, and launched Fox and Miles as moderately bankable stars. Bogarde garnered well-deserved universal critical acclaim and a British Academy Award as Best British Actor.

The moody theme song, *All Gone*, written by Pinter and performed by Cleo Laine in various atmospheric John Dankworth arrangements, is possibly the first use of song lyrics as part of a script. It is not only the film's warning voice of the gathering darkness surrounding Susan and Tony, but it also draws attention to Tony's growing emotional and possible sexual dependence on Barrett as cleaner, cook, companion, 'mother' and supplier of 'substances'.

The Servant moves Bogarde's screen homosexuality beyond the well-bred boundaries of *Victim*. Though he is clearly having some kind of liaison with Vera, we are quite plainly meant to view Barrett as predominantly queer. His prissy walk and accent, his talent for cooking, interior decoration and flower arranging all suggest this. He has also pinned a collection of hunky and homoerotic body builder pin-ups on his bedroom wall! For a popular British matinée idol, even post-*Victim*, playing this role was an act of some bravery. Bogarde plays the unapologetic villain to the hilt. There is no explanation whatsoever for his evil doings. They are acts of pure pleasure spiked with class revenge! Unusual for 1963, the film ends with Susan's – and heterosexuality's – complete defeat. Barrett will continue to corrupt Tony as the 'master' continues his downward spiral. No doubt Susan will marry a property developer/stockbroker, and Vera will hoist her mini-skirt even higher and be passed from aristocrat to aristocrat.

The Servant is a 'swinging London' film made two years before that phrase was coined. It works effortlessly as a classy chiller and as an exercise in satanic satire. Losey would never again work with quite so perfect a script and with such clever casting. However, excellent though Wendy Craig is as Sloane Ranger Susan, it would have been fascinating to see how Bogarde's *Victim* co-star, Sylvia Syms – who had to withdraw through pregnancy – would have handled the role, and interacted with Bogarde a second time under such different circumstances.

The Servant is not an easy film to watch because there is no one the audience can identify with. However, it is a seductive film, and one of great sophistication and intelligence. Though critically acclaimed, and still recognized as a 'classic', and a landmark in British cinema, it is a pity it is not seen or appreciated more widely. For example, for years film-study courses have encouraged students to look at such major works as Eisenstein's *Battleship Potemkin*, Orson Welles's *Citizen Kane*, John Ford's *The Searchers* and Hitchcock's *North by Northwest*, but most British films, especially complex ones like Losey's *The Servant*, continue to be ignored.

Bogarde won the British Academy Award for Best British Actor against tough competition. The other nominees that year were Tom Courtenay in John Schlesinger's *Billy Liar*, Albert Finney and Hugh

Griffith in Tony Richardson's *Tom Jones* and Richard Harris in Lindsay Anderson's *This Sporting Life*. In addition to Bogarde's award, James Fox was voted the Most Promising Newcomer (the nominees included Fox's co-star Wendy Craig). Another award went to Douglas Slocombe for his black-and-white cinematography while other nominations were received for Best British Film and Best Film from any source (losing both to *Tom Jones*) and Sarah Miles as Best British Actress (she lost to Rachel Roberts in *This Sporting Life*). The Variety Club of Great Britain also named Bogarde Best Film Actor and Fox Most Promising Newcomer, and in Italy Joseph Losey received the 1965 Nastri d'Argento Silver Ribbon for Best Foreign Director. In America Harold Pinter received the 1964 Best Screenplay award from the New York Film Critics Circle.

This Sporting Life

In *This Sporting Life* Richard Harris gives an outstanding performance as Frank Machin, an aggressive ex-miner who becomes the star attraction of a rugby team. He strives to achieve something worthwhile, but goes about it the wrong way. In a desperate search for his own identity he succeeds only in destroying everything and everyone around him.

Scripted by David Storey from his own novel, the film is a fascinating study of sexual power games, and retains some of the homoerotic charge of its source. For example, Storey's novel opens with the following paragraph:

> I had my head to Mellor's backside, waiting for the ball to come between his legs. He was too slow. I was moving away when the leather shot back into my hands and, before I could pass, a shoulder came up to my jaw. It rammed my teeth together with a force that stunned me into blackness.[2]

The scene in the changing room after the rugby match at the beginning of the film displays a homoeroticism rarely seen in a British film. The naked men are lovingly composed and photographed, displaying their gladiator-like bodies and bare bums while tightly packed together in steam-filled spaces. In the bath they are completely uninhibited. Playing, splashing and handling each other without a care in the world. One man is even seen with a look of satisfaction on his face as he rubs a towel on the back of another player, who grins with pleasure. In the bath a naked man grabs a passing team-mate and pulls him down on top of him. For the gay spectator it is a pleasurable, and sexually exciting experience. There is nothing being hidden here. It is a vision of masculinity and male camaraderie which is overtly sexual, but it is hardly surprising that most writers who have acknowledged and praised this film classic have avoided, or missed, its overtly homoerotic content.

This Sporting Life was directed by the late Lindsay Anderson who never married, and whose sexuality is open to question. Anderson was a director who, like his contemporary Tony Richardson, was uncompromising, non-conformist and 'difficult'. Following Anderson's death in 1994, Gavin Lambert revealed the following in an article in *Sight and Sound*:

> Like Hitchcock (it's their only point of resemblance), Lindsay played out his erotic fantasies on the screen, not in life. In *This Sporting Life*, his first feature, there's a powerful but indirect response to the physicality of the footballer and his world, the tussles on the field and the emotional steam of the locker room .... Lindsay came to be the Great Outsider of British films.[3]

A great deal of critical attention has been given to this film, especially the performances of Richard Harris and Rachel Roberts. But there has been hardly any acknowledgement of the film's gay characters, especially 'Dad' Johnson, a sad, lonely, pathetic creature. He's movingly played by William Hartnell, just before he became nationally famous as BBC television's space traveller, Dr Who. Wearing a flat cap, glasses, an overcoat and scarf, 'Dad' is a scout for the rugby team. Attentive and loyal to Frank, he follows the young rugby player everywhere. In one scene he's even referred to as Frank's 'little dog'. A conversation between Frank and his landlady, Mrs Hammond (Rachel Roberts), reveals Johnson's sexual attraction to Frank, and her hostility towards the old man. 'He looks at you like a girl,' she sneers. Frank, in a defensive and protective mood, explains that Johnson is only interested in his rugby playing, but Mrs Hammond is not convinced: 'I'd say excited. . . . Just look at his hands. He's got awful hands. They're all soft.' Sadly, Frank drops Johnson after he becomes a rugby 'star'.

In *This Sporting Life* Johnson isn't the only man interested in hunky

Frank. Gerald Weaver (Alan Badel) is the powerful, influential and slightly effeminate chairman of the City Rugby League Club. Weaver obviously desires Frank and, when he takes him for a ride in his Bentley after signing him to a contract, he grabs his knee. Weaver's relationship with his wife (Vanda Godsell) is platonic, and this is revealed when she lusts after Frank. Meanwhile, when Weaver invites Frank to one of their parties, his wife reveals that her husband enjoys the company of young men. 'I think he sometimes keeps them too much to himself,' she says, obviously jealous. When Frank is introduced to Mr Slomer (Arthur Lowe), Mrs Weaver explains: 'Mr Slomer is your newest fan. You seem to have the kind of charm that appeals to him.' Clearly Frank is popular with older, influential men in the rugby world, men whose sexuality is open to question. Mrs Weaver explains: 'The only reason you're in the team is because Mr Slomer wants you there.' Gradually Frank begins to realize there is a 'hidden agenda', but he doesn't play ball. Gerald Weaver and Mr Slomer play games with Frank, battling with each other for 'ownership' of him. And the tension gets too much for Frank. When he takes Mrs Hammond to a restaurant, he embarrasses her by drinking too much and insulting some of the customers. This is observed by the Weavers who are sitting at the bar. Says Mrs Weaver: 'I don't think she's getting quite what she expected.' Replies her husband: 'No. But then does anybody with Machin?'

Apart from the acting nominations received by Harris and Roberts (see above), *This Sporting Life* was nominated for British Academy Awards for Best British Film, Best Film from any source and Best British Screenplay (David Storey). All three awards were won by *Tom Jones*. In America the film received Oscar nominations for Best Actor (Harris) and Actress (Roberts), and was listed as one of the National Board of Review's ten best films of the year. At the Cannes Film Festival Harris was named Best Actor, and Anderson received the International Critics Prize.

The Leather Boys

In *The Leather Boys* a teenage couple called Dot (Rita Tushingham) and Reggie (Colin Campbell) get married, jump on a number 49 bus to the wedding reception, go to Butlins of Bognor Regis for a rain-soaked honeymoon, and split up when Reggie tires of Dot's constant nagging.

Later, Reggie settles down with his biker friend Pete (Dudley Sutton), a kind and understanding gay man who takes over Dot's role. It is Pete who provides Reggie with the time, consideration and emotional support lacking in his marriage. 'You need looking after,' says Pete, but his love for Reggie is unrequited. When Dot discovers the two men waltzing around their motor bikes, she sneers sarcastically: 'Men? You look like a couple of queers!' Needless to say, Reggie realizes that he cannot return Pete's affection, and ends their relationship after a bizarre encounter with some of Pete's gay 'friends' in a dockside pub.

For Dudley Sutton, the role of Pete provided him with an opportunity to portray a different kind of gay man on the screen. He remembers:

> When I came to do *The Leather Boys* in 1963, I was interested in homosexual law reform. Growing up in Britain I found myself surrounded by men who were being victimized, or who lived their lives in fear, and I hate fear. So in *The Leather Boys* my whole purpose as an actor was to play a lover, not a wrist-flapping, camp stereotype. I thought that if I played Pete as a lover with emotions, feelings and depth, and I concerned myself with nothing else, I could offer something honest and true.

Fortunately Sutton worked with a sympathetic screenwriter, Gillian Freeman, and director, Sidney J. Furie, who gave him free rein, but he recalls the producer was less understanding: 'He wanted to see my wrists flapping, but I refused. I knew that Shelagh Delaney's *A Taste of Honey* had been ruined in New York by having the actor playing the gay role flap his wrists. So I'm very glad I resisted.'

Gillian Freeman based *The Leather Boys* on her novel. Says Dudley: 'Gillian had to use a pseudonym for her novel. She called herself Eliot George because in those days homosexuality was illegal, and a very difficult subject to write about. She was a brave, tough woman. The eleven-month delay in the release of the film was because of its subject matter. No question.' Sidney J. Furie gave Dudley total freedom to inform his part:

> We had worked together on a previous film about anti-capital punishment called *The Boys* and we trusted each other implicitly. Sidney gave me freedom I have never enjoyed since. I would walk on to the set and he'd get rid of the crew and we'd work out what

the scene was going to be. Splendid! We didn't worry about censorship. We just kept our heads down and got on with it.

In the late 1950s and early 1960s we had the kitchen-sink dramas. There was a radical change in theatre and film and everything we did at that time was new and brave and fresh and politically motivated. Not politically obvious, but underneath it were deep convictions. The whole country was alive. *A Taste of Honey* came from Joan Littlewood and she was the source of a lot of political power in the country and it wasn't left-wing, socialist stuff, it was a real, intelligent, deep intellectual thing.

In spite of its sympathetic portrayal of a gay man, *The Leather Boys* has often been criticized for its final scene. When Pete takes Reggie to meet some of his friends in a gay pub, we are suddenly confronted with a freak show. The gay men are portrayed as a group of predatory aliens. No wonder Reggie runs away from Pete at the end of the film! But Dudley defends this scene:

> Quite a lot of it was based on truth. I don't think it was false. The bald merchant seaman, played by Oliver MacGreevy, was based on a character I knew very well in the RAF who'd been a merchant seaman. The only false note in the film, where they did sell out to the producer, was the very last shot when Colin Campbell as Reggie walks away from me in the pub and back into heterosexuality. This positive upbeat ending suggests he is going back to his wife.[4]

The World Ten Times Over

After playing 'controversial' roles as a stripper (*Expresso Bongo*), the wife of a gay barrister (*Victim*) and the fiancée of a Jamaican school teacher (*Flame in the Streets*), it seemed only a matter of time before Sylvia Syms would play the role of a lesbian. The opportunity came in 1963 with *The World Ten Times Over*, written and directed by Wolf Rilla. It's the story of Ginnie and Billa, two nightclub hostesses who share a flat and give each other the emotional support they cannot find in the outside world. Until then, no lesbian relationship had ever been shown in a British film, and it was only one year earlier that Cicely

Courtneidge played one of the first explicitly lesbian roles. Though Ginnie (June Ritchie) has a capricious, lively but exasperating personality, she is also deeply insecure, especially about her relationship with the wealthy son of a property tycoon, separated from his wife. Billa (Syms) is older, wiser, cynical and very protective towards Ginnie. By the end of the film Billa has discovered she is pregnant (but she doesn't know who the father is), and Ginnie, after rejecting her lover's genuine declaration of love, fails in her suicide attempt. Alone in their flat at night, this incident shocks the two women into an awareness that their only chance of happiness lies with each other.

The World Ten Times Over desperately tries to imitate the French New Wave, but Wolf Rilla is not in the same class as Godard, Truffaut, Varda and Resnais. Ultimately he fails to create a British entry in the *nouvelle vague* because he skirts around the lesbian relationship instead of exploring it. It's a shame, because this could have been a great film, and an honest attempt at depicting a lesbian relationship. However, Rilla and his two stars do succeed in showing the reasons why Billa and Ginnie depend on each other, and their relationship is explored with some insight. Rilla certainly has the support and commitment of his stars, especially Sylvia Syms who, in a complex role, gives one of her best film performances. Said *Variety* : 'Miss Syms, long one of Britain's most underrated screen actresses, gives an intelligent and often moving performance.' Throughout the film Syms tries to indicate that she loves Ginnie, for example, in the opening scene, when she looks at Ginnie's photograph fixed to their dressing table mirror, or later when she rubs Ginnie down with a towel after her bath.

After Billa has told Ginnie she is pregnant, she suggests that they take care of the child together. She says: 'You and me. It'll be fun. We can dress it up and show it off to our friends. Take it for walks in the park. It'll be something to have.' This is the first time the possibility of lesbian parenting is proposed in a British film. At the end of the film, after Ginnie has slashed her wrists, a long-term lesbian relationship is suggested. Billa, angry with Ginnie, says: 'Didn't you give one thought to me? You're all I've got. Didn't you know that?' Ginnie, in bed and crying, responds: 'The flat was empty and I thought you'd gone.' Billa runs to Ginnie and hugs her. They start laughing and Billa rubs Ginnie's hand. 'Damn 'em all, eh?' she says, referring to men. 'Damn 'em all,' repeats Ginnie. Leaning over Ginnie, Billa pulls the blankets over her and strokes her hair. Protective and loving towards her companion, the following close-up of Billa's face reveals a slight but tender smile. The film ends with a closing shot of the two women asleep together in the double bed, and Ginnie turning over, and resting her arm on Billa. The synopsis in the film's publicity release said: 'To each of them comes the realization that their only chance of happiness lies with each other.'

For Sylvia Syms, *The World Ten Times Over* was a frustrating experience. She later recalled that she wanted to portray Billa as a woman in love with another woman who was neither 'butch' or predatory:

> As far as I was concerned my character was in love with June Ritchie and I wanted to play it that way, but in those days one could only suggest lesbianism. One could not be too explicit. To suggest the character's lesbianism I wore a leather coat to help make her look tough, but I also felt that it was important for her to be feminine. If this film had been made in a freer atmosphere, perhaps the relationship between the two women would have been developed.[5]

The Haunting

The Haunting is one of the scariest ghost films ever made, and has rightly become a cult classic. The story is set in an oppressive, haunted Gothic mansion called Hill House, in New England. Led by Dr Markway (Richard Johnson), a team of investigators agree to stay in the house and assist him with his exploration of the paranormal. The group includes Eleanor (Julie Harris), who has experienced an encounter with a poltergeist, Luke (Russ Tamblyn), the sceptical nephew of the owner of Hill House who will inherit the mansion, and Theodora (Claire Bloom), a lipstick lesbian who has extrasensory perception.

Writer Nelson Gidding based his screenplay on Shirley Jackson's novel *The Haunting of Hill House*, published in 1959. Many critics have claimed that Theodora's character was not a lesbian in Jackson's novel, but Gidding disagrees: 'There are many hints and many things about her that suggest that she might be [a lesbian]. The relationship of the two women is suggestive of that. Don't forget in those days, in movies and literature, one had to be careful. Everything, as it were, was in the closet!' Says Julie Harris: 'It wasn't really overt. There was no mention of her homosexuality. The censors said that Claire must never touch my character because they didn't want that implied. Then a few years later they made *The Killing of Sister George*!'[6]

In her appearance, Theodora differs from most other screen lesbians that have come before her. Beautiful, chic and glamorous, she is outwardly confident, but reveals vulnerability and confusion. In one scene she admits that she is afraid of 'knowing what I *really* want'. Her approaches to Eleanor could be interpreted as being predatory, and Eleanor calls her 'unnatural', but by the end of the film the two women have become friends, comforting each other when they are being terrorized. Apparently there may have been a scene cut from the film showing Theodora in her flat at the beginning of the story. She sweeps all her ornaments off the mantelpiece in a fit of rage and frustration, and at the same time smashes a photograph of a girlfriend.

Other films of interest released in 1963

Gay icon Judy Garland made her last film appearance in *I Could Go On Singing*, a London-based melodrama with songs, and clearly autobiographical. Said critic Philip Oakes: 'She is a star; the genuine outsize article. She is an actress of power and subtlety; a singer whose way with a song is nothing short of marvellous. She is a great artist. She is Judy. She is the very best there is.' Garland's remarkable *tour de force* was matched by superb underplaying from her leading man, Dirk Bogarde; in the James Bond thriller *From Russia with Love* Lotte Lenya played the lesbian killer spy Rosa Klebb, a colonel in the KGB, who tries to seduce Tatiana (Daniela Bianchi), the beautiful agent Bond has bedded. In a memorable sequence Klebb attacks Bond with a spike-tipped shoe. Later, Klebb is shot to death by Tatiana; at a party sequence in *The Comedy Man*, starring Kenneth More, an innocent young blonde woman dances with a tall man. A short queen interrupts them and takes him away to dance. Surprised, the woman looks around to see if any of the party revellers have noticed, but they haven't. They couldn't care less! The expression on the short queen's face shows that he is overjoyed to be dancing with the tall man. Both men are wearing suits and ties and look like a pair of accountants!; Michael Winner directed the screen version of Gilbert and Sullivan's *The Mikado*, retitled *The Cool Mikado*. A camp cast is headed by Frankie Howerd as Ko-Ko, Dennis Price and Lionel Blair; the pop musical *Live it Up* featured songs by gay Joe Meek and a guest appearance by lesbian journalist, novelist and television personality Nancy Spain; Anthony Asquith directed *An Evening with the Royal Ballet* starring Rudolph Nureyev.

Notes

1. Robin Maugham in *Talking to. . . Peter Burton* (Third House, 1991), p. 111.
2. David Storey, *This Sporting Life* (Popular Library, 1961) p. 5.
3. Gavin Lambert, 'Lindsay Anderson: Unrequited Lover'. *Sight and Sound*, vol. 4, no. 10, October 1994, p. 18.
4. Dudley Sutton, interview with the author, London, March 1995.
5. Sylvia Syms, 'A Chorus of Approval', interviewed by Stephen Bourne in *Gay Times*, June 1989, p. 34.
6. Nelson Gidding and Julie Harris interviewed by Judy Sloane in *Film Review,* June 1995.

1964

A Hard Day's Night

Though at first they presented themselves as squeaky clean, The Beatles quickly became an unconventional and uncompromising 'pop' group, four young working-class men who took the 1960s by storm and helped revolutionize popular music. Their millions of adoring fans included gay men, and this was acknowledged by George Harrison in the television series *The Beatles Anthology*, shown in December 1995. During the group's first trip to Paris in January 1964, Harrison remembered 'slightly gay-looking boys at the stage door shouting "Ringo! Ringo!"'. Throughout their first feature film, *A Hard Day's Night*, scripted by Alun Owen, and directed by Richard Lester, young men are clearly visible amongst the screaming fans who chase the fab Liverpool four all over the train station, and blast their eardrums in the TV studio. One can only speculate how many of them were gay. But, sadly, the gay *characters* who exist in this film are objects of ridicule. They exist only for comic relief and, no doubt, to reaffirm the 'Fab Four's' heterosexuality. The Beatles may wear their hair long, but they're *real* men!

Uncredited on the cast list, Kenneth Haigh plays Simon, the camp head of an advertising agency which promotes 'clothes for teenagers'. Simon is helped by his gay assistant Adrian (Julian Holloway). Simon takes a shine to George Harrison and tries to persuade him to model some new shirts. But heterosexual George doesn't want to know. He prefers 'birds'. Later, Victor Spinetti pops up as a bossy, wrist-flapping television director. This obnoxious screaming queen is dressed in a fluffy sweater and orders his effeminate floor manager (Robin Ray) about the TV studio. When George notices Spinetti being followed by a pretty blonde woman he says to John: 'I bet his wife doesn't know about *her*.'

Replies John, who is obviously more sexually 'aware' than George: 'He hasn't got a wife. Look at his sweater!'

In spite of the film's homophobia, it must have been very liberating for gay men to see these attractive, talented and anarchic young rebels behaving badly in their first film. Who can forget the standout sequence at the beginning of the film? Travelling to London on a train, a man wearing a bowler hat (memorably played by Richard Vernon), joins the boys in their carriage. They politely say hello, but he just looks disapprovingly at them. He closes the window, but Paul asks if he can open it again. The man refuses but John says they outnumber him four to one, and bats his eyelids at him. Ringo turns on his transistor radio but the man turns it off. He glares at John who promptly leans forward and says, quite unexpectedly, 'Give us a kiss!' This is a wonderful moment in the film, played out by the sexually playful (though somewhat sinister) John Lennon. Says the man, in desperation: 'I fought the war for you lot.' But he has already lost this particular war. The Beatles have arrived, and life will never be the same again, for anyone. Says Ringo to the man: 'I bet you're sorry you won!'

Ferry Cross the Mersey

In 1960 a young writer called Tony Warren created a new television drama series called *Coronation Street*, set in a close-knit working-class community in Manchester. It has since become one of the most successful and popular television series of all time. At the start, Warren was responsible for writing the first thirteen episodes. He was twenty-three and people often asked him how he could know so much about life. Warren later explained in an interview with Melvyn Bragg in the *South Bank Show* shown in November 1995 to commemorate the thirty-fifth anniversary of the series: 'Believe you me, a gay guy who's been out on the scene since the age of sixteen, at twenty-three he *is* Elsie Tanner!'

However, Warren's contribution to the series as a script writer was shortlived, and he went on to reveal to Bragg that when homophobia reared its ugly head at script conferences, he knew it was time to quit:

> The blokes took over. They came in and most of them had never seen anything like me in their lives before. And here was I, and I had invented it. It got very unpleasant because I was openly gay

at a time when it was not considered sensible to be openly gay but somebody had to stand up and say 'Yes, I'm gay.' But they ganged up, they really did gang up, and I don't think they even knew they'd done it until there was a terrible morning when there was a story conference and I sat there and I listened and then I got to my feet – nobody got to their feet to address story conferences – and I said: 'Gentlemen, I have sat here and listened to two poof jokes, to an actor who is referred to as a poof, to a line dismissed because it is poofy, and I would remind you that without a poof none of you would be in work this morning.' Nothing was quite the same after that.

After leaving *Coronation Street*, Warren wrote his first stage play. It was about a female impersonator and he called it *Strumpet's Daughter*. The play went on tour but failed to reach London, folding prematurely in Sheffield. Turning his attention to films, he was approached by Brian Epstein, gay manager of The Beatles and several other rising pop groups, to write a screenplay for Gerry and the Pacemakers. Epstein was promoting them at the time and wanted to capitalize on the success of the Beatles' first film, *A Hard Day's Night*.

Epstein and Warren agreed on a title, *Ferry Cross the Mersey*, and Warren began working on the script. He spent three weeks with Gerry Marsden and the boys in the band, accompanying them on a tour of one-night stands. But Warren quickly realized they were very inexperienced and he felt it was unfair to put them in front of film cameras. Consequently, he spent two-and-a-half months desperately trying to write an amusing and entertaining film for them. He tore up five rough versions before collapsing from nerves and tension.

Epstein and Warren agreed to part on friendly terms, and Epstein brought in another writer to take over the script. When the film was completed there was hardly a word of Warren's script in the finished version but when he saw *Ferry Cross the Mersey* he was shocked to discover his name splashed across the cinema screen with the rest of the film's credits. . . 'Based on a story by Tony Warren'.

Happily, Warren has found success and popularity as a novelist and in December 1995 he was affectionately described by Judy Finnegan in television's daytime series *This Morning* as 'Manchester's answer to Armistead Maupin'.

Other films of interest released in 1964

In *Becket* a sexual relationship between Richard Burton's Thomas Becket and Peter O'Toole's Henry II was implied; in Walt Disney's *The Moon-Spinners* Pola Negri, the glamorous, exotic star of the silent screen, made a brief, but memorable movie comeback after an absence of twenty-one years. She camped it up as the wealthy jewellery expert Madame Habib. In the script she was to have a pet siamese cat, but Negri suggested the substitution of a cheetah, which made her appearance all the more fun. Negri made headlines when she threatened to sue her companion, a Texan heiress, when the latter married. After the heiress divorced, the ladies were reunited; in *Goldfinger* gay icon Shirley Bassey memorably belted out the theme song, and James Bond bedded and 'converted' the strikingly beautiful leather-loving lesbian Pussy Galore (Honor Blackman); in the Second World War drama *633 Squadron* Bergman (George Chakiris) was captured by the Nazis and interrogated by a mannish lesbian with a butch haircut, her leather jacket slung over her shoulder, and an evil grin. When Bergman refuses to talk, she rips off his shirt, and begins to torture him, but luckily the RAF arrives in time, and saves Bergman from a fate worse than death – a direct hit!; in *The Beauty Jungle* Janette Scott played Shirley Freeman, a typist who becomes a beauty contest winner. Her gay hair stylist Lucius (Peter Ashmore) is a throwback to the old-style pansy, popular in pre-war comedies. He fusses and fawns over Shirley, but at first he insists that he can do nothing with her hair. 'Who am I? God?' he asks. 'You can see for yourself it's like old mattress stuffing. No lustre in it. No life. No lights. It's the colour of compost!' When Shirley wins the 'Miss Rose of England' beauty contest (the judges include Norman Hartnell, a cigar-smoking Duchess of Bedford and Linda Christian, the actress who was once married to bisexual Hollywood star Tyrone Power), Lucius stands up, cries 'My Queen!' and, overcome by the excitement, faints; in *Children of the Damned*, based on John Wyndham's novel *The Midwich Cuckoos*, a gay couple (Alan Badel and Ian Hendry) have to work together – one's a biologist, the other a psychologist – to outwit an international group of other-wordly children. This is the first and, so far, only mainstream film to show male lovers as respected professionals working *together* to solve a major problem. The producer, Ben Abeid, often chose projects about male bonding (*Eagle's Wing*) or sensitive outsiders (*Private Potter*). But perhaps he is best-known for *The Hireling* which was named Best Film at the Cannes Film Festival in 1973. Badel had played a whole range of non-100 per cent heterosexual men in films (i.e. *The Stranger Left No Card*). Intense and sexy, the two men are split not, as many reviewers would have it, by Hendry falling in love with one of the children's mothers, but because of divergent professional approaches and priorities.

1965

Darling

In 1965 director John Schlesinger and screenwriter Frederic Raphael made use of relaxed censorship rules, and created a new, sexually 'liberated' screen heroine in *Darling*. The idea for the film originated with the gay writer and journalist Godfrey Winn. He suggested it to Schlesinger and producer Joseph Janni when they were making *Billy Liar* in 1963. However, what appealed to Schlesinger:

> was not primarily a satirical view of society, but the more personally haunting theme of loneliness and disenchantment. '*Darling* was really about choice,' he later reflected, 'about a girl who had the possibility of always thinking there was something better round the next corner, but was never capable of settling for anything, whether emotional stability or professional career. . . I think it was very much a disease of the age.'[1]

Lesbian, gay and bisexuality crops up throughout *Darling*, though not always in a positive light. The film begins with a sequence in which Dirk Bogarde, as television news reporter Robert Gold, interviews members of the public in the street. These include a 'Tory'-type gentleman who complains to Bogarde: 'How rife homosexuality has become in London itself. . . a few years back you were very blatantly approached by different people in different places.' Replies Bogarde, unmoved and unconcerned: 'Really?' Clearly this brief exchange is included in the film as a reference to the public debate which would result in the partial decriminalization of homosexuality in 1967.

Later, at a charity gala organized by John Basildon (James Cossins), the racist attitudes of the English aristocracy are exposed through an unpleasant gay lord, Alex Grant (Peter Baylis). Seen talking to his handsome, younger boyfriend, he is interrupted by Miles Brand (Laurence Harvey) and John Basildon. Says Lord Alex: 'I like your black boys, John,' referring to the black youngsters who have been employed to wait on the guests. 'It's a pity I can't wrap one up and take him home.' Says Miles: 'They're all numbered, Alex, and I wouldn't try to change your luck if I was you.' Clearly upset by this remark, Alex walks away with his boyfriend, looks down at one of the black boys, and is then seen walking past a large portrait of Queen Elizabeth II. Though Alex is a nasty, reprehensible character, the film's treatment of him is homophobic. The inclusion of the Queen's portrait is used solely to point out Alex's gay sexuality, and to poke fun at it.

Lesbians are also the target for some homophobic treatment in Raphael's screenplay. When Diana Scott (Julie Christie) accompanies Miles to Paris, she readily agrees to go to a party with him, eager to taste the bohemian, decadent life. But the free-spirited Diana is in for a shock. At the party, Miles introduces her to Billie Castiglione (Annette Carell), 'one of the best sculptresses in Paris'. A predatory lesbian, she embodies all the unpleasant characteristics of the stereotype. Unattractive and vampirish, Billie tries to seduce Diana. 'You've got a beautiful head,' she says, 'Wonderful bones. Truly.' Taking her coat off, she adds 'it's very hot in here' (a cliché if ever there was one), then an unnecessary close up reveals the lesbian's face staring intently at Diana, making the 'innocent' young woman (and the audience) feel very uncomfortable. When the party turns into a bizarre 'orgy', with the men and women swapping clothes, Diana Scott sheds her inhibitions and begins to have a good time, except when Billie keeps pestering her.

The most interesting – and realistic – gay character in *Darling* is Malcolm, the smart, amiable magazine photographer. He's played by Roland Curram, a superb but under-used character actor who later became well-known on British television for his gay roles in *The Crezz* and *Eldorado*. Malcolm is responsible for helping Diana secure a lucrative modelling contract. She becomes famous as the 'Happiness Girl' and, when they are together, Diana and Malcolm have lots of fun. They thieve in Fortnam and Mason, and Malcolm willingly accepts her offer of a holiday on the Isle of Capri. As Diana and Malcolm are both 'outsiders', it is inevitable they become close friends. 'Brother and sister till death us do part,' he says. On Capri Malcolm cruises a handsome, virile young waiter called Gino (Dante Posani), and competes with

Diana for his favours. Both end up enjoying holiday flings with him. At first it seems that Malcolm is going to be portrayed as just another 'fag' friend of a movie heroine, a desexualized sidekick. But when they are on Capri, *Darling* unexpectedly, and triumphantly breaks away from convention by allowing Malcolm to have a sexual liaison (even if we don't see them being intimate with each other). Also, Malcolm clearly has a life of his own. He's not just an appendage to Diana. This brief but frank depiction of a happy, well-adjusted gay man is light years away from Billie, the predatory lesbian.

In Italy Diana marries Prince Cesare Della Romita (José-Luis de Villalonga), a middle-aged widower with six children. At this point in the film one cannot help recall another film success from 1965, the enchanting musical *The Sound of Music*. But Diana Scott is no Maria, and this is not an enchanting situation. It is a nightmare. She has married the Prince because she wants security, but all she finds is more loneliness. His children do not need her. There is no fun or music in her life. When she tries to contact her new husband in Rome, she is told this is only possible 'by telegram'. Coming close to a breakdown, she flies back to England. But she fails in her one, last desperate bid to get back with her former lover, Robert. He promptly rejects her, and sends her back to Italy and the Prince.

Darling was an international success, but it is not a great film. Its success was due almost entirely to the presence of its young, beautiful leading actress, Julie Christie. She made a huge impact on audiences, especially in America where critic Pauline Kael found her 'extraordinary – petulant, sullen, and very beautiful'. In Britain, *Darling* was nominated for several British Academy Awards including Best British Film (it lost to *The Ipcress File*) and cinematography. Raphael's screenplay won an award and, surprisingly, Dirk Bogarde received his second Best British Actor award for one of his least interesting roles (beating Rex Harrison in *My Fair Lady*). Unsurprisingly, Christie walked off with the Best British Actress award and, in America, an Oscar. The film also won Oscars for Raphael's screenplay and Julie Harris's costume designs. Nominations were received for Best Film (it lost to *The Sound of Music*) and Director (Schlesinger). Also in America *Darling* received three New York Critics Circle awards (Film, Director and Actress).

Dream A40

In 1958 the Jamaican actor Lloyd Reckord made a big impression on West End theatregoers with his performance in Ted Willis's highly-charged play *Hot Summer Night*. Subsequently Reckord enjoyed a short but busy career as an actor in this country, though he secretly wished to become a director. In the 1960s Reckord wrote and directed two experimental short films: *Ten Bob in Winter*, which was funded by the British Film Institute, and *Dream A40*.

In *Dream A40* a young gay couple, one dark-haired and attractive (Michael Billington), the other slightly younger and blonde (Nicholas Wright, who also played an uncredited 'bit' role, with one line, at the beginning of *Darling*), drive along one of Britain's new highways. But a trivial incident triggers a disturbing guilt fantasy in the older man.

In the car the couple are warm, affectionate and playful towards each other. The older man strokes the younger one's arm. The men even hold hands. But when they pause at some traffic lights they are seen by a little girl, a passenger in another car, and the older man quickly drops his partner's hand (after all, this is 1965 and homosexuality is still a criminal offence). The younger man thinks it is funny, but the older one doesn't share his sense of humour.

The couple break their journey to eat in a restaurant and the younger man touches the older man's arm, causing him to panic and run out. The couple drive off but after the older man drives through a red light and is stopped by a policeman on a motorcycle, the dream begins.

The policeman leads them off the motorway and along a deserted road to a desolate warehouse. Here the two men discover a group of young men sitting and waiting. The older man sees a noose hanging nearby and leaves the younger man. 'I'll soon be back,' he tells him. He runs into a room which is full of men of different ages who immediately crowd around him. Panic-stricken, and feeling suffocated, he runs out. Discovering that he can buy his way out by paying a fine, he returns to his lover but he is too late, the younger man has been hanged. Holding his lover in his arms, the older man finds he is still alive, but only just. He kisses him on the lips – but as he does this, the lover dies.

Dream A40 is a strange, but compelling experimental drama which explores a gay man's fears about his sexuality and attraction to another man. The younger man, though daring, is somewhat precocious, but completely uninhibited. He shows his feelings, while the older man represses his. It is rare to find a British film made before the 1967 Act which explores a gay man's sexual repression in a frank and honest way. There are similarities to be found here with Cocteau's *Orphée*, and Lloyd Reckord's unselfconscious approach to his subject matter is similar to that of the British black gay film-maker Isaac Julien. He directed *Looking for Langston* and *Young Soul Rebels* more than twenty years later. Says Reckord:

I'd been living and working in Britain for about twelve years when I made *Dream A40*. It was not a film I was ashamed of then, or now. I made it because I wanted to get into television production but the film was entirely ignored, perhaps because I was too frank about homosexuality.

The story came from a dream I had and I built on that. It was a rather frightening dream. *Dream A40* is a frank statement on homosexual guilt. That was what I wanted to make. Instead of fantasizing about boy meets girl, the usual thing that everybody does, I thought, well, let's try to be honest and make an interesting statement from my own experience. I'd had this dream, and I developed the story from it.

I wanted to cast two good-looking actors in the roles and Michael Billington and Nicholas Wright seemed right. They had no anxiety about playing gay roles. They liked the script and wanted to do it. They worked well together. I didn't use black actors in the main parts though I talked to a few of them about it. I know that the black actors I spoke to would have had a more difficult time afterwards than the white actors for playing gays. I approached quite a number of black actors about appearing in the film and they told me 'I like your script. I like your ideas. But it wouldn't be good for business.' Also, being gay in the Caribbean is less acceptable than in Britain.

In reality there *were* gay men like these two characters. Some wanted to be bisexual but others, like the blonde man, said: 'I'm gay and that's it.' There *were* gay men around like him who didn't care if people knew they were gay. They openly defied the law. We called them screamers. But young people in the 1960s were open about everything. They didn't care what people thought.

There was no law about making a film about gays, and I was interested in making a film that made a mark, that said something about the times we were living in, and the fear and guilt some gay men felt. I *was* being defiant.[2]

Sadly, though Reckord had made two impressive short films, he discovered that there was no place for a black director at the BBC at that time. He later recalled:

I remember going to the BBC and talking to a young director who had come in as a trainee. Originally he had been a young actor in the theatre and had worked with me as a walk-on at the Old Vic. Now, here he was, one of the BBC's latest recruits on a directors' programme. This sort of thing made me a little unhappy because I thought, 'I haven't heard that so-and-so directed anything, or showed initiative by going out to make a film with his own money, which I have done twice.' Yet nobody, at any time, offered me a break as a trainee director in television. Talking to people today, they tell me that it isn't much better. . . . I eventually left Britain for good in the late 1960s because I'd had enough.[3]

Other films of interest released in 1965

After an absence of twelve years from the screen, the legendary bisexual stage and screen actress Tallulah Bankhead came to Britain to appear in a minor Hammer horror called *Fanatic* (known as *Die, Die, My Darling* in the USA); in Otto Preminger's underrated chiller *Bunny Lake is Missing*, Martita Hunt gave a memorable performance as the nursery school headmistress who lives with her partner Madge, and loses herself in recordings of children's fears and nightmares.

Notes

1. Alexander Walker, *Hollywood, England: The British Film Industry in the Sixties* (Harrap, 1974) p. 278.
2. Lloyd Reckord interviewed by Stephen Bourne, 14 August 1991.
3. Lloyd Reckord interviewed by Stephen Bourne in *Black and White in Colour: Black People in British Television Since 1936* (British Film Institute, 1992) p. 55.

1966

The Family Way

Sir John Mills is one of the finest screen actors of his generation who, for more than sixty years, has symbolized the best of British cinema: decent, understated, seemingly effortless. Even if he did miss out on being cast in showy roles in films like *The African Queen* (once announced for Mills and Bette Davis) and *Separate Tables* – which won Oscars for Humphrey Bogart and David Niven respectively – there are many terrific performances by Mills which should be given greater critical attention.

Mills is always at his most interesting when cast against type, for example, as the Nazi spy in Anthony Asquith's *Cottage to Let* (1941). He's also splendid when playing military men living on the edge in films like *Ice Cold in Alex* (1958) and *Tunes of Glory* (1960). For the latter he won the Venice Film Festival Best Actor Prize and was named Film Actor of the Year by *Films and Filming*. It seems incredible that Sir John has *never* won a British Academy Award, and has only received three nominations. Though he made his screen debut in 1932, he had to wait until 1995 before the British Film Institute gave him their Life Achievement Award. It is regrettable, also, that only one serious critical appreciation of his work exists. This is Ian Johnson's tribute in *Films and Filming* (June 1962).

The Family Way (1966) contains what is, arguably, Sir John's best screen performance. Set in a working-class community in Bolton, Bill Naughton based the screenplay on his own stage play, *All in Good Time*. Also that year Naughton was responsible for writing the screenplay for the hugely popular *Alfie* which catapulted Michael Caine to international stardom as a cockney Casanova. Both films were produced in the middle of the 'Swinging Sixties', when Britain was experiencing great moral and social upheavals. The Beatles' impact on popular music and culture had been phenomenal, and Paul McCartney was enlisted to compose the music score for *The Family Way*. The 'new morality' and political protests were rapidly changing the way people were thinking and feeling at this time and *The Family Way*, though meant to be a light-hearted comedy, succeeds in reflecting some of the more serious concerns of its time. It may have been a coincidence, but Naughton's clever observation of working-class male sexuality was very topical. After all, the film was released just a few months before the 1967 Sexual Offences Act partially decriminalized homosexuality in Britain.

The Family Way is a landmark in British cinema, for it is one of the few films to portray working-class family life with warmth and humanity. The family are seen as intelligent human beings, not caricatures. With humour and sensitivity, Naughton explores a young couple's failure to consummate their marriage. Unhappily for them, speculation arises regarding the husband's masculinity and sexuality. The couple, Jenny and Arthur, are played by twenty-year-old ex-Walt Disney star Hayley Mills in her first 'adult' role, and newcomer Hywel Bennett, but far too much media attention was given to Hayley's brief 'nude' scene. More attention should have been given to the most interesting character in the film, Arthur's father, Ezra Fitton (John Mills). He works in belt and braces at the local gasworks, and is always putting his foot in it when all he wants to do is help. On the surface he's loud and crude, but underneath he's a big softie who loves his son, even if he doesn't understand him.

Ezra is also a deeply troubled and confused man. As a youngster he had a close and intimate relationship with his pal, Billy Stringfellow. 'Best mate a man ever had,' he says. Together they enjoyed what was, for Ezra, the most satisfying friendship of his life. Throughout the wedding reception Ezra constantly refers to Billy, until his annoyed wife Lucy (Marjorie Rhodes) asks: 'Do we have to keep bringing up Billy tonight? Nobody here knows him, and nobody wants to hear about him.' Replies Ezra: 'I bloody knew him, didn't I? So did you.'

When Ezra and Billy grew up they were inseparable. Billy even accompanied Ezra and Lucy on their honeymoon in Blackpool, and the two men danced together. 'Leaning against the bar – drinking!' explains Lucy. She reveals this to Jenny's parents, and asks them: 'Would you say there was anything odd or queer about a fellow that went on his honeymoon and took his pal with him?' With this revelation, Ezra becomes very defensive and angry, and tries to explain why Billy came with them: 'I'd never taken a holiday without him. Did you expect me to leave him alone during holiday week just because I'd got wed to you? I was raised with him. I used to play in the gutter with him, making mud pies. We were scrubbed off together in the same wash tub in his Mam's back yard. We went to school together. We worked together. It takes a lifetime for a man to make a proper friend.'

In another emotional, poetic sequence, Ezra stands in the backyard looking up at the stars, remembering the first morning of his honeymoon when he strolled along the beach at Blackpool with Billy. Lucy listens at the kitchen window. 'That first morning,' he says, 'standing at the edge of the sea. I remember a little frothy ripple of tide rolling right over our new brown leather boots, then off again like water off a duck's back. Then the sun came out, and our boots were covered with little drops of water, all glistening away. Do you know what Billy said? 'You can't beat nature for beauty, Ezra.' I never forgot it. That were the big moment of my honeymoon.'

Then, one day, Billy disappeared. It is suggested that he might have had a brief affair with Lucy, and fathered Arthur. But this is ambiguous. Far more interesting is the suggestion that Billy was gay, and realized that his relationship with Ezra had to be terminated. Ezra never saw Billy again, or found out the reason for his departure. At the end of the film, after Arthur and Jenny have resolved their marriage difficulties, they go off on their delayed honeymoon. Lucy and the younger son, Geoffrey (Murray Head), see them off in a taxi, but when they come back into the house, they find Ezra in tears. Arthur has reminded him of Billy, the pal he loved and lost. 'It could have been him,' he says. Lucy holds him, and Ezra grabs her hand. Confused, Geoffrey asks his father what the problem is. Ezra replies: 'It's life, lad. It might make you laugh at your age, but one day it'll make you bloody cry.' This heartbreaking scene reveals that Ezra still misses Billy, and longs for his companionship again. Lucy is sympathetic, and understanding. At the beginning of the film, Ezra is portrayed as a man who believes he has to 'put on a show' to prove his masculinity. Loud and vulgar, he guzzles beer, takes part in arm-wrestling competitions, and tries to dominate every situation he is in. But by the end of the film, he has revealed a more gentle, sensitive, even poetic side, and become something of a tragic figure. He is a man who has lost a companion he loved dearly, and doesn't understand why. He wants him back, but doesn't know where to find him. Life has been cruel to Ezra.

John Mills captures Ezra's different moods perfectly, and reveals an extraordinary emotional range. His portrayal of this particular working-class man is quite remarkable for it offers something different. Until then, with few exceptions, in British films working-class men were usually caricatured as passive, forelock-tugging 'dads', villains or brutes. The beauty of *The Family Way* is that it offers an alternative image of a working-class man, one that is accurate and believable. In one lovely scene, Ezra is glued to the television set, watching an episode of *Coronation Street*. Lucy is not interested in the programme at all. Yet in most working-class homes at that time, *Coronation Street* was seen as a 'woman's programme'. Men did not watch it (or at least they didn't *admit* to watching it). Therefore it is unusual to find the 'man of the house' viewing it. *The Family Way* also treats its characters with respect. For example, though the family are poor, they are not scruffy. The actors in the film respond to this, especially Marjorie Rhodes and John Mills.

The Family Way did not receive a single British Academy Award nomination, and it is unforgivable that John Mills and Marjorie Rhodes were overlooked in the acting categories. But in America Marjorie Rhodes's superb performance as Lucy Fitton was much admired by the critics. The scene in which she defends her son, when it is suggested he might be gay, is breathtaking. 'Suppose he were?' she shouts at Ezra. 'Is it something to get at the lad for? Nature would have done it. A father should help and protect a lad like that – not turn on him like the mob when it sees somebody different.' Says Vito Russo in *The Celluloid Closet*: 'This is the only speech in which a parent defends the possibility that a homosexual child might not be turned away from the fold. The mother's suggestion that queerness might be a natural thing, something one could live with, works here because the heterosexuality of her son is never really in doubt. It is the father's relationship with his friend that is at issue.'[1] In America in 1967 Rhodes deservedly received Best Supporting Actress awards from both the National Board of Review and National Society of Film Critics. The National Board of Review also named the film one of its 'Ten Best' (four other British films,

Schlesinger's *Far from the Madding Crowd*, *The Whisperers*, *Ulysses* and *Accident*, were also listed).

Other films of interest released in 1966

Though *Khartoum* was co-directed by Basil (*Victim*) Dearden, the gay sexuality of General Charles Gordon (Charlton Heston) was completely ignored; the revue artist and female impersonator Douglas Byng made one of his rare screen appearances in *Hotel Paradiso*; in Joseph Losey's *Modesty Blaise* a blonde Dirk Bogarde camped it up as an effeminate villain; director Tony Richardson filmed Jean Genet's *Mademoiselle*.

Notes

1. Vito Russo, *The Celluloid Closet:
Homosexuality in the Movies*
(Harper & Row, 1981), pp. 148–9.

1967

Dance of the Vampires

Roman Polanski's *Dance of the Vampires* (known in America as *The Fearless Vampire Killers*), is an engaging horror spoof in which Professor Abronsius (Jack MacGowran) and his young assistant Alfred (Polanski), rescue an innkeeper's daughter from vampire Count Von Krolock (Ferdy Mayne). On arriving at Von Krolock's castle in Transylvania, they are introduced to his gay vampire son, Herbert (Iain Quarrier). The predatory Herbert immediately takes a fancy to Alfred, and is determined to seduce him. When Alfred discovers Herbert in his nightshirt, the gay vampire gently leads him to a bed, insisting that he looks pale and needs a 'rest'. When Herbert gets too close for comfort, and tells Alfred his eyelashes look like 'golden threads', Alfred starts to panic. Putting his arm around Alfred's shoulder, Herbert prepares to attack his victim, and a close-up shows the vampire's grotesque face. Opening his mouth wide he reveals his fangs but he is prevented from taking a bite when Alfred shoves a book into his mouth. The half-naked vampire chases the terrified Alfred about the castle, and at one point he catches him and wrestles him to the floor. They roll about and at one point Herbert straddles Alfred and looks as if he is raping him. But Alfred escapes after biting the vampire's ear.

Two notable gay film critics were divided on their view of the film. In 1976 in *Gay News,* Jack Babuscio described Polanski's film as

> one of the best and certainly the funniest of the vampire farces
> . . . . The Count – and would that all our fathers were equally understanding – is determined that his son's fancy for Polanski be satisfied in marriage. 'Your young assistant,' he says in his most insinuating tones to Jack MacGowran, 'will make an *excellent* companion for my boy.' And so he does. For in *Dance of the*

Vampires we at last have a film in which the suckers of blood are truly triumphant![1]

A few years later Vito Russo damned the film in *The Celluloid Closet*:

The incidental flaming faggots and bull dykes who passed through films in the 1960s to liven up the action were the same 1930s window dressing, but now they were nastier and ugly as sin in their newfound certainty. Roman Polanski's *The Fearless Vampire Killers* featured a gay vampire so viciously stereotyped that Polanski should have called his film *Dracula's Hairdresser*.[2]

Other films of interest released in 1967

At the height of his success, writer Joe Orton attempted to script a film for the Beatles called *Up Against It*. The result was an anarchic comedy set in a dark, sexually ambivalent world, but the Beatles were deemed too loveable and commercial for such a project. One week after the group rejected Orton's script, producer Oscar Lewenstein approached director Richard Lester to prepare a version of the screenplay for Mick Jagger and Ian McKellen, but nothing came of this either; in *Pretty Polly*, based on a story by Noel Coward, ugly duckling Polly (Hayley Mills) found romance in Singapore with gorgeous Amaz (Shashi Kapoor) and was transformed into a beautiful swan. While they sit drinking in a bar, she recognizes her silver-haired gay hair stylist who minces over and, after looking at her hair, exclaims in disappointment, wrists flapping in the air, 'Oh, you've absolutely ruined it. After all the time I spent on it. It's sacrilege!' After Polly apologizes, the queen introduces her to his handsome companion, a German hunk called Gunther who works as a 'chief engineer on an oil tanker and doesn't speak a word of English'. Joining Polly and Amaz, the gay hair stylist raises his glass, and toasts Polly. 'Let's drink to the only *real* lady among us!' he says; in the atmospheric thriller *Deadfall*, written and directed by Bryan Forbes, jewel thief Henry Clarke (Michael Caine) falls in love with the beautiful young wife of Richard Moreau (Eric Portman), a French crook. It is a marriage of convenience, as revealed by the wife, Fe (Giovanna Ralli). 'Is he bent? Is he queer?' asks Clarke. Replies Fe: 'I didn't know it was so obvious. Don't you like queers? Is that it?' Says

Clarke: 'I don't have to. I'm not married to one.' At the climax to the film, Moreau commits suicide by shooting himself in the head; Tony Richardson and Christopher Isherwood collaborated on the screenplay of *The Sailor From Gibraltar*, based on the novel by Marguerite Duras.

Notes

1. Jack Babuscio, 'Brutes, Beasts and Vampires' in *Gay News,* no. 110, 1976, p. 21.

2. Vito Russo, *The Celluloid Closet* (Harper & Row, 1981; revised 1987) pp. 53–4.

1968

If...

Lindsay Anderson's *If...* is set in what the director once described as 'a fictitious, but extremely authentic public school. . . a microcosm of the [English] social system'. It is here that a violent revolution takes place, staged by a group of young student rebels. The leader of the group is Mick Travers (Malcolm McDowell), a character modelled on James Dean in *Rebel Without a Cause*. It is difficult to put into words the impact Lindsay Anderson's *If...* had on audiences when it was released. In some ways it acted as a war cry to young people who were being increasingly smothered by commercialism, but feeling isolated from political power which, in spite of a Labour government, was still in the hands of a small, secretive establishment. The timing couldn't have been more perfect. Just before Anderson completed the film, the 1968 student riots broke out in Paris. So into this climate Anderson, working closely with writer David Sherwin, dropped his small, but deafening grenade.

According to film critic David Robinson, *If...* is a film that:

> must be acknowledged as a peak in British cinema history. As no other British film before or since, it caught – and perhaps moulded – the spirit of a time. Anderson used a public school as a microcosm of British society; but his observation of that society discovered something universal.
>
> Other films of the day and of the Swinging Sixties that preceded it were determinedly modish. *If...* was not, and perhaps that was its strength. Anderson wrote: 'The heroes of *If...* are, without knowing it, old-fashioned boys. They're not anti-heroes, or dropouts, or Marxist–Leninists or Maoists or readers of Marcuse. Their revolt is inevitable, not because of what they

think, *but because of what they are.*

Mick [Malcolm McDowell] plays a little at being an intellectual ('Violence and revolution are the only pure acts', and so on) but when he acts it is instinctively, because of his outraged dignity, his frustrated passion, his vital energy, his sense of fair play if you like. If his story can be said to be 'about' anything, it is about freedom.[1]

British cinema is full of public-school stories about tyrannical masters and rebellious boys. What Anderson did was to tell it from the boy's point of view and draw strongly, if ultimately superficially, from a political manifesto that was out there on the streets of Paris, and later on American campuses.

The leading actors in the film, Malcolm McDowell, Richard Warwick (later to appear in Derek Jarman's *The Tempest*) and David Wood, became instant heroes because they were playing upper-class boys with a working-class agenda. McDowell gets all the best lines (and numerous close-ups) and deservedly so, because he was a force to be reckoned with. So much so that Anderson featured him and his character – Mick Travers – in two other films: *O Lucky Man* (1973) and *Britannia Hospital* (1982).

The villains of the piece are the school bullies who are also exploiters of the younger boys, and enthusiastic participants in the war games played in the school regiment. The masters are depicted as an unholy gang of fools and pedants. There are no surprises here. The casting of familiar British character actors like Arthur Lowe and Mona Washbourne help to make the film 'acceptable' to a wider audience who would normally have been repelled by the bolshie message, choppy editing, swerves from colour into black and white, and semi-explicit sex.

In a highly charged moment, mixing reality with wishful thinking, Travers engages in a tigerish fight with a young waitress. This is followed by a lingering scene of adolescent love when a young boy observes Richard Warwick exercising on the parallel bars in the gym. A full frontal nude shower scene may have been cut after press screenings, but the eroticism in this dreamy, poetic sequence was unmistakable. So dreamy – and so right – that a later scene, with the same boy sleeping beside Warwick – caused little outrage, though it was a first for British cinema.

The film's total acceptance of gay love and sex is discreetly but firmly conveyed. Neither McDowell or Wood ever demean Warwick, probably because they are in love with him too, or had been. The nasty, unnatural side of public school life is clearly depicted by the school prefects who ritualistically have the fags run errands and do their (off-screen) sexual bidding. The beating of the three rebels is plainly meant to represent their perverse desires linked not to passion, but to power.

For a gay audience, *If. . .* is particularly fascinating for the way Anderson takes homoeroticism a stage further than his 1963 film *This Sporting Life*. For Gavin Lambert, *If. . .*

is more openly and highly charged, with its naked adolescents in the shower, dialogue loaded with sexual interplay, and – one of the most purely lyrical homoerotic scenes in any movie – the sequence in subliminal slow motion of the pretty junior schoolboy watching the handsome senior exercising in the gymnasium. And from his first appearance, black scarf masking his face below the eyes, black hat on his head, body wrapped in a loose black overcoat like a cape, there's a halo of glamour around Malcolm McDowell's Mick Travers, the sardonic and beautiful rebel hero.[2]

If. . . was only nominated for two British Academy Awards: Lindsay Anderson for Best Director and David Sherwin for Best Screenplay. Both lost to America's *The Graduate*. Surprisingly, though it was one of the most innovative and critically acclaimed British films of the decade, it did not receive a Best Film nomination, neither was Malcolm McDowell – in his first film role – nominated for Most Promising Newcomer. Likewise, in America, the film did not receive a single Oscar nomination, though in 1969 it received the Golden Palm Best Film prize at the Cannes Film Festival, and was shortlisted for Best Film by the New York Film Critics Circle. Anderson and Sherwin were also shortlisted.

The Lion in Winter

In *The Lion in Winter*, which James Goldman adapted for the screen from his own stage play, Peter O'Toole gives an outstanding peformance as King Henry II, the head of a family at war. For Christmas 1183,

Henry brings together his wife Eleanor of Aquitane (Katharine Hepburn), imprisoned for a decade for meddling in affairs of state, his three surviving sons, Geoffrey (John Castle), Richard (Anthony Hopkins) and John (Nigel Terry), his mistress Alais (Jane Merrow), and Alais' brother Philip (Timothy Dalton), the young King of France.

At the beginning of the film, Henry II confesses to Alais that 'I've known contessas, milkmaids, courtesans, novices, whores, gipsies and little boys – but nowhere in God's western world have I found anyone to love but you.' But when Eleanor, the 'mother from hell', arrives from her prison in Salisbury Tower, Henry and Alais find themselves caught up in a fierce battle for the inheritance of Henry's throne.

Anthony Hopkins makes an early screen appearance as Richard, the legendary Lionheart. Bearded, handsome but treacherous, he describes himself as 'a constant soldier, a sometime poet'. Determined to succeed to the throne, he tells everyone 'I *will* be King!' Enter Philip, the effeminate King of France, and former lover of Richard. He plots with Geoffrey and John to get Richard out of the running.

When Richard goes to see Philip in his chambers, he reveals that he is still attracted to him, but Philip is angry. After Richard had abandoned Philip some years earlier, the young King says 'I spent two years in every street in hell.' Philip offers his hand to Richard, and he takes it. 'You haven't said you love me,' he says. He leads Richard to the bed, but they are interrupted by Henry who has come to see Philip to continue 'negotiations'. Richard hides behind a curtain, but just when Henry thinks he has won the argument, Philip says: 'I learned how much fathers live in sons. . . . Well, what's the official line on sodomy? How stands the crown on boys who do with boys?' As he says this to Henry, there is a shot of Richard in hiding, closing his eyes in shame. Replies Henry: 'Richard finds his way into so many legends, let's hear yours and see how it compares.' Philip then describes how, when he was just fifteen, he and Richard expressed their love for each other. However, it was a lie, for Philip always intended to use this information against Henry. At this point, Richard bursts out from behind the curtain screaming 'No! It wasn't like that. You *loved* me!' Replies Philip callously: 'Never.'

In his performance, Anthony Hopkins tries to create sympathy for Richard, expressing pain when he discovers Philip has used him. But he is a pitiable figure, and the film works against the actor, suggesting that

Richard is gay because Eleanor raised him. He is a 'mummy's boy'. Says Henry to Eleanor: 'He was the best, but from the cradle on you cradled him. I never had a chance. You threw me out of bed for Richard.' *The Lion in Winter* is one of the few films to portray Richard the Lionheart as gay. Usually he is seen as a romantic, heterosexual figure, most recently in Kevin Costner's *Robin Hood, Prince of Thieves* (1991) where he was played by Sean Connery.

The Lion in Winter was an international success, and for her performance as Eleanor, Katharine Hepburn won her third Best Actress Oscar (sharing with newcomer Barbra Streisand in *Funny Girl*). Hopkins was nominated for a British Academy Award as Best Supporting Actor, and James Goldman was nominated for Best Screenplay (in America he won the Oscar).

Other films of interest released in 1968

Franco Zeffirelli's ravishing version of Shakespeare's *Romeo and Juliet* included a magnificent performance by John McEnery as the flamboyant, troubled Mercutio who may be in love with Romeo. He's played by the beautiful Leonard Whiting, with whom the camera seems to be having a love affair. In his nude scenes with Juliet (Olivia Hussey) it lingers on his bare bottom. McEnery was nominated (with Anthony Hopkins in *The Lion in Winter*) for a British Academy Award as Best Supporting Actor, and Zeffirelli was nominated as Best Director; in the appalling *Baby Love*, a sexually promiscuous teenager Luci (Linda Hayden) seduced her mother's ex-lover, his son and his wife (Ann Lynn); the cast of *Boom!*, adapted from Tennessee Williams's *The Milk Train Doesn't Stop Here Anymore*, included Noel Coward as the Witch of Capri. Directed by Joseph Losey, the stars of the film were Richard Burton and Elizabeth Taylor; Losey and Taylor came together again for *Secret Ceremony* in which a prostitute (Taylor) 'mothers' a seemingly innocent waif (Mia Farrow).

Notes

1. David Robinson, 'A Film That Shook the World' in *The Times*, 1 September 1994.
2. Gavin Lambert, 'Lindsay Anderson: Unrequited Lover'. *Sight and Sound*, vol. 4, no. 10, October 1994, p. 18.

1969

The Killing of Sister George

In 1967, when Angela Lansbury was starring on the Broadway stage in the hit musical *Mame*, director Robert Aldrich considered her for the role of soap star June Buckridge in the lesbian drama *The Killing of Sister George*. Based on the highly acclaimed stage play by Frank Marcus, the role of Buckridge had been created by Beryl Reid. Adapted for the screen by Lukas Heller, he later recalled: 'We met with her (Lansbury) in her hotel suite. When Bob offered her the part of the lesbian, Miss Lansbury became quite offended. "No, I think not," she told him, "I have my fans and reputation to think of."' A few years later, in 1976, Keith Howes interviewed Lansbury for *Gay News* and asked her why she turned down the role. She replied:

> I didn't want to play a lesbian at that time. I wasn't mad about the play either – I'd only read it, not seen it – but not very many women played immediately recognizable lesbian roles in 1968. They do today but they didn't then and I suppose that had a bearing on my decision, and I was doing something else at the time. Now I think the truth is filtering down to all of us but I still don't think I'd play the part.[1]

After Lansbury turned him down, Aldrich approached Bette Davis whom he had directed in two box office hits: *What Ever Happened to Baby Jane?* (1962) and *Hush. . . Hush, Sweet Charlotte* (1964). 'I have no qualms about playing a lesbian,' she is reported to have said. 'I have been married four times so I think my track record speaks for itself.' There was even talk of casting Bette's friend, and *Sweet Charlotte* co-star, Olivia de Havilland, in the role of the predatory BBC executive Mrs Mercy Croft. With Hollywood legends Davis and de Havilland in the cast, one can only speculate how *Sister George* would have turned out. Surely these movie queens would have transformed the material into a glorious camp spectacle, and box office smash. Unfortunately, Aldrich and Heller turned Marcus's stage play into an overblown exploitation flick, and almost succeeded in destroying Beryl Reid's magnificent *tour de force*. Aldrich later admitted: 'It just didn't work. Beryl Reid had every right to expect a lot of things from that picture. That's an extraordinary performance she gave.'[2] At first, Beryl Reid didn't expect to appear in the film version:

> Bette Davis had been to see me after one of the performances, and had said '*Nobody* must do the movie but you. You're the *only* person to do it'. . . . Then, in every paper the next day, it said, 'Bette Davis to play George'. . . . I blame this totally on the press, because I found Bette wonderful, and don't think she would ever have behaved like that intentionally. . . . The press reports I'd read even went on to mention Olivia de Havilland and, I think, Stella Stevens for the parts of Mrs Mercy Croft and Childie.[3]

Before *Sister George* Beryl Reid was best-known as a comedienne. She welcomed the opportunity to extend her range with a strong dramatic role in the theatre. But, like most of the country, her knowledge of lesbians was almost non-existent. At that time few lesbians had been seen on British television, and audiences had been fed a diet of false and damaging stereotypes. In drama, lesbians were usually portrayed as sick, sinister and predatory, or in comedy they were butch stereotypes. It was not until the mid-1960s that documentary programmes began to acknowledge the existence of lesbians, and give them air time. Few of these women felt comfortable on-camera. Most preferred to be interviewed in silhouette. But, in spite of this breakthrough, when Associated Rediffusion's *This Week* devoted a whole programme to lesbians in 1965, the *Daily Express* pleaded with its readers on the day of the transmission: 'to stop this filth entering your living-room'. One can only speculate how far programmes like *This Week* and the BBC's *Man Alive* (1967) changed viewer's minds. So it is hardly surprising to find that when Beryl Reid visited the popular lesbian club, Gateways, with director Robert Aldrich, she was shocked:

The Killing of Sister George was the first play I'd ever done. I liked the script. I thought 'Oh yes, I can do that.' Yet when I did the film and Robert Aldrich took me to Gateways, the club in Bramerton Street, Chelsea, I nearly had a fit. I said, 'If I'd been here before I did the play, I'd never have done it.' I didn't realize they held each other's bums and went to the gents' loo. What did they do in the gents' loo? And Archie, the chucker-out with all these tattoos on her arms! But she was lovely. They all were, although they frightened me a bit to begin with because I didn't know exactly what it would be like.

My mother was terribly funny. Somehow she got to know all those kind of things before I did because she used to look at some woman and say, 'I think that's a collar-and-tie job, Beryl'. Collar-and-tie job! I'd never heard anything like it.[4]

To quote Bette Davis in *All About Eve*, the stage version had suffered a 'bumpy ride' on its pre-West End tour. Says Reid:

The tour was a disaster. We were pathfinders. In the British theatre nobody before had spoken about lesbianism, and this really destroyed the people we were playing to: in Bath we were deafened by the old chaps in their bathchairs being wheeled out by their nannies, their urine bottles rattling as they went, saying, 'Disgusting, disgusting'. . . . Hull was the biggest disaster of all. The people of Hull would barely serve us in the shops, they were so horrified.[5]

But when the play opened in London at the Duke of York's theatre, it was another story. It was a huge success, both critically and commercially, and Eileen Atkins received the *Evening Standard* Award for Best Actress. The play was a triumph on Broadway too, and Reid won the prestigious Tony Award for Best Actress in a Dramatic Play in 1966–67. Atkins was nominated in the same category and Frank Marcus was nominated for Best Dramatic Play.

In the screen version of *The Killing of Sister George* June Buckridge is the much-loved star of *Applehurst*, a popular, long-running BBC television soap set in Somerset. She has played the district nurse, Sister George, for six years, and is confident her popularity with viewers will keep her in the role for many more years. But off-screen, Buckridge unexpectedly experiences tensions in her professional and personal life, and the threat of losing her role in *Applehurst* looms when the show starts losing its audience.

The plot was vaguely similar to a true-life story. Ellis Powell (who was at one time married to the character actor Ralph Truman) had enjoyed a long run as Mrs Dale, the middle-class doctor's wife, in a BBC radio soap opera called *Mrs Dale's Diary*. Launched in 1948, the BBC decided to revamp it in the early 1960s, and sacked Powell. Her replacement was Jessie Matthews, a matronly character actress who had once been the popular 'Dancing Divinity' of pre-war British screen musicals. Says Matthews's biographer, Michael Thornton:

> On 19 February 1963, a plump and embittered fifty-six-year-old character actress called Ellis Powell walked out of Broadcasting House for the last time. She was not a star. In fact she had earned less than £30 a week. But her voice was as well-known in Britain as that of Queen Elizabeth II, for it was heard twice a day by seven million devoted listeners. Miss Powell was Britain's most sacrosanct fictional paragon, Mrs Dale, in the radio serial *Mrs Dale's Diary*. And now, after fifteen years in the role she had created, the BBC had summarily fired her – partly because of her drinking habits, and partly because it was felt that the role, and also the entire programme, was in need of a facelift. 'The BBC have chucked me out like an old sock,' protested Miss Powell as she made her sad exit. . . . Three months later, at the age of fifty-seven, she died. . . her friends believed she never recovered from the shock and distress of her summary dismissal by the BBC. In the last weeks of her life she worked as a demonstrator at the Ideal Home Exhibition and as a cleaner in a hotel.[6]

In the film Buckridge is a middle-aged, butch, abusive, cigar-smoking alcoholic who shares her home with her young girlfriend, the 'feminine' wife/child, Alice 'Childie' McNaught, played by Susannah York. Essentially both women are lonely and insecure, afraid that one of them will destroy their long-term relationship. Throughout the film they exist on a knife-edge, indulging in screaming matches, but there are a few moments of tenderness. For instance, when Buckridge remembers her first encounter with 'Childie' in a boarding-house, Reid's heartfelt playing is tremendously moving: 'One night I went into the bathroom just after you'd had a bath and the mirror was all steamed up and the bath mat was all wet and glistening where you'd been standing on it and there was a smell of bath crystals and talcum powder. It was like an enchanted wood.'

With Aldrich's exploitative, sensationalized and voyeuristic approach to the lesbian theme constantly working against her, Bery Reid just about manages to surface in triumph with a remarkable performance. She beautifully conveys Buckridge's highly charged emotionalism. One minute she is tough and foul-mouthed, the next vulnerable, and in need of protection. Reid is clearly treating the subject with the sensitivity and respect it deserves. She is also hilarious in several comedy scenes, insulting the tall Australian dyke Mildred ('You miserable looking cow'), assaulting two young nuns in a taxi ('Well, hello girls – out on a mission are we?') or describing to Mrs Croft (Coral Browne) why, as Sister George, she looks so cheerful on a motor bike ('You'd look cheerful too with fifty cubic centimetres throbbing away between your legs!').

On the other hand, Reid's co-star, Susannah York, an otherwise fine actress, gives one of the worst performances of her career. Looking unattractive with her scruffy haircut and greasy, shiny skin, she reinforces the perverted image of lesbians the general public had at that time. Later that year York redeemed herself with a much admired portrayal of a blonde flapper in 1930s Hollywood in *They Shoot Horses Don't They?*, and in 1972 she gave another outstanding performance in Robert Altman's *Images*.

It was inevitable that *The Killing of Sister George*, the first explicitly lesbian commercial film, would run into censorship difficulties. More so after Aldrich had turned it into nothing more than an exploitation flick. The infamous seduction scene between Coral Browne and Susannah York did not appear in Frank Marcus's original, and Aldrich's decision for the encounter between the two women to be sexually explicit was very controversial. Says Tom Dewe Matthews:

> Critics accused the American director of gratuitous sensationalism, and certainly lesbian kissing, breast fondling and nipple sucking were without precedent in a film scene. But the censor had already anticipated the furore and taken steps to restrain Aldrich's sense of sexual adventure on the screen. 'We are not prepared as yet to accept lesbian sex to this point,' said

Trevelyan in a letter to the film's distributor. 'You can arrange to try another re-editing of the scene, but I can hold out little hope that it will be acceptable if submitted here'. . . . The inevitable compromise was reached. The kissing was reduced, but the breast manipulation (in which a body double had been substituted for Susannah York) remained. . . . In America, the doyenne of film critics Pauline Kael had previously remarked, in respect of another film, that 'lesbians needed sympathy – because there isn't much that they can do.' When she saw in *The Killing of Sister George* exactly what lesbians could do her review of the film appeared under the title 'Frightening the Horses'.[7]

Unlike *Victim*, which could be described as its 1960s male-counterpart, *The Killing of Sister George* has not found favour in lesbian or gay critical circles. In *Gay News* in the 1970s Jack Babuscio said it 'presents the lesbian world as a grotesque collection of the sick and the predatory'. Around the same time, Caroline Sheldon said in *Gays and Film*:

There is certainly little or no solidarity between any of the women, consistent with male assumptions about women not getting on together (rooted in their fears about women allying). Lesbianism here is not woman-identification in any way. The voyeuristically necessary seduction scene is as nasty as the women: though it is hard to work out what is happening, the dark setting and strange musical score indicate that it is certainly perverted. The events and the portraits of the three women, drawn as quite emotionally repellent, make no attraction to the idea of lesbianism possible. Little threat is implicit in these women's presence in the world since they are destructive of themselves and each other.[8]

The Killing of Sister George was an American film, mostly shot in Hollywood, but with some location work in London (including the Gateways sequence). It is included here because of its British setting. Sadly, Beryl Reid's *tour de force* did not earn her nominations for a British Academy Award or an Oscar. However, in America, she did receive a Hollywood Foreign Press Golden Globe nomination for Best Actress, and was one of the runners-up for the New York Film Critics Circle Best Actress award.

The Virgin Soldiers

Set in 1951 in the 'Panglin Barracks' in Singapore, *The Virgin Soldiers* follows the (hetero) sexual exploits of a National Serviceman, Private Brigg (Hywel Bennett). After an unsuccessful encounter with a local prostitute, he courts Phillipa (Lynn Redgrave), the daughter of his Sergeant Major. But in spite of its promising credits (John Hopkins, John McGrath and Ian La Frenais collaborated on the screenplay, based on Leslie Thomas's novel; Ned Sherrin co-produced), and an excellent cast (in addition to Bennett and Redgrave, there's Rachel Kempson, Nigel Davenport and Nigel Patrick), the humour of *The Virgin Soldiers* barely rises above the level of a bad *Carry On* film.

However, though it fails to deliver the goods, *The Virgin Soldiers* does include Foster and Villiers, a fairly well-integrated and well-adjusted gay couple who exist amongst the 'virgins'. Foster is played by Gregory Phillips who, several years earlier, played the son of Judy Garland and Dirk Bogarde in *I Could Go On Singing*. So the on-screen son of a world-famous gay icon and the star of *Victim* grew up to become a gay soldier! Foster's lover, Villiers, is played by none other than the soon-to-be dazzling classical and jazz dancer, Wayne Sleep.

Foster and Villiers sleep together in the dormitory, but only Sergeant Driscoll (Nigel Davenport) disapproves, though he doesn't do anything to stop them. When he sees them holding hands on the parade ground, he admits it 'turns his stomach', but he doesn't take any steps to prevent the couple being together, and being openly affectionate. One can only speculate how often this happened in reality. Presumably men like novelist Leslie Thomas and co-producer Sherrin had witnessed this in their National Service days? However, this 'toleration' only goes so far. For example, Foster and Villiers do not attend the soldier's dance. Instead they remain, dancing together, in the dormitory. Either they prefer to do so, but it is more than likely they know they wouldn't be welcome.

While on active service in the jungle, Foster and Villiers are seen wearing pyjamas, and being reprimanded for holding hands. But, though they hardly speak, a snatch of dialogue is hilarious, and very camp. A soldier asks the gays if they saw the film set in the jungle. Replies Foster: 'Yes. Rhonda Fleming played the nurse.' Chips in Villiers: 'I wish I knew how she kept her uniform so clean!' On the negative side, the gay couple are effeminate and weak, and used for unecessary comic relief. In the scene when Foster wounds his lover with his bayonet, Villiers faints, and Foster faints on top of him. But, compared to the *Carry On* films, they're progressive in a way because, unlike Hawtrey and Williams, they are not desexualized. They are identified as gay, and they're also portrayed as a *couple*, extremely rare in British films. *And* they're in the army!

At the end of the film, when the 'virgin' soldiers come to the end of their National Service and depart for home, it is revealed that Foster and Villiers' periods of service overlap. So they have to keep signing on for another six months in order to be together! They seem happy about the situation. Says Lantry (Geoffrey Hughes): 'That is *definitely* love!' But at no time is it suggested that, if the gay couple *had* returned home with the others, they could not have lived together without fear of arrest and imprisonment.

The Italian Job

Gays are all over the shop in the entertaining thriller, *The Italian Job*, but the star of the film, Michael Caine, isn't one of them. He plays Charlie, the crook who inherits a plan to steal four million dollars in gold. At the beginning of the film he shares a scene with Simon Dee as an effeminate gay 'shirtmaker' called Adrian. It's brief, but Charlie has a nice, relaxed relationship with Adrian, and there's a bit of ad-libbing between the two actors. Throughout the film, Caine's Charlie is presented as a virile, masculine 'macho man', and the rapport he has with effeminate gays like Adrian, and queer villains, such as Tony Beckley's 'Camp Freddie', serves to reinforce his heterosexuality. However, on close inspection it is revealed that Charlie has, on his wall, a large poster of leather-clad gay icon Marlon Brando in *The Wild One*.

The most peculiar character in the film is Mr Bridger, played by Noel Coward. He's a criminal mastermind, serving a prison sentence. In spite of this, Mr Bridger lives a life of luxury in gaol. He is a queer in control who commands respect from the inmates *and* warders. He's also a patriotic queen, sitting regally under a portrait of Queen Elizabeth II in his cell, reading the *Illustrated London News*. 'There's more to life than breaking and entering,' he says. Coward's off-screen friend and companion Graham Payn plays Keats, Mr Bridger's prison 'companion'.

In one of the great moments of gay movie history, a happy, smiling Noel Coward parades through the prison like Queen Elizabeth II herself. As he gives a 'royal' wave to the enthusiastic inmates, they loudly chant 'England!' as if they were at a football match. It's a wonderful, fitting tribute to one of the stately homos of England (to borrow Quentin Crisp's description of himself).

Other films of interest released in 1969

Years before he came out of the closet and became a gay activist, Ian McKellen entered films as the outlaw Roger in *Alfred the Great*, and Sandy Dennis's lover in *A Touch of Love*; years before she became television's most famous agony aunt, Maureen Lipman played a lesbian inmate of a remand home in *The Smashing Bird I Used to Know*; spotty public schoolboys are all over the place in the stylish musical remake of *Goodbye, Mr Chips* which Terence Rattigan based on the 1939 classic. A wonderful cast, headed by Peter O'Toole, included a scene-stealing Siân Phillips, camping it up as Petula Clark's friend Ursula Mossbank (in America she won the National Society of Film Critics Best Supporting Actress award). Swishy gays, and at least one suit-wearing dyke, appeared briefly at Clark's party in Chelsea; Ken Russell's *Women in Love* included the famous homoerotic wrestling match between Alan Bates and Oliver Reed; in the homophobic comedy *The Magic Christian* Yul Brynner, in drag, sang Noel Coward's 'Mad About the Boy' to Roman Polanski; in *Staircase*, an American–British–French co-production (set in London but filmed in France) Richard Burton and Rex Harrison gave a pathetic account of an ageing gay couple. Said Vito Russo: 'For two hours they moan and piss about their sad, wasted lives, never showing a sign of love or affection.'⁹

Notes

1. Angela Lansbury interviewed by Keith Howes in *Gay News*, no. 91, 1976, reprinted in *Outspoken: Keith Howes' Gay News Interviews 1976–83* (Cassell, 1995).
2. Robert Aldrich, Andy Warhol's *Interview*, no. 35, August 1973.
3. Beryl Reid, *So Much Love* (Hutchinson, 1984), pp. 141, 151.
4. Beryl Reid, 'Sheer Bloody Magic' in Carole Woddis (ed.), *Conversations with Actresses*, (Virago Press, 1991), p. 235.
5. Reid, *So Much Love,* pp. 129–30.
6. Michael Thornton, *Jessie Matthews* (Hart-Davis, MacGibbon, 1974), p. 27.
7. Tom Dewe Matthews, *Censored* (Chatto & Windus, 1994), pp. 184–5.
8. Caroline Sheldon, in Richard Dyer (ed.), *Gays and Film* (British Film Institute, 1977), p. 13.
9. Vito Russo, *The Celluloid Closet* (Harper & Row, 1981; revised 1987), p. 192–3.

1970

Performance

With *Performance* Donald Cammell (screenwriter and co-director) and Nicolas Roeg (co-director) set out to redefine British cinema. When the film was made, much publicity centered upon the screen debut of Mick Jagger. He plays Turner, a reclusive pop star, living with two androgynous women (Anita Pallenberg and Michèle Breton) in a large North London house. This is kitted out with all manner of North African furnishings and a recording studio. At the beginning of the film, Jagger makes one brief, unexplained appearance – possibly to reassure his fans and the American studio (Warner Brothers) that put up the money. But the first third of the film concentrates on Chas Devlin (James Fox), a nicely turned out East End gangster who walks with confidence and flair. It is strongly hinted that he owes his current good fortune to his looks, as much as his personality.

The first time we see Chas he is naked and having sex with a woman which involves some infliction of pain. Afterwards, he spends a great deal of time taking care of his body, face and clothes. Probably for the first time cinemagoers were shown a man's underpant drawer, perfectly neat, clean and ordered. Chas is good at sex and good at his job – intimidation. It seems very likely that Chas was once the bed mate of the local Mr Big, Harry Flowers (Johnny Shannon), a grinning, would-be tycoon with a fondness for well-muscled, none too bright young men. Chas is a fast learner, and he has picked up – and tailored to his own tastes – Harry's lavish standard of living and utter ruthlessness. But there is a rival to be considered. Joey Maddocks (Anthony Valentine) is less of a pretty boy like Chas, but tough and resilient. There is tension between them, and not only because each wants to be top dog after Harry Flowers. Love and sex was once part of the equation, and Joey has still got it bad. Their feelings culminate in Joey and his goons ambushing Chas in his flat, daubing the walls with queer taunts, and beating Chas's bare buttocks. Seizing a momentary lapse in concentration, Chas picks up a gun and kills his former friend. From then on, Chas is a dead man in Harry's eyes.

Changing his appearance (red paint on his blonde hair) the hunted gangster rents a room in a house owned by a faded pop idol. At first, Chas – who is unsettled by the obvious bohemianism of the set-up – humours the suspicious Pherber (Pallenberg), but the decadence and drug-taking increases Chas's unease. He is, of course, completely 'normal', not in any way a 'pervert'. Ushered into the presence of the long-haired, androgynous Turner, Chas's fate is sealed. Fascinated, repelled, bewildered and totally dependent on this strange trio, he is drawn into the world of magic mushrooms, transvestism and group sex. His vision and perception are blurred. The careful barriers he has erected around himself and his sexuality begin to crumble. Betrayed by a friend, Harry Flowers's men descend on the little kingdom. Turner is shot, and Chas is taken away for eventual execution and dumping. But the face we see through the car window at the end of the film is not that of Chas, but of his recent host.

No synopsis can hope to do justice to the richness of design, the interrelation of subterranean worlds (guns and gangsters) and the fearsome violence that represents Chas. Never before in a British film had the strange, queer bedfellows of the East End bully boys and the British establishment (police, judges, politicians) been so starkly spotlighted. There had been queerish thugs before, of course. Peter Sellers appeared to have the hots for Adam Faith, as well as Carol White, in *Never Let Go* (1960). And there were hints in the press about one of the Kray twins. But they were very guarded hints. After all, nobody wanted to end up with bits missing. *Performance* let cinemagoers have it with both barrels. Corruption and violence in the highest echelons of society. And sexual borders smashed. What exactly was the relationship between Mick Jagger, Anita Pallenberg and Michèle Breton? Were the two women lovers? And how far did Chas go in showing his appreciation to the trio for giving him a guided tour through sex, drugs and rock 'n' roll? And what exactly was the meaning of Turner's song, delivered by a devillish Jagger in a sleek suit with slicked-back hair, surrounded by gangsters, and ending with total male nudity (through a distorted lens)?

Not that the *Performance* the audience saw – nearly two-and-a-half years after it was made – was the film intended by its makers. Warner Brothers had viewed the footage with alarm. 'Even the bath water is dirty,' complained one executive. Sequences were cut (including the bed scene where Jagger exposed his sizeable genitalia – frames were helpfully printed in *Private Eye*!). Scenes in the first half were re-edited, and Chas's sado-masochism was toned down.

The participation of Jagger – a major factor in securing American finance – was not quite the drawcard that had been expected. His own 'performance' is strangely abstracted. The big build-up he receives in the dialogue is not quite justified by the pale figure who emerges out of all the carpets, cushions and heavy make-up. By contrast, Anita Pallenberg is totally in control, and sardonic, as Pherber.

The revelation is James Fox. With prissy, self-righteous energy, he's cocky on his own patch, completely out of his depth among the denizens of everything he has been taught to distrust: men who look like women, and vice versa, mind-altering drugs, foreign ideas, cluttered rooms full of 'old' things. It's a brilliant piece of casting. The former 'boss' of Joseph Losey's *The Servant*, on the other side of the class divide, is now completely taken over by forces beyond his control: dangerous, intoxicating and pleasurable. The power of *Performance* owes much to the sympathetic playing of Fox. He doesn't play for sympathy, but he allows the viewer to experience his fear, fascination and wonder at the new worlds opening up to him. He has a chance of redemption, a means of escape from a limited, cruel world. Whether he achieves his dream must be left open because the film employs one of those mystifying endings.

The Private Life of Sherlock Holmes

The opening credits of *The Private Life of Sherlock Holmes* reveals a sepia photograph of Sherlock Holmes standing behind Dr Watson, who is sitting in a chair. Holmes's hand rests on his shoulder. It resembles a Victorian studio portrait of a husband and wife, teasingly suggesting that the relationship in the film between Conan Doyle's heroes might offer something new. But this is not to be. Though they're bosom buddies, and Watson (Colin Blakeley) is very protective of Holmes

(Robert Stephens), he is unequivocally presented as heterosexual. Holmes, on the other hand, is something else entirely.

The film's director, Billy Wilder, had already made a big impact with his sparkling, sophisticated gender-bending comedy *Some Like it Hot* in 1959. He intended to go a stage further and make a gay version of Sherlock Holmes. But he faced opposition from the son of Conan Doyle. He said:

> I should have been more daring but, unfortunately, the son of Conan Doyle was there. I wanted to make Holmes a homosexual. That's why he is on dope. Look, we have been freed now from the Breen Office or the Johnson Office or that stupid thing. In many respects, it's terrifying because now any idiot and any pornographer can do anything. But for the ones who are a little bit discriminating, who do it delicately, a grand new thing has opened. But that was after *Private Life*. The saddest thing about the film is that it was a waste of a year and a half of my life.
>
> When you get to be my age, you say, 'Shit, if I just had the time back that I wasted on pictures that were failures.' But I'm not ashamed of it. There are many pictures I wish I could scratch out, but this I'm not ashamed of. It was just a failure. It just did not work.[1]

In spite of Wilder's disappointment, Holmes's sexual ambivalence is hinted at. Not only does Robert Stephens resemble Oscar Wilde with his long hair, heavily made-up eyes and effete personality, he gives a camp performance *par excellence*. In one hilarious sequence the great Russian ballerina Petrova (Tamara Toumanova) invites Holmes to make her pregnant. She wants to have a baby by a 'brilliant' man, but her first two choices were not up to it. Tolstoy was 'too old' and Tchaikovsky a 'catastrophe'. Explains Petrova's translator Rogozhin (Clive Revill), women are not Tchaikovsky's 'glass of tea'. Holmes is not interested in fathering Petrova's child either, and backs away. 'I am not a free man,' he explains. 'I am a bachelor living with another bachelor for the last five years. Five very happy years. Tchaikovsky is not an isolated case.' Asks Rogozhin: 'You mean Dr Watson is your glass of tea?' Replies Holmes: 'If you want to be picturesque about it.' Meanwhile, rampant heterosexual Watson is having the time of his life dancing with the female ballerinas. However, his fun ends when Rogozhin spreads the news that Watson is gay. Immediately the ballerinas abandon Watson on the dance floor, and the now-interested gay ballet dancers move in. Sadly, what should have been an inoffensive comedy scene becomes homophobic and out of step with the rest of the film. The gay ballet dancers are shown as nothing more than a bunch of predatory, grotesque-looking movie stereotypes.

When the penny finally drops, a horrified Watson vents his anger on Holmes. 'You wretch. . . you blaggard. . . of all the unspeakable fabrications. . . how could you invent such a dastardly lie?' he screams. Holmes apologizes, and explains that he didn't want to hurt Petrova's feelings, but Watson is in a panic, claiming that he will be dishonoured, disgraced and ostracized. 'We must stop this talk,' he says. 'We must get married!' Replies Holmes: 'Then they'd *really* talk.' He adds: 'Of course we can continue to meet clandestinely in the waiting rooms of suburban railway stations.' This is a direct reference to Noel Coward's *Brief Encounter* as well as an acknowledgement of the 'secret' liaisons of gay couples. Watson claims: 'I can get women from three Continents to testify for me. And you can get women to vouch for you, too, can't you, Holmes? Can you, Holmes?' Holmes simply replies: 'Good night, Watson.' Watson responds: 'I hope I'm not being presumptuous. There have *been* women in your life?' The conversation ends with Holmes saying: 'The answer is yes. You're being presumptuous. Good night.'

At this point in the film Holmes is saying to Watson that his sexuality is a private matter. The fact that Watson has been an intimate friend of Holmes for years, but cannot recall any relationships he's had with women, is significant. The scene is beautifully played by Robert Stephens whose entire performance in the film is superb. In spite of the stereotyping of the gay ballet dancers, *The Private Life of Sherlock Holmes* is a stylish, sophisticated comedy-drama which deserves greater attention and recognition. Says Parker Tyler in *Screening the Sexes*:

All the resources of superlatively cute scriptwriting have been needed to exonerate him [Sherlock Holmes] from something he lightly, deliberately takes on himself and Dr Watson quite early in the film: the public onus of pederasty. Of course, Dr Watson himself denounces it as a 'damned lie' to Holmes's own face. And it would seem, indeed, it has been a *blague* of the great detective to get out of a ticklish situation with a Russian prima ballerina, who has selected him to be the father of a child she wants. Yet the style in which Holmes is acted by Robert Stephens proves that any other *blague* by the name of jolly will laugh as sweet if the rose itself has style and wit, which it has. In one unexpected stroke, a classic detective, long enshrined on film, becomes a Hollywood funny fellow *and* a professional sissy. Welcome, Mr Holmes![2]

Walk a Crooked Path

Barry Perowne was responsible for writing the screenplay for *Walk a Crooked Path,* a truly appalling melodrama, set in a public school for boys. It concerns a disruptive teenager's charge of a sexual assault against one of his masters. According to the 1969 edition of *The British Film and Television Year Book*, Perowne's previous credits as a screenwriter included such films as *The Crunch*, *Seawolf in Lisbon*, *Head in Hand* and *The Sunset Gun*. But none of these films is listed in Denis Gifford's comprehensive *British Film Catalogue*, so it can only be assumed they were never produced.

It is a pity that such fine character actors as Tenniel Evans and Faith Brook became involved in this production. They play schoolmaster John Hemming and his wife Elizabeth, a middle-aged couple who live within the stifling confines of the public school. He's lonely and pathetic, she drinks like a fish, and their humdrum lives are disrupted by the appearance of Philip Draper, an unpleasant, evil American pupil who describes himself as 'cosmopolitan'. He's played by Clive Endersby in what can only be described as one of the worst performances ever put on screen.

The stale, sterile look of the film and Hemming's character are almost indistinguishable. It is hardly surprising he's passed over for the job of headmaster after seventeen years of service to the school. When Draper claims Hemming has molested him: 'He kept squeezing me and putting his arms around me. He was all over me,' it is obvious a more complicated plot is being hatched. But not only does the plot become more incomprehensible, it is downright silly.

Elizabeth Hemming is killed in a car crash. We discover that Hemming has been having an affair with Nancy, another master's wife.

The assault on Draper *did* take place, but it was a set-up. However, the 'assault' has triggered off something in Hemming, bringing his long-repressed gay sexuality to the surface. He describes to Nancy an experience he had many years ago in France when he swam naked with some other boys, and she realizes his true nature and abandons him. At the end of the film Hemming asks Draper to join him in France for the summer, but Draper demands an Italian car, an apartment in Cannes and a speedboat. 'I was thinking of a quiet summer,' says Hemming. 'That's too bad,' replies Draper. He tells Hemming he is 'going places' but 'not with a washed-up schoolmaster.' Hemming throws him out of the house.

After *Victim* and the 1967 Sexual Offences Act it is tragedy that such a truly reprehensible and depressing film about gays was produced by the British film industry. A blessing, then, that it has hardly been seen. At the end of the story, Hemming is left alone in his empty house, gazing out of a window at an empty future. The message of the film appears to be a warning to gay men in 1970 to watch out, especially those who think they may have found 'freedom' after the passing of the 1967 Act. Thank goodness for the birth of the Gay Liberation Movement the year after this film was released.

Other films of interest released in 1970

Film versions of Joe Orton's *Loot* and *Entertaining Mr Sloane* were produced. The latter was adapted for the screen by Clive Exton, and provided Beryl Reid with one of her most outrageous roles. She gave a memorable performance as the vulgar, middle-aged Kath who vies for the attentions of young Mr Sloane (Peter McEnery) with her creepy brother Ed, played by gay actor Harry Andrews; Hammer Films struck box office gold with *The Vampire Lovers* in which the beautiful Carmilla (Ingrid Pitt) seduced a household of women. There followed a brief cycle of lesbian vampire films including *Lust for a Vampire* (1970) and *Twins of Evil* (1971) which, says Andrea Weiss in *Vampires and Violets*, fully exploited 'the pornographic value of the relationship between the vampire and her victim';[3] in Ken Russell's *The Music Lovers* Richard Chamberlain played the tortured gay Russian composer Tchaikovsky.

Notes

1. Billy Wilder quoted in Doug McClelland, *Hollywood Talks Turkey: The Screen's Greatest Flops* (Faber, 1989), p. 279.
2. Parker Tyler, *Screening the Sexes: Homosexuality in the Movies* (Holt, Rinehart & Winston, 1972), pp. 338–9.
3. Andrea Weiss, *Vampires and Violets: Lesbians in the Cinema* (Cape, 1992), p. 88.

1971

The new decade began with an honour from one Queen to another. In January 1970 seventy-year-old Noel Coward was granted his long-overdue knighthood. Better late than never. For years the rumour spread that Coward had been denied recognition because he was gay. Says Graham Payn, his friend and companion:

> The accolade meant so much to him, though he was almost the last of his generation to become a theatrical knight. Olivier, Richardson, Gielgud, Redgrave, Guinness (the latter two much younger) had all preceded him, so when the news was made public, it was Alec (Guinness) who expressed the slightly embarrassed relief felt by his peers: 'We have been like a row of teeth with a front tooth missing. Now we can all smile again.'[1]

Not only did the Queen acknowledge Coward's contribution to the arts, but a knighthood was subsequently bestowed on Terence Rattigan in 1971. This royal 'approval' of gay men in the arts coincided with the birth of Britain's Gay Liberation Front. The first gay rights demonstration in Britain took place on 27 November 1970 when about 150 people marched across Highbury Fields in North London to protest against the prosecution of a gay man for allegedly importuning there. Although not yet known as a Gay Pride celebration, this demonstration is widely seen as the beginning of the annual events in Britain. In August 1971, 225 people took part in the first march in London organized by the fledgling Gay Liberation Front. 1972 was the year of the first official Gay Pride march. Two thousand people took part and threw a party in Hyde Park.

Come Together was a short documentary directed by John Shane 'for' the London Gay Liberation Front. It included footage of GLF members speaking at meetings, as well as sequences of activism and personal testimony. Says Richard Dyer:

Come Together organizes its material as a move from the personal experiences of being gay before GLF through the change it has made in people's lives to the political agenda for Gay Liberation. The opening sequence cuts between footage of meetings and talking heads, people recalling their life before GLF, then talking about what GLF has done for them. . . . Affirmation documentaries tend to conceal their interviewee's involvement in the movement or present it as an optional extra that some get into after they come out; in *Come Together* it is the movement itself that allows people to come out and feel good about themselves. As the film develops, the individual perspective expands into a collective one, with one form of gay collectivity, the gay scene, contrasted with the new one of gay liberation.[2]

Come Together captured the birth of the Gay Liberation Movement and was given an enthusiastic review in the eighth issue of *Gay News*. 'It is colourful, confused and rather appealing like GLF itself,' said Mike Coulson. 'By its warmth and vitality, the film should (if they ever manage to see it) convey a message of hope to timid provincials wistfully longing to escape from their closets.'

It is hardly likely that any closeted 'provincials' were able to see *Come Together* or, for that matter, mainstream British cinema audiences. They were more likely to have been exposed to an unexpected range of lesbian and gay images which were served up in an odd collection of films. The darkest James Bond thriller featured two of the nastiest gay killers ever seen on the screen. The Artful Dodger fell in love with Oliver in one of the most homoemotional of David Puttnam's films. In Sherwood Forest closet gay comedian Frankie Howerd had a brief encounter with a sissy Robin Hood. Peter Straker made a wonderfully camp but sexually ambiguous appearance in an underrated Ned Sherrin comedy. The Burtons indulged themselves in some queer activities. Liz bitched with her faggot confidante, and bedded Susannah York. Dick played a vicious gay thug who loves his mum. John Schlesinger, Peter Finch, Glenda Jackson and Murray Head were at their best in a mature, emotional melodrama and, finally, an artist called Derek Jarman was given his first movie job as a set designer on a Ken Russell production (*The Devils*). A few years later, as a director himself, he helped change the face of gay cinema.

Diamonds Are Forever

After a four-year absence, Sean Connery returned to the role of James Bond in *Diamonds Are Forever*. It starts with a catchy theme song belted out by gay icon Shirley Bassey, and two of the nastiest gay villains ever seen in the movies. Right at the beginning of the film we are introduced to overweight, balding Mr Kidd (Putter Smith) and his lover Mr Wind (Bruce Glover) who talks like Peter Lorre and sprays himself with perfume. Bond decides to call it aftershave. Observing a scorpion in the desert, 'one of nature's finest killers', Mr Wind says to his companion: 'One is never too old to learn from a master.' The deadly duo take great pleasure in forcing the scorpion down the back of a victim, the first in a series of killings. They survive until the end of the film, when they finally get their come-uppance from Bond. Posing as waiters on a ship, they prepare to serve a meal, complete with a time-bomb hidden inside a cake, to Bond and his female companion, but Bond recognizes Wind's 'perfume'. The gay killers come to a nasty end when Bond sets fire to Kidd, and shoves the bomb up Wind's arse, flinging him overboard just before it explodes. Looking pleased with himself, Bond says: 'Well, he certainly left with his tail between his legs.' This is one of the most horrific, and homophobic sequences in the history of cinema. As far as the heterosexual audience is concerned, the gay killers deserved to die. *Diamonds Are Forever* is one of the nastiest Bond films of all.

Melody

Filmed on location in Hammersmith and Lambeth, *Melody*, which was later given the alternative title *SWALK*, is a gentle, funny film about young love. It was conceived as a vehicle for Jack Wild and Mark Lester after they had achieved international stardom with the hit musical *Oliver!* The credits include David Puttnam (producer), Waris Hussein (director) and Alan Parker (story and screenplay), and the supporting cast featured wonderful comedy performances by the likes of Sheila Steafel, Kate Williams and Roy Kinnear. Set in South London, Wild plays Ornshaw, a scruffy, cheeky but lonely drummer with the local Boys' Brigade. He forms an attachment to the younger, prettier but decidedly middle-class Daniel Latimer (Lester). They attend the same school, and Ornshaw is keen to indulge in after-school activities with Latimer. One afternoon, while standing in a bus queue, he persuades the young boy to join him on an adventure 'up west' instead of going home. There follows scenes of the two lads larking about Trafalgar Square and Piccadilly Circus, eating popcorn, and Ornshaw taking the piss out of a street busker. On the soundtrack of this delightful sequence the Bee Gees sing a song called 'Give Your Best to Your Friends'.

When Latimer begins to take an interest in Melody (Tracy Hyde), a girl his own age, and the other kids taunt him about it, Ornshaw intervenes and protects him from them. At the school disco Latimer and Melody dance happily together, but they are shocked at Ornshaw's unexpected show of hostility towards girls. Finally, after Ornshaw and Latimer get into trouble and are punished by the headmaster, Ornshaw waits outside for Latimer. Melody is waiting too, but Ornshaw tries to get rid of her. When Latimer comes out of the headmaster's office, Ornshaw finally expresses his jealousy: 'I don't know why she's hanging around. Tell her to buzz off.' Latimer goes to Melody but Ornshaw tries to persuade the younger boy to stay with him. When Latimer and Melody run off together, Ornshaw is left alone, shouting: 'Danny! Danny! Danny!' It is a heartbreaking scene. By the end of the film, Ornshaw has reconciled himself to the fact that Latimer and Melody are an 'item'. He even arranges a mock 'wedding' ceremony for them, attended by a gang of schoolchildren, in a railway arch by some wasteground. But Ornshaw's attachment to Latimer is more than just friendship. It is emotional and, possibly, sexual. This is a theme which has surfaced in subsequent David Puttnam films. Says his biographer, Andrew Yule:

> When I commented on the homophilic aspects of many of David's movies to one of his friends and colleagues, I received a thought-provoking reply: 'David and women are a whole complex subject. This industry is full of men who fancy themselves with women. David's unique in that he charms men as well. Others can't be bothered. When David's making a film, the director in effect becomes his mistress. There's homoeroticism, buddies, in all Puttnam movies. That's because he had a very happy childhood with lots of other boys and he wants to relive that in his movies. He's like the writer who spends his whole life trying to figure out what happened in the first sixteen years, trying to recapture that

simplicity and innocence. That's the root of his interest in the friendship of male-bonding.'³

Up the Chastity Belt

Up the Chastity Belt was a sequel to the television comedy 'spin-off' *Up Pompeii*, but there were few laughs to be had. Its closeted gay star, Frankie Howerd, was light-hearted and cheeky but the script, co-authored by Sid Colin, Ray Galton and Alan Simpson, didn't deliver the goods. However, gay favourite Eartha Kitt provided some of the little fun there was by singing a song during the credits ('A Knight for My Nights') and making a brief appearance, and Godfrey Winn popped up as the Archbishop of Canterbury.

Set in the Middle Ages, the citizens of Nottingham think Lurkalot (Howerd) is King Richard and attempt to burn him at the stake, but he is saved by a swishy Robin Hood (Hugh Paddick) and his gay Merry Men. They're all screaming queens and, in Sherwood Forest, at Robin's camp, they chase each other in and out of the trees. Meanwhile Robin engages in an outrageous conversation with Lurkalot. 'Well, duckie, what do you think of our camp?' he asks. Replies Lurkalot: 'Oh, I think that's the word for it.' Says Robin: 'I designed them [clothes] myself. Mind you, I prefer our winter outfits best. Black leather. Cut very tight across the hips. Open-thonging up the chest. Of course we're not looking our best at the moment. Lost most of our sequins.' When Robin asks if he would like to meet the rest of the lads, Lurkalot replies: 'You mean the boys in the band?' Enter Mutch (Christopher Sandford) who is in a terrible state because he has laddered his tights. Robin offers to darn them for him. Finally, Lurkalot tells Robin he thinks it's marvellous the way he and his men rob the rich and give it to the poor. Replies Robin: 'You must be joking! We keep it all ourselves. How do you think we get all this bona drag? It doesn't grow on trees, you know.'

Girl Stroke Boy

The producer of *Up the Chastity Belt* was Ned Sherrin who was also responsible for producing (with Terry Glinwood) another comedy that year, *Girl Stroke Boy*. He also co-authored the screenplay with Caryl

Brahms, basing it on David Percival's play *Girlfriend* which starred Margaret Leighton and had a short run in London's West End in 1970. In the screen version Joan Greenwood replaced Leighton as Lettice Mason, a successful authoress – and mother from hell. 'Darling, I hope you will choose to do what you think is right, as long as you discuss it with me,' she tells her son Laurie (Clive Francis).

Lettice and her headmaster husband George (Michael Hordern) prepare a small dinner party to welcome home hunky Laurie. He arrives at their snowbound country retreat with his black partner, Jo (Peter Straker), but the Masons are unable to determine whether or not Jo is female. Jamaican-born Peter Straker, who starred in the original cast of the 1960s hit rock musical *Hair*, made his film debut as Jo. He was billed simply as Straker to preserve the ambiguous sexual identity of his character.

Lettice refuses to accept the possibility of her son being gay. 'In my day you wondered which man was going to ask you to dance, not which one was the man!' she says. When Peter Straker appears as Jo it is obvious he is an effeminate gay man, though he is supposed to be androgynous. Nevertheless, George believes Jo is a woman. Throughout the film, Laurie and Jo enjoy a tender, loving relationship. They are affectionate, warm and passionate towards each other. They kiss on the lips several times and Jo says to Laurie: 'We care for each other and show others we care.' Clive Francis and Peter Straker give convincing performances as the gay lovers and, together with John Schlesinger's better-known *Sunday, Bloody Sunday*, also released in 1971, this film broke new ground in the portrayal of gay relationships on the screen.

Girl Stroke Boy received a hostile reception from the critics which ensured that it was never seen again (except for one brief appearance on television in 1978 as a 'Saturday Adult Movie'). In the *Evening Standard* Alexander Walker called it a 'tedious, ill-made, appallingly-acted and directed piece of mindlessness' while Richard Afton said in the *Evening News*: 'It's difficult to understand how *Boy Stroke Girl* [sic] ever got made. It was one of the most stupid films I have seen. A one-word description would be putrid. . . it disgusted me. Seeing men kissing each other and making love is not my idea of entertainment.' But this witty, funny film has stood the test of time and should be revived more often. Said Ned Sherrin in his autobiography:

The plot sounds sleazy but the play handled it tactfully and amusingly and the parents and the lovers (played by Clive Francis and Peter Straker) gave elegant high comedy performances under Bob Kellett's direction. It has remained one of my favourite films and I could not understand the very severe press criticism it received. *Girl Stroke Boy* seemed to delight audiences until the press show, when dismay set in.[4]

Clive Francis had previously been seen as the young lodger in the 1968 television version of Joe Orton's *Entertaining Mr Sloane*. Co-starring Sheila Hancock and Edward Woodward it was, in many ways, superior to the 1970 film version.

Zee and Co

In *Zee and Co* (known as *X, Y and Zee* in America) Robert Blakeley (Michael Caine) is a successful architect married to the garish, loud-mouthed, party-loving Zee (Elizabeth Taylor). When he is introduced at a party to Stella (Susannah York), an attractive young designer, who is also a widow with two children, he is only too willing to respond. But after they fall in love, Zee takes several dramatic measures to get her husband back, not realizing they will result in an unexpected revelation from Stella.

Edna O'Brien's screenplay also includes two gay characters, though neither of them was of any use to the Gay Liberation Movement. Gordon (John Standing) is Zee's confidante, a nasty faggot who willingly agrees to assist Zee in destroying her husband's affair. 'He thinks he's really in love with this cow,' spits Zee. 'Then do it to *him*, dear,' Gordon responds. 'Have an affair with a gorgeous man!' Replies Zee: 'If your lot would stop increasing and multiplying, maybe there'd be someone left to do it with!' Says Gordon: 'There's no need to get personal or I shan't do your hair nicely.' Zee informs Gordon that Stella has a gay assistant working for her in her boutique who might prove useful. 'She's got this poncy little fag working for her and I want you to chat him up!' Gavin, the 'poncy little fag', is played by none other than Michael Cashman. He later found fame as gay Colin in the BBC television series *EastEnders*, and as a spokesperson for gay and lesbian equality.

After Zee has attempted suicide, Stella visits her in hospital. Zee encourages her to reveal the reason why she was expelled from school. In the following 'seduction' scene, Stella plays straight into Zee's hands. 'I fell in love with one of the nuns,' Stella tells her. 'What a silly thing to be expelled for,' Zee says. 'I kissed her while she was making me up for one of the school plays,' Stella explains. When she offers to peel Zee an orange, Zee says seductively 'I think I could get quite used to having you as my personal slave.' Replies Stella: 'Only available for limited engagements.' Then the two women hug each other.

Later, when Zee realizes that Robert is going to leave her for Stella, she visits Stella at her flat and *really* seduces her (off-camera). Asks Zee: 'A girl has to be quite grown up for kissing a nun. A child can't be expelled for falling in love. Were there other girls at school you fell in love with?' Zee starts stroking Stella, but not in a predatory way like Mercy Croft in *The Killing of Sister George*. The two women hug each other for the second time in the film, but Zee's seduction of Stella only goes so far. The two women do not kiss.

When Robert returns to the flat he is welcomed by a triumphant Zee. 'I'm just paying a little social visit,' she explains. Robert discovers Stella in bed. 'Leave me alone,' she tells him. He recognizes Zee's neck chain on the side table and asks Stella what has happened. 'I don't know,' she says. Zee enters and tells him: 'Don't worry. She's a bit confused. She'll be all right in a few days. Come on, daddy. Baby wants something to eat. It's been one hell of a day.'

Throughout the film, Zee is determined to keep her husband, and goes to extraordinary lengths to seduce her rival. But Elizabeth Taylor's 'seduction' of Susannah York is tentative, and lacks the passion of the attention she lavished on some of her former co-stars, like Lassie, Montgomery Clift, Paul Newman and Richard Burton. Otherwise Taylor's performance is outrageous enough to hold the attention of the audience. American critic Pauline Kael suggested that the film marked the 'coming out' of Taylor:

> A world-famous woman change[s] status and, I think, maybe get[s] in touch with the audience in a new egalitarian way. Her range has become even smaller. . . she's not enough of an actress to get by with the bruised and hurting bit. She's got to be active and brassy and bold; she's best when she lets her gift for mimicry and

for movie-colony sluttiness roll out. . . . The aging beauty has discovered in herself a gutsy, unrestrained spirit that knocks two very fine performances right off the screen. . . . She's Beverly Hills Chaucerian and that's as high and low as you can get.[5]

For her performance in *Zee and Co*, Elizabeth Taylor shared Italy's David Di Donatello prize for Best Foreign Actress with Glenda Jackson, who was named for *Sunday, Bloody Sunday*.

Villain

While Elizabeth Taylor was bedding pretty Susannah York in *Zee and Co*, her husband Richard Burton (as Vic Dakin) was bedding handsome Ian McShane (as Wolfe) in the crime thriller *Villain*. Dick Clement and Ian La Frenais based their screenplay on James Barlow's novel *The Burden of Proof*, and there is more than just a touch of East End villainy and violence to satisfy audiences with a lust for blood. Burton plays Dakin with an appalling cockney accent (it's even worse than Dick Van Dyke's in *Mary Poppins*, and that's saying something). He's an evil, sadistic brute who takes pleasure in beating and slicing up men, but he is kind to his elderly bedridden mother. There are parallels with the lives of the East End Kray twins, but too often *Villain* lapses into crude melodrama and, when it depicts violence, it is nothing more than an exploitation flick. There is no subtlety here. In one very disturbing scene, Dakin takes Wolfe upstairs to his bedroom where the younger man takes off his jacket and tie. The expectation is that Dakin will embrace him, but instead he punches him in the stomach and on to the bed. Standing over him, Dakin takes off his shirt and says: 'Take you to town tomorrow and get you some good suits.'

After making *Villain*, Richard Burton worked with Peter O'Toole on the screen version of Dylan Thomas's *Under Milk Wood*. He later recalled: 'A wicked devil that O'Toole. *Villain's* my second time in the part of a queer and he said to me, "It looks as though you've cornered the limp wrist market, duckie."'[6] It is sad to find a wonderful actor like Burton, who revealed enormous talent as a young man, ending up playing queer stereotypes in second-rate films like *Villain*. Needless to say, *Villain* was popular enough in Britain for him to be voted the number one box office attraction of 1971.

Sunday, Bloody Sunday

Sunday, Bloody Sunday was the first film directed by John Schlesinger after he had won an Oscar for his first American film, the homoemotional buddy movie *Midnight Cowboy* (1969), starring Jon Voight and Dustin Hoffman. In one way or another Schlesinger's earlier films had been concerned with the search for freedom from oppression. In his first feature, *A Kind of Loving* (1962), Schlesinger explored the limitations felt by working-class Vic (Alan Bates) after he gets married. Another working-class hero, *Billy Liar* (1963), played by Tom Courtenay, discovers freedom of expression through fantasy. With intelligence, sensitivity and honesty, *Sunday, Bloody Sunday* explores an emotional, bisexual triangle, involving three people in a painful search for love and happiness.

Alex Greville (Glenda Jackson), a divorced business consultant, is in love with the young bisexual designer and 'free spirit' Bob Elkin (Murray Head). However, their relationship is under considerable strain since Bob is also the lover of a middle-aged Jewish doctor, Daniel Hirsch (Peter Finch, a last-minute replacement for Ian Bannen who fell ill with viral pneumonia). When the emotional pressures on Bob become too great, he decides to leave them both.

When Glenda Jackson was sent Penelope Gilliatt's original screenplay, she knew straight away it was something special. In 1981 she said:

> I took the part simply because it was the best script I think I've ever seen. I admired John Schlesinger's work, so obviously I was keen to work with him and I was interested and sympathetic to the woman I played in the film.[7]

From the start it is clear this film is going to offer something different, especially in its depiction of a gay man. Dr Hirsch lives alone with his books, Mozart's *Cosi Fan Tutte*, middle-class respectability and Jewish faith. But, though he appears to be the familiar stereotype of an isolated gay man, on closer inspection it is evident this warm, compassionate man is resourceful. He copes *and* survives. At the end of the film, after he has been deserted by Bob, he talks directly to the camera. 'I miss him,' he says. 'But I *am* happy. Apart from missing him. All my life I've been looking for someone courageous and resourceful. He's not it. But something. We *were* something.' So *Sunday, Bloody Sunday* is not a gay film as such, it is a film about two mature people hanging on to a love affair with someone younger in the hope that it will bring eternal happiness, and one of them happens to be gay. At the end of the film they are left with their memories which, for them, is better than nothing. Schlesinger saw the film as a positive statement because it deals with people coping with life.

Hirsch is a kind, gentle man who is well-liked and trusted. When we see Hirsch and Bob together, it is clear the older man is head over heels in love, and their tender kiss on the lips, and subsequent lovemaking, is portrayed as something that is natural. It works because Peter Finch and Murray Head are totally unselfconscious and believable as the lovers. Head later recalled the atmosphere on the set when they came to film the kissing scene:

> The kiss! To me it was an infinitely simple gesture which caused ruptions right, left and centre. . . . I looked around and there were four or five photographers instead of the usual two. And a tenseness on the set. Everybody getting jumpy and I started to pick up the vibes of uneasiness. I thought, Sod them! This is ridiculous to get into this pitch over such a simple gesture of affection! So we began shooting and Peter was the easiest person in the world to get on with and do that sort of thing without any fuss. But there came a point in the shooting – I've never heard of it happening before – when the cameraman turned round and said to Schlesinger, 'John, is this really necessary?' and John snapped, 'Yes, of course it is!'. . . . So I started to think about the older generation. . . where the roles had to be clearly defined. . . they suppressed things in themselves so much, that when confronted with a symbolic gesture like the kiss, what really disturbed them about it was that it could happen with such *ease*.[8]

Until 1971, male kissing and lovemaking had not been seen in a mainstream film, and it was upsetting for some people. One of them was Shirley Bassey, a former lover of Peter Finch, and a woman whose career as an internationally acclaimed singer would not have been possible without the support of her gay fans. When the film was released, it was reported that the sight of Finch and Head kissing had made her feel sick to her stomach, forcing her to leave the cinema. One can only applaud Schlesinger for his determination not to make any compromises. He later said: 'The male kiss shocked everybody. I overheard a remark by a couple sitting behind me at a preview as they walked out: "Harry, this is not a film for nice people!" It was ahead of its time.'[9] It is difficult to agree with this statement because *Sunday, Bloody Sunday* was very much *of* its time, and a major turning point in the depiction of gays in British cinema.

It seems fitting that *Brief Encounters* should end with an intelligent film which has a leading gay character. It is also a 'gay' British film which has received more international film awards than any other. These include five British Academy Awards for Best Film, Director, Editing, Actor (Finch) and Actress (Jackson). Nominations went to Screenplay (Gilliatt, she lost to Harold Pinter who won for *The Go-Between*), Cinematography and Sound. In Britain, Finch won the Variety Club of Great Britain Award for Best Film Actor. In France, Finch and Jackson received L'Etoile de Cristal (Crystal Star) awards for Best Foreign Actor and Actress. In Italy, Jackson shared the David Di Donatello prize for Best Foreign Actress with Elizabeth Taylor (*Zee and Co*) and Schlesinger was named Best Foreign Director. In America, Finch and Gilliatt were honoured by the National Society of Film Critics, and Gilliatt shared the New York Film Critics Circle Best Screenplay award with Peter Bogdanovich and Larry McMurty (*The Last Picture Show*). *Sunday, Bloody Sunday* also received a Golden Globe for Best English-Language Foreign Film, and four Oscar nominations (Schlesinger, Finch, Jackson and Gilliatt).

Notes

1. Graham Payn with Barry Day, *My Life with Noel Coward* (Applause, 1994), p. 239.
2. Richard Dyer, *Now You See It: Studies on Lesbian and Gay Film* (Routledge, 1990), pp. 260–61.
3. Andrew Yule, *Enigma: David Puttnam, The Story So Far* (Mainstream Publishing, 1988), p. 409.
4. Ned Sherrin, *A Small Thing: Like an Earthquake* (Weidenfeld & Nicolson, 1983), p. 208.
5. Pauline Kael, *New Yorker*, 12 February 1972.
6. John Cottrell and Fergus Cashin, *Richard Burton* (Coronet, 1974), p. 377.
7. Glenda Jackson interviewed by John Preston in *Radio Times*, 19–25 September 1981.
8. Elaine Dundy, *Finch, Bloody Finch* (Michael Joseph, 1980), pp. 310–11.
9. John Schlesinger interviewed by Mat Snow in *Empire*, March 1991.

Appendix
The *Victim* letters

St John Adlard

I saw *Victim* in King's Lynn, Norfolk and I did at that time feel that it was a film about London gays. In London it was much easier to be 'out' as far as one could in those days. In the provinces it was a case of remaining firmly in the closet and the lack of gay bars reinforced this. Indeed, there was only one known gay bar in the whole of Norfolk – the Mischief Tavern in Norwich.

A gay subculture definitely did exist at the time of the film's release. In the provinces this existed mostly in the form of teas at gay households and, of course, cruising and trips to London to partake of the entertainments offered by the huge number of pubs and clubs, underground as it may have been.

I saw the film on my own and I think I knew about its contents from reading film reviews in the serious press. I cannot recollect any particular audience reaction and was only able to discuss it with my one gay friend in King's Lynn, and with gay friends in London when I went there. The film had a huge effect, for the good, on the thinking of those who saw it.

I feel that I can now accept Bogarde's claim that he made the film to show up the dreadful stigma attached to gays at that time, after all, he was a leading heart throb and the film could have seriously damaged his career. However, I have always been uncomfortable with him, even in *Victim*. To my mind, since making that film, he has done immense damage to the advancement of gay rights in that he is the acceptable face of gayness to most heterosexuals.

R. A. Atcherley

I can confirm that *Victim* was a tolerably accurate picture of life for homosexuals around 1961. It was a bit too upper class in emphasis, and the figure of the blackmailer was very far-fetched. But certainly fear of blackmail was an important factor for professional people. No one in those days would have dared to 'come out'. That started in the early 1970s with the Gay Liberation Front.

In London there was a 'scene' – quite a few gay clubs/bars where gays could meet each other; somewhere, if you were so inclined, you could pick up a 'rent boy'. Everything, however, was quite covert and secret and surrounded by fear, shame and guilt.

John Bennett

I remember very clearly the day in 1957 when the Wolfenden Report was issued. I was thirteen at the time and my paper delivery round took an hour longer than usual as I read every word in every paper.

When *Victim* was released I was seventeen and at school in Farnham in Surrey. It was there that I went, rather bravely, to see it. My first impression was an overwhelming sense of identification with the gay characters. The diversity of types portrayed was very liberating for me. The second point was that the film was, in my view, very well done with some superb acting which gave it so much more reality. The sad ending was no surprise given the culture of the time.

While it took me a number of years after that to sort myself out as a gay man I am certain that *Victim* had a very positive effect on me as a teenager. Incidentally I saw a re-run on television some two years ago and ended up crying for most of the last half hour! It is a wonderful reflection of life in 1961.

Douglas Brown

I saw *Victim* at its West End première in 1961. The grapevine had it that the then taboo topic would be ventilated. Inside the atmosphere was exciting and there was an obviously 'vested interested' audience, i.e. a gay majority audience. I viewed it with a homosexual friend. We enjoyed the arts generally. I cannot remember precisely how I knew it would deal with the theme of homosexuality, maybe my friend mentioned it as he moved more in those circles? I think there had been the odd leaked press item that the film would be 'controversial' and important to Bogarde's career.

Bogarde was always a superb actor. He was just right for the part of Melville Farr in *Victim* as was Peter McEnery as Barrett. Tactful, moving, understated, they brought near tears to the eyes. The discreetness, the fact that they did not obviously look like homosexuals was, in fact, how it was in real life then – and now! I was a civil servant all my life, sober-suited, dull looking (my verbal according to company is quite otherwise!). I was the very model of a model civil servant. I couldn't help my looks. I couldn't help my basic persuasion.

The atmosphere was electric when Dirk Bogarde, as a married barrister, taxed with his homosexual relationship, paused, then blurted out: '. . . because I *wanted* him!' At the end there was a prolonged applause. We felt some kind of breakthrough had been achieved. On leaving the cinema I was given a new magazine, *Manpower* (akin to *New Society*) containing a plea for law reform on male homosexuality – and volunteers were needed. Acutely aware of the mental anguish caused by the current law and very much in sympathy with those wishing to alleviate such distress which often led to suicide, I went along.

(After attending the première of *Victim*, where he received a copy of *Manpower*, Douglas Brown joined the newly formed Albany Trust (The Homosexual Law Reform League) as a 'modest voluntary helper'.)

Christopher Coates

A friend and I saw *Victim* at the Odeon, Leicester Square one Saturday afternoon. Reviews had been favourable, even respectful (it was no secret what *Victim* was about) and we both felt a bit bold going to see a film which had an X certificate because it was about 'us'.

The makers of the film steered a careful course. They wanted to agitate, not shock. They also wanted to entertain. *Victim* is a plea for tolerance as well as for a new law. It works well as a thriller too. Furtiveness and terror are well conveyed. I would definitely classify *Victim* as a landmark movie.

In some ways attitudes haven't changed. The scene where Farr meets the well-to-do set who confess their secret passion and advise him to lie low could still happen in the 1990s. In 1961 homosexuality was never mentioned or discussed in my middle-class environment. If it was, it was viewed as nasty, disgraceful, unacceptable.

I can't remember discussing the film with anyone else (certainly not in depth) except the friend I saw it with. I think we hoped it might change the law. Subconsciously we were sick of being 'criminal'. A female colleague at work did remark (having seen *Victim*) that she thought 'men like that' shouldn't be imprisoned.

I remember sitting near a schoolboy on the upper deck of a bus. As we passed a cinema near Golders Green which was showing *Victim*, he whispered hoarsely to his chum: 'That's a film about. . . (pause). . . *queers!*'

Dave

I came into the gay scene in 1947 and by the time 1957 had arrived I was well established in the homosexual world. I was then twenty-six years old. As I see it today, while the expressions for homosexuality are much more varied and open, nevertheless the basic approach and contact with gays remains pretty well the same. That is to say via the age-old system of the sports club, toilets and well-known open-air spaces, these are now what they were then, the main areas of contact.

People were the same then as they are today: two-faced, hypocritical and full of shit about homosexuals. The medical attitude was that it was an illness, that if treated successfully, the homosexual would become normal, whatever that meant, like have sex with their sons as so many, so-called normal fathers did. I know because I have slept with men who have been abused by their fathers, the same as I have slept with policemen and priests.

In 1959 I was sent to prison for five years for robbery and there I met young men who had been given prison sentences for up to four years for homosexual acts. What a stupid place to send them. To me that was a shocking thing to do to people, and even now I feel sick that such a thing could have been allowed. The fear of the police was very strong. People suffer in the same way today as they did then, not so much for being caught, but being exposed as homosexuals to their families and friends, neighbours, and the community in general. The acceptance of homosexuals is very difficult for people today as it was then. Perhaps we have more freedom, but acceptance I don't think so.

It took ten years from the report of the Wolfenden Committee for those little shits in Parliament to pass the Act. In that ten-year space of time countless lives were unnecessarily ruined and destroyed. To us homosexuals going about our daily lives the Act made very little difference as it seemed we had been doing what the Act said we could do all the time.

Eddy

In 1957 I had just left secondary modern school at sixteen knowing, as I had always known, that I was very definitely homosexual, and not in the least bit bothered by the fact! I am very lucky in that my sexuality has never caused any problems for me.

The gay scene in those days was much nicer than it is now. There were so many 'characters'. I think that we were much more respectable, in our own way, in those days. There was much more fun being gay then. We didn't take being gay so seriously as people do now. And – thank goodness – we didn't clone. My personal view of clones is that they have done as much for homosexuality as Cromwell did for church architecture! Another feature of being gay in the late 1950s and early 1960s was the fact that we were always impeccably dressed.

As a lad I did get something of a shock when, in the Red Lion in Preston, I saw other men openly wearing make-up. In the Preston, and nearby Blackpool areas, there were a constant round of parties to go to, and to be gay in those days was almost a kind of freemasonry. It was to be someone rather exclusive! I well remember a straight friend (who didn't know I was gay) being very envious of the parties to which I was invited, and pleading with me to take him along. I can't recall how I explained that one away!

Someone once said that television had killed the art of conversation. Rubbish! Discos did that. The gay scene in the 1950s and 1960s was much more a matter of friends meeting for a drink, a good old gossip, and slagging off all and sundry, including each other. It was riotous! Individuality seems all too rare on the gay scene these days.

I saw *Victim* in Blackpool which was then, and even more so now, the gay 'capital' of north-west England. I viewed the film alone, and did not tell anyone that I was going to see this particular film. On entering the cinema everyone was given a close scrutiny by two men who I assumed were plain clothes police. During the film, several members of the public walked out of the cinema complaining. The response to the film from homosexuals at the time was predominantly sympathetic, although some older homosexuals objected to any exposure of the subject. I only discussed the film in homosexual bars and in the workplace, with fellow homosexuals. Discussion of the film in any other circumstances would have been unthinkable in 1961. We, in north-west England, certainly did not regard London as the only place where homosexuals existed! I felt very strongly that the film represented homosexuals throughout the country.

It never occurred to me that the motives for making the film were to exploit the publicity surrounding the Wolfenden Report. I am sure the motives of the producer and director were genuine, and that they were serious about making a film which was genuinely sympathetic and positive towards homosexuals. Yes! They did succeed.

Dirk Bogarde's participation in the film was most welcome. For such a 'heart-throb' star of that era to create the role he did was very courageous. One can only allow oneself a private, personal view as to his motives! His portrayal of the character was, as with everything he has done, considered and considerate, honest, accurate and sympathetic.

Victim did portray gay life in those days quite accurately. I saw the film several times, and also read the book of the film. I also remember, as a teenager, reading a book entitled *A Way of Life* by Peter Wildeblood, which made a big impression on me.

To sum up, there has always been, and I suppose always will be, prejudice against gays, but it didn't seem so prevalent in the 1950s and 1960s. Then again, the popular press was much more responsible, generally speaking, than today. Nor did there seem to be so much police harrassment then, if we kept ourselves to ourselves, and were well-behaved. The 'scene' was much more friendly, close-knit, with more characters and much more individuality. I have often heard older gays bemoan the fact that we were partly de-criminalized in 1967. No doubt the 'little boys stealing apples' syndrome! Presumably the thrill of doing something illegal made for more fun!

Alan Goodrum

In 1957 I was eighteen years old. So in my youthful years, being homosexual, I was officially a 'criminal'. I was brought up in a fairly small town (Lowestoft in Suffolk) and it was difficult in those years to contact anybody else who was gay. There were no pubs or clubs to visit and no gay organizations to contact. Obviously because of the legal position you could not openly state that you were gay or openly appear to be. I tried to make sure that nobody would guess that I was a homosexual. . . . The ironical thing is that although homosexuality was still illegal between 1957 to 1967 I think there was more public understanding and support for a change then than there is now and people are more anti-gay now as far as I can see.

Yes, I think the film *Victim* with Dirk Bogarde was fairly accurate in its representation of gay men at that time. Blackmail was quite common against gay men which was a strong reason for changing the law. In the film Dirk Bogarde plays the part of a married gay and I think there were more married gays in those days than now because (a) it took suspicion away from them that they might be gay and made them appear more respectable and 'normal' and (b) it was considered by most so-called 'experts' to help men to become 'normal' if they married (of course it did no such thing).

John Hall

I declared my irrevocable homosexuality in 1946 – long before we became legal. I'm happy to say that my admission never lost me a friend! I did not consider that one only found queers in London. But I had to go to London – during a leave from the army – to realize my own homosexuality. But I then recognized all the opportunities I had not understood during my life in Nottinghamshire, and I deeply regretted at least 50 per cent of them!

My partner and I had been together for eight years in 1961, and were together for twenty-seven years until he was unfaithful to me by dying in 1980! At least 60 per cent of our friends were heterosexual who, since neither of us had ever been 'in the closet', were able to talk to us. They were all sympathetic – happy that we had no fears greater than our love – and sorry for those who couldn't overcome the pressures of convention and were condemned to pseudo-bisexuality. Both mentally and physically.

My partner and I saw *Victim* in 1961 and knew the homosexual content before seeing it. We were grateful to Bogarde for his courage in accepting the role. We saw it in a comfortable West End cinema – sort of opposite the Adelphi in the Strand. It no longer exists. I remember the audience as mixed – and quiet, subdued or thoughtful. Comments seemed to be quiet and private also. After all, it wasn't a musical and queers can't whistle anyway. The homosexuals we knew all found the film sympathetic and helpful – some of the more outrageous wished there had been a few more overt actions – kissing, a bed, a bare bum – not realizing how this would have ruined the film and public acceptance.

John Hawker

I did see *Victim* on its initial release and was much moved by it at the time, especially by the Peter McEnery character. Of course it's dated now but quite a good social document for all that and not to be derided, I think. I went especially to see the film in the West End rather than see it in a local (Purley) cinema on release. I was on my own. I was aware of the homosexual content before I saw it from reviews (Dilys Powell, in the *Sunday Times*, spoke well of it). I never discussed the film, or heard it discussed either at the time I saw it, or after. It was my belief that homosexuals found the film sympathetic. I didn't know about a gay sub-culture in 1961 but I think I would have taken the view that homosexuals who went to university would have had 'wider knowledge', and since most of them would have come to university via public school, I daresay that helped.

Kenneth Keenan

I saw *Victim* alone in St Martins Lane in London, and again in Salford, Manchester. Before I went I was not at all aware of its homosexual content. I went to see *Victim* because I was in love with Dirk Bogarde! Homosexuals (known to me) found the film sympathetic, helpful and, above all, totally realistic. My view too! At the time of its release I was not able to discuss it in public at all. Only in private, in a friend's house in Wigan. Six of us discussed it. We all lived near each other, but were definitely in the 'closet'.

I don't think that Dearden and Relph exploited us. I am sure their motives were genuine and they succeeded in making a positive film about us. Dirk Bogarde (my hero!!!) made a very accurate portrayal of homosexuality.

Derek Metheringham

I went to a public school and I was always mad on the theatre – going each week for some forty years. Films were only seen in the main because I fancied the leading man – Tyrone Power, Gregory Peck, etc. My only other passion was, and is, Bette Davis.

I had left home in 1951 at twenty-four and for a few months ended up in a den of iniquity in Hackney. I remember the owner saying one set of neighbours were sympathetic – the others not. We all were very low key and dressed conservatively (small 'c'). If we had done half of what goes on today we would have been inside. I remember feeling how diabolical it was that the police could enter one's home at any time. I remember police entrapment was rife.

I saw *Victim* in London in a West End cinema. I saw it on my own. I was probably aware of the homosexual theme as Bogarde received publicity for being 'courageous'. It was advertised as a thriller and I went along because I enjoyed *Sapphire* by the same team, not because I was a Bogarde fan in any way. I found the film sympathetic. My oldest and campest friend says it was a talking point, a great breakthrough and Bogarde was brave to do it. It was a reasonable portrait of the times. I suppose in retrospect it was quite daring – whether one believed in it depended on one's lifestyle. Censorship at that time was pretty pathetic.

Don Minifie

Dearden and Relph (and their writer Janet Green) were known for tackling controversial subjects – racism in *Sapphire* and religious bigotry in *Life for Ruth*, but the conventions of the day only allowed them to put their topics into thriller-style formats. In *Victim* the liberal viewpoint which they appeared to hold was given to the sympathetic, non-controversial police inspector played by John Barrie. I think they were wholly sincere. Indeed they were amongst the only British film-makers of the time to tackle thorny subjects, and shrewd enough to see that the only viable approach for the early 1960s was to put the screenplay into a whodunnit form. The two blackmailers in *Victim* are, after all, horrid old witch-and-stock, 1960s villains. Neither of them are people the audience can sympathize with. Green could have made them nicer people but she didn't.

Films and Filming (October 1961) found *Victim* to be brave and crusading but not very good as a film. Oddly, given that in the 1960s and 1970s *Films and Filming* was a 'closet' gay magazine, an unofficial gay, er, organ. Hardly a copy went by without a photo showing you whether Alain Delon or Udo Kier 'dressed' to the left or right.

A letter about the film was published in the magazine pointing out, interestingly, that Dearden and Relph had bought the screen rights for Simon Raven's novel *Feathers of Death* which had a gay theme. For whatever reason, perhaps because they did not want to be pigeon-holed as gay film-makers, Dearden and Relph never saw this project through.

Tony Newton

I saw *Victim* in early 1962 when I was seventeen in Sussex. I went alone. Though that part of Sussex was near to Brighton, where undoubtedly there was a gay milieu, (a) I was still at school (b) I had no money and (c) I was still very unsure of myself in pubs of any kind.

I had never had a conversation with anyone about homosexuals which wasn't purely adolescent and in which I was concealing my own gayness. I can't recall the view being expressed that 'you only get gays in London'. I suppose in a sense I didn't think you got them anywhere, as the whole world seemed to be against the idea.

I did not at all see *Victim* as being about London homosexuals. It could have been set in Anytown, England, but one thing was for sure: it wasn't Bexhill or Hastings!

I was most certainly highly aware of the content of the film. As a trainee *Observer* reader, I probably read the film review in 1961, but my main information would have been from reading between the lines in the trailer the week before (you know how soon a young gay learns how to read between the lines!). Therefore I went to see *Victim* as a film about homosexuality, and I didn't have to account to my parents at all because it was a thriller with Dirk Bogarde. I went to the pictures a lot anyway.

I have no recollection of hearing any reactions. I remember thinking that many people would find the idea of homosexuals disgusting but that was based on my reading in the media and the general disdain I picked up in school about 'bum-boys', etc. I don't think I talked to anyone about *Victim* until about 1966 when I first came into the gay milieu in my last year at Oxford. Even then I think it was largely based on speculation about Dirk Bogarde's sexual orientation.

The reality of the film was still a late-1960s reality. Gay liberation seemed a long way off and people were conditioned to secrecy. The film cannot, therefore, be regarded as helpful in any political sense, though it may have been reassuring that one was not alone. I certainly reacted that way. I was glad to know that I was part of a scene. Otherwise it was upsetting. The message was about 'stop being homosexual', homosexuals commit suicide, or get blackmailed. The fact that the police inspector was in favour of the Wolfenden recommendations did very little to reassure me that I was safe being gay.

The success of *Victim* was in creating a reality – it was realistic. It must have helped to shape opinion in favour of law reform. The decision to use popular actors like Dennis Price and Donald Churchill as the gay characters was obviously deliberate, as was the exclusion of any really offensive stereotypes. In that sense they performed a real service. Blackmail was real (and continued to be real well after the 1967 Act). The most positive message was that the police would deal with blackmailers. It was realistic about the fear gays had of the police in revealing that they were victims of extortion.

Dirk Bogarde's presence obviously fetched in audiences, despite his not having had a very big film success for some time before. By appearing in *Victim* Bogarde got to play other sexually ambiguous characters in adult movies. He always was the best-looking British film star of the 1950s and 1960s and his film persona was established as being sensitively heterosexual. Lots of other stars would just have been too bluff (Richard Todd, Kenneth More, Peter Finch) or too young, or too old. Bogarde was just so right as someone that a person could worship from afar, as Barrett was supposed to have done. The character finally came out and he was brave, dashing and very decorative. It was good to have a hero.

David Nott

I came to London from the provinces and yes, I suppose London was seen as 'sin city', but I can't think that anyone other than the most naive thought it was the only place where homosexuals congregated. There was a feeling, especially from the kind of working-class background that I came from, that queers were decadent, upper-crust type people. I wouldn't say that people who go to university have any wider knowledge of the arts, gay culture or literature, than anyone else. In fact a lot of them have less. You may recall the case of Lord Montague who was imprisoned along with his friends for having a jolly time with boy scouts and young 'working-class' airmen. Yes, I think the Wildean, Victorian concept of gays lived on in the 1950s and early 1960s when it very definitely all began to change!

I recall seeing *Victim* the first time it came out. It was seen as a breakthrough in film-making, the first film that discussed homosexuality. It was somewhat overrated but it was a start. I thought the film was a bit patronizing. It perpetuated the class thing, about nice middle-class people who didn't do such nasty things, while the unfortunate youth in the film was very working class. I remember that. It was well acted, and good British actors were used, but it was all a bit turgid. It must have been like that in many middle-class homes. I remember a German film called *Third Sex* which was of more interest.

Ken Rhodes

I first saw *Victim* at the Odeon cinema in Leicester Square, the day it opened its initial run in 1961. I went along straight from work at about 5.30pm only to find a long queue stretching round the alley beside the cinema. As I walked to the end of the queue I found myself nodding to numerous acquaintances I had made during my then, fourteen years in London. It was rather amusing but they had also rushed to see this film, full of curiosity as to how it would deal with its subject matter, homosexual life in London, then very rare on screen.

I was alone and I was aware of the subject through film magazines and press reviews of the film. Naturally its homosexual subject was referred to as this is what made it stand out from the average thriller. There had been a lot of discussion about it in the press.

The film was made by a very respectable producer/director team (Relph and Dearden) and was done with discretion and sincerity. There were no scenes put in just to shock. As a result it was well received by the press and public. I heard no adverse remarks from the audience.

Most homosexuals seemed to find it both helpful and sympathetic and giving a fair impression of various types in that world. The girls at my factory who saw it were not shocked or surprised but saw it as a good film with a (then) unfamiliar theme. It was not a subject of any special discussion amongst my friends and co-workers, just discussed as any film would be with perhaps a slight emphasis on Dirk Bogarde's courage in taking on such a role.

I definitely feel that the film-makers' motives were genuine and that they were serious in their endeavours. It was a successful breakthrough.

Bogarde was playing a bisexual, a married barrister who tried to hide a relationship he had with a young man. His playing of the part did seem honest and sincere and he was praised in the press for his courage for taking on such a role and risking the loss of his adoring female following and for displaying hitherto hidden depths as an actor.

I wouldn't say there was a gay sub-culture in Britain at this time. From my experience, provincial cities from as far back as the 1940s had their bars frequented by homosexuals as had London where there were also several gay clubs. As far as I know there were no gay newspapers or magazines. There were gay novels and most gays (of all classes) heard of them and, if they were readers, read them. There didn't seem to be any class barriers in the gay world and in these bars and clubs you would find men from all walks of life mixing happily.

Most gays seemed to know of the gay writers, actors, artists, musicians, etc. in the arts, possibly because it was a small world and rife for gossip. If you went to the theatre and concerts or opera and ballet, you were naturally more interested in hearing who in those worlds were gay.

Michael A. Rutt

Of all the films of the early 1960s which dealt with gay topics, perhaps *Victim* was the most heralded and awaited, with great expectations, by the gay community. We were still 'criminals' in the eyes of the law, even when living together in loving one-to-one relationships.

The impact of seeing this film in Leicester Square on its initial West End release was an experience which stays in the memory. Not only was it superbly acted by Dirk Bogarde and Sylvia Syms, and indeed the rest of the cast, but tackled the 'taboo' subject of homosexuality with a previously unseen candour and authenticity. This movie did much to bring about the 1967 Act.

P. M. Scott

In the early 1960s I was an under-age youth, having escaped the stifling life of a small market town in East Anglia for the 'freedom' of London life.

I vividly remember what it was like to be gay in those days. Yes, we were well and truly 'in the closet' but we were united by a common bond which, on reflection, has been disappearing under waves of gay liberation and gay politics.

To be gay in the 1960s was very much a Jekyll and Hyde kind of life. One knew that to be gay was to be different. To socialize and find one's own kind was of major importance. The mecca of this was the drinking club. Quite a few of these were tucked away in dingy West End streets.

There were also gay pubs which were overflowing with gay strangers who were given open invitations to join many of the parties that were held at weekends. Many gays talked in a slang 'in' language and were much more jovial and 'camp' than they seem today.

I remember seeing *Victim* on its initial release at an Odeon in North London. I went to the cinema at least twice a week in those days. I remember seeing the trailer to *Victim* which had a certain fascinating ambiguity about it. This was made much clearer when I read an article in a movie magazine highlighting the subject matter – referred to as the 'twilight world' – and how Dirk Bogarde was taking on the most daring role of his career. I remember walking round the block several times before I could pluck up the courage to go in. I knew the majority of the audience would be gay but to face the cashier to buy a ticket was my first 'coming out' statement.

In those days to even discuss a film like *Victim* would have made me feel nervous and scared that the finger would be pointed and that I would be held to ridicule.

The film authentically captured the deception and fear which were the guiding factors of the life of gays at that time. It seemed sympathetic even if its 'hero' was a married man caught up in a blackmail ring. All the gays portrayed were hiding in fear of being 'found out' – all were victims leading double lives, made to feel they were criminals and leading bad lives. A scene where an elderly hairdresser was threatened by a blackmailing thug and had a heart attack was, I remember, very frightening. I recall that fear very vividly together with the damp palms to this day.

If nothing else, *Victim* did highlight the unhappy lot of the gay man at that time but it also used it for its provocative background to highlight a daring theme for entertainment purposes, in a climate where homosexuality was thought to be something 'unnatural' and not spoken of.

Looking back on it, its most positive attitude was to portray gay men coming from all classes of society and all walks of life – something I had not seen portrayed before.

David J. Sherlock

A very happy childhood (born 1947) in Cheshire coincided with a boarding school education in North Wales (1956–65) and so I was sheltered considerably from the profound social changes going on around me. However, a liberal schooling enabled me to grow up in an atmosphere of trust and confidence that most of my fellow men were OK and that many of them were gay and were quite successful and well adjusted.

Out in the big wide world the move towards a liberal attitude was very strong after the Vassall spy scandal and the horrors of McCarthyism. There is a link with the spy scandals and Washington's British Embassy purges (likewise London's American Embassy was 'purged' of gays, thought to be a security risk). This infuriated Liberals, Tories and Labour alike as did the use of *agents provocateurs* when gay men were cottaging. Sir John Gielgud was arrested for cottaging while appearing in a play in the West End and after he was released, Edith Evans said to him, the assembled cast and the audience before the play started: 'John, we hear you've been a very naughty boy. Let us hear no more of it. Shall we get on with the play?' When Gielgud made his entrance he was given a standing ovation. That gives a little insight into the period and the general reaction to witch-hunting.

I was into theatre, and the Royal Shakespeare Company in Stratford were making big strides with new actors who were working class. In 1961, when I was a fourteen-year-old schoolboy, I attended the RSC season with two school friends (and no parental guidance) and saw

Peter McEnery as Laertes, Tybalt and Clarence on consecutive nights. I fell in love with this guy – still with his short haircut from playing the working-class lad in *Victim*. I was fully aware of the film although I had not seen it, but I read the reviews. The two Oscar Wilde films and *Victim* did stimulate debate.

I was so starstruck during my first time in Stratford I collared Peter McEnery in the High Street and told him I thought he was a brilliant actor. I begged him for his autograph and he looked *terrified!* I was only fourteen for God's sake! He was receiving a great deal of attention from the press at the time, for *Victim* and his first season at Stratford, and here he was, being accosted by a very forward youth in his best short haircut and wearing a white mac with a scarlet lining – the nearest thing a would-be 'mod's' mum would let him buy! Peter McEnery saved himself from this embarrassing predicament by grabbing the nearest passing actress and arming her down the High Street! I was so embarrassed on seeing his reaction but it made my day, in fact week, month, year!

Afterwards I realized this was probably the reaction he was getting from a number of young men who had seen him in *Victim*, and fancied him, though, of course, I hadn't seen the film. I saw it much later. I still have photos of him from that period.

George Toland

I arrived in London in March 1961 from west Devon to find work. I had no idea about any homosexual sub-culture, and had no idea how to go about meeting other homosexuals. I have turned up my diary for 1961 to see what I, then just twenty-two years old, wrote about the film *Victim*, which I saw in a West End cinema.

Thursday, 31 August 1961

Victim – and for me a lesson in how not to become one. That is the title of the film and it presented – for me – an eyeopener on the world of which I am, by nature, a part. The fear created by blackmail must be terribly great and I am all too well aware of how close to that fear and danger I am likely to come. I am hardly worth blackmailing from the financial point of view, and I've little to lose anyway. However, the film is a perfect warning to all concerned how to avoid the pitfalls. It was letters which exposed the Wilde–Douglas affair, and in this film it was the same. I'll never commit anything to paper in that aspect, and destroy all I may receive.

It was a brave film to make and the actors showed a reckless kind of bravado in appearing in such a film. It could not have been easy for Dirk Bogarde or Dennis Price, of whom I have heard things mentioned.

I have seen the film a number of times over the years since then, and realize that it is dated in many ways, but for me as a callow twenty-two-year-old in 1961 it really was a watershed in my awareness of gay life.

Late in 1962 I was seduced (willingly) by a policeman's son at Heathrow, and have gaily trod the primrose path to ruin ever since. I really 'came out' in 1970 when the Campaign for Homosexual Equality began in London, and I became a leading light within it.

Anon

I often feel that I have lived a lie all my life and that I will be relieved to reach the end of it without discovery. Consequently, I do not fear the thoughts of dying – I am more afraid of living. I have a saying which often crosses my mind – 'that I have been dead most of my life'. I cannot 'come out' – it is too late to bother anyway. I have been married twenty-seven years and produced two beautiful daughters so you see I have to carry on this charade to the end.

I wish I could say 'I lived *my* life *my* way' (how courageous that would have been) but I have lived it anyone's way *but* mine. It is a great shame for my gayness is me at my best – then I sparkle!

Appendix
The critics' reaction to *Victim*

Britain

The Rank Organization is to make a film about homosexuality starring Dirk Bogarde. But my information is that the subject will make its central character, a middle-aged barrister, only a potential homosexual. The reason: The studios are afraid that their top contract star for fifteen years would lose his female following if he played an honest queer. . . . If *Victim* at least points to the plight of millions who, because of Parliament's refusal to amend the law, are open to blackmail because their promiscuity is homosexual rather than adulterous it may do some good. But if it implies, as is the case of some cheap literature, that homosexuals exist only among a low-life criminal group, then it will add little to public enlightment.

(Peter Warren, *Films and Filming*, April 1961)

The homosexuals in the picture are criminals in no sense other than that they break the law by the very fact of their homosexuality. The film puts forward the same point of view as the Wolfenden Committee, that the law should be changed. Contrary to suggesting homosexuals 'exist only among a low-life criminal group', the film shows that homosexuality may be found in otherwise completely responsible citizens in every strata of society.

(Michael Relph, *Films and Filming*, May 1961)

I should like to correct a very false and inaccurate remark made in your April issue. The Rank Organization is *not* making *Victim* and merely has a financial interest in the subject with no controls. The film is being made by Allied Film Makers, that is, Michael Relph and Basil Dearden. The script was sent to me early in December and I accepted this as it stood with no changes or alterations whatsoever, neither has the Rank Organization requested any on my behalf.

The subject in question is not an 'examination' of homosexuality but deals simply with the break-up and destruction of a man's marriage and life owing to the fact that he is flawed by homosexual tendencies.

It is distressing, in a paper of your kind, to read such inaccurate reporting, especially for once when one is trying to get out of the Simon Sparrow category (however excellent and delightful he was to play) and join forces with a team who are honestly trying to develop with a new and exciting trend in the cinema today.

(Dirk Bogarde, *Films and Filming*, May 1961)

We are grateful to Mr Relph and Mr Bogarde for clarifying and correcting our studio report. By dispelling our contributor's fears that the subject would avoid many vital issues relevant to homosexuality in Britain today, and by emphasizing the film's overall support for the Wolfenden Committee recommendations, Mr Relph gives promise of a courageous and important production. We wish it well – and look forward to the time it is ready for release.

(Peter G. Baker, editor, *Films and Filming*, May 1961)

Victim, as everybody knows by now, is about queers. And about the way they are 'prey' to 'normal' society. . . exploited by publicans, bullied by landladies, ridiculed by 'decent people' and, as a last resort, blackmailed. 'Once,' says a young man to his friend somewhere in the film, 'it was witches. Now it's us.'

This, then, is one of those rare things in British cinema, a film that unabashedly has a message. Change the law, it argues, and let homosexuals live at peace with society freed from the dangers of blackmail. It is a film which took courage to write, courage to act, courage to direct and produce and – in fairness to the often criticized Rank Organization – courage to distribute to British cinemas.

But, for reasons which I will try to explain, whereas it is a notable piece of propaganda it is not a very good film. . . . Unfortunately there is too much argument and too little visual action. . . . Propaganda drama needs more than logic on its side, it needs emotional involvment. And this is what *Victim* lacks.

Basically I think the characters fail to come to life because there is no humour. And anyone who has ever come close to queer society must surely admit it, whatever his or her prejudices, that they are not lacking in a sense of humour. ('Gay' is perhaps the most apposite word in the queers' vocabulary.) There are, of course, far more homosexuals (and lesbians!) than most people would think, not to count bisexual behaviour and the diseased state of perversion created by the frustrations and pressures of society. But it is a pity that almost every central character in *Victim* is queer, or a blackmailer (and even the blackmailer's strong-arm man has a drawing of Adonis on his wall!). . . . On the other hand the film has many merits. I can think of no other instance in which a dramatist has so accurately handled homosexual relationships (certainly not the hysterical Tennessee Williams) except, of course, the historical reconstruction in Ken Hughes' *The Trials of Oscar Wilde*. It is perhaps expecting the censor – and the public – to accept too much if these men were seen actually to embrace each other; but in its own way there are moments when the film reflects the homosexual's capacity to love and to be loved. . . . Dirk Bogarde plays Mel with great strength. Here is a man living in the law that upholds social justice, convinced that one aspect of it is unjust, and quietly resolved to hit back, whatever the cost. Bogarde finally succeeds in giving Mel some of that quality of greatness that Finch got into his Wilde. . . .

Victim, for all its faults, is a landmark in British cinema. The British have stopped being hypocrites and the censor has indicated that no subject, responsibly treated, is taboo. And when, as inevitably will happen, the law is changed and a man is no longer penalized for expressing his senses and sensibility as he will, *Victim* will have made its contribution to that understanding. And we'll have to find a new name for 'queer'.

(Peter G. Baker, editor, *Films and Filming*, October 1961)

As the successful barrister who must confess his own homosexuality if he is to trap the blackmailers, Dirk Bogarde gives the commanding performance one has long expected from him. With a fine control of gesture and tone he conveys both the suffering of the man condemned by nature and the resolve of the man bent on sacrifice.

(Dilys Powell, *Sunday Times*, 3 September 1961)

. . . the major triumph is Bogarde's. He suggests the anguish behind the sombre barrister's façade brilliantly. Though it may not be how his fans prefer to see him, the integrity of his performance should impress everyone. A bold, brave picture which is also gripping entertainment. It deserves to do well.

(*Daily Cinema*, 31 July 1961)

The rumour that Janet Green had used homosexuality as a mere peg on which to hang a whodunit turns out to be unfounded. In fact she uses a rather rickety, ill-carpentered whodunit as a peg on which to hang her humane, observant and often very moving plea for tolerance towards the homosexual. Hitherto the novel, the stage and the screen have done their damnedest to establish these people in the public eye either as comic cissies or tragic neurotics. This film seeks to establish them primarily as inconspicuous human beings. . . . That none of them looks happy is not to be taken as diagnostic: for in the film we are never allowed to see them at ease among their fellows, but only in solitude and under stress. The stress is caused by their common blackmailer, whose identity remains a secret until the end. Only a moron could listen unmoved.

(Paul Dehn, *Daily Herald*, 1 September 1961)

USA

But what seems at first an attack on extortion seems at last a coyly sensational exploitation of homosexuality as a theme – and, what's more offensive, an implicit approval of homosexuality as a practice. Almost all the deviates in the film are fine fellows – well dressed, well spoken, sensitive, kind. The only one who acts like an overt invert turns out to be a detective. Everybody in the picture who disapproves of homosexuals proves to be an ass, a dolt or a sadist. Nowhere does the film suggest that homosexuality is a serious (but often curable) neurosis that attacks the biological basis of life itself. 'I can't help the way I am,' says one of the sodomites in this movie. 'Nature played a dirty trick.' And the scriptwriters, whose psychiatric information is clearly coval with the statute they dispute, accept this sick-silly self-delusion as a medical fact.

(*Time*, 23 February 1962)

Time should really be very happy with the movie, because the hero of the film is a man who has never given way to his homosexual impulses; he has fought them – that's part of his heroism. Maybe that's why he seems such a stuffy stock figure of a hero.

(Pauline Kael, *I Lost it at the Movies*, Little, Brown, 1965)

Although the Motion Picture Association of America's Code Administration refuses its seal to practically nothing these days, it did refuse a seal to this piece of undisguised propaganda for homosexuality. Made in England, where sexual perversion is said to now infect 4 per cent of the population, *Victim* blatantly pleads for a change in the law which makes homosexuality a crime, on the ground that such a law abets blackmailing. The biological, social and psychological evils resulting from homosexuality are never mentioned. The false contention that homosexuality is congenital is stressed throughout. And though the corruption of the young by older perverts is impugned, the ways in which it is so are perfunctory.

(Anonymous reviewer [all the other film reviewers in the magazine are identified] *Films in Review*, February 1962)

Bibliography

Barr, Charles, *Ealing Studios*. Studio Vista, 1977; revised 1993.

Barr, Charles (ed.), *All Our Yesterdays: 90 Years of British Cinema*. British Film Institute, 1986.

Dewe Matthews, Tom, *Censored*. Chatto & Windus, 1994.

Durgnat, Raymond, *A Mirror for England: British Cinema from Austerity to Affluence*. Faber, 1970.

Dyer, Richard (ed.), *Gays and Film*. British Film Institute, 1977.

Dyer, Richard, *Brief Encounter* (Film Classics Series). British Film Institute, 1993.

Gifford, Denis, *The British Film Catalogue 1895–1985*. David & Charles, 1986.

Hadleigh, Boze, *The Lavender Screen: The Gay and Lesbian Films: Their Stars, Makers, Characters, and Critics*. Citadel Press, 1993.

Howes, Keith, *Broadcasting It: An Encyclopaedia of Homosexuality on Film, Radio and TV in the UK 1923–1993*. Cassell, 1993.

Howes, Keith, *Outspoken: Keith Howes' Gay News Interviews 1976–1983*. Cassell, 1995.

Landy, Marcia, *British Genres: Cinema and Society, 1930–1960*. Princeton University Press, 1991.

McFarlane, Brian (ed.), *Sixty Voices: Celebrities Recall the Golden Age of British Cinema*. British Film Institute, 1992.

Minney, R. J., *Puffin Asquith*. Leslie Frewin, 1973.

Murphy, Robert, *Sixties British Cinema*. British Film Institute, 1992.

Murray, Raymond, *Images in the Dark: An Encyclopedia of Gay and Lesbian Film and Video*. TLA Publications, 1994.

Richards, Jeffrey, *The Age of the Dream Palace: Cinema and Society in Britain 1930–1939*. Routledge, 1984.

Robertson, James C., *The Hidden Cinema: British Film Censorship in Action, 1913–1975*. Routledge, 1989.

Roen, Paul, *High Camp: A Gay Guide to Camp and Cult Films vol. 1*. Leyland Publications, 1994.

Russo, Vito, *The Celluloid Closet: Homosexuality in the Movies*. Harper & Row, 1981; revised 1987.

Shipman, David, *The Great Movie Stars: The Golden Years*. Hamlyn, 1970.

Shipman, David, *The Great Movie Stars: The International Years*. Angus & Robertson, 1972.

Tyler, Parker, *Screening the Sexes: Homosexuality in the Movies*. Holt, Rinehart & Winston, 1972; revised Da Capo Press, 1993.

Vermilye, Jerry, *The Great British Films*. Citadel Press, 1978.

Walker, Alexander, *Hollywood, England: The British Film Industry in the Sixties*. Harrap, 1974.

Weiss, Andrea, *Vampires and Violets: Lesbians in the Cinema*. Cape, 1992.

Index of Film Titles

Index of Names